The New Department Chair

The New Department Chair

100 Daily Reflections for Mindfully Designing Your Term

W. Benjamin Myers

ROWMAN & LITTLEFIELD
Lanham • Boulder • New York • London

Published by Rowman & Littlefield
An imprint of The Rowman & Littlefield Publishing Group, Inc.
4501 Forbes Boulevard, Suite 200, Lanham, Maryland 20706
www.rowman.com

86-90 Paul Street, London EC2A 4NE

Copyright © 2025 by W. Benjamin Myers

All rights reserved. No part of this book may be reproduced in any form or by any electronic or mechanical means, including information storage and retrieval systems, without written permission from the publisher, except by a reviewer who may quote passages in a review.

British Library Cataloguing in Publication Information Available

Library of Congress Cataloging-in-Publication Data

Names: Myers, W. Benjamin, author.
Title: The new department chair : 100 daily reflections for mindfully designing your term / W. Benjamin Myers.
Description: Lanham, Maryland : Rowman & Littlefield Publishers, 2025. | Includes bibliographical references and index.
Identifiers: LCCN 2024039629 (print) | LCCN 2024039630 (ebook) | ISBN 9798881805081 (cloth) | ISBN 9798881805098 (paperback) | ISBN 9798881805104 (ebook)
Subjects: LCSH: College department heads—United States—Handbooks, manuals, etc. | Universities and colleges—United States—Departments—Administration—Handbooks, manuals, etc. | Educational leadership—United States—Handbooks, manuals, etc.
Classification: LCC LB2341 .M94 2025 (print) | LCC LB2341 (ebook) | DDC 378.1/11--dc23/eng/20241011
LC record available at https://lccn.loc.gov/2024039629
LC ebook record available at https://lccn.loc.gov/2024039630

To Tasha, Henry, Esben, and Zenon. You all are not only the inspiration for this project, but also the reason it was not completed sooner. Thank you for all the motivation, laughter, and tempting invitations to do something fun that seemed to come each time I found my writing groove. I wouldn't trade our wonderful chaos for anything. I love you all.

Contents

Foreword		xiii
Acknowledgements		xv
Introduction		xvii
1	Your New Professional Identity	1
2	You Don't Have to Be a Reluctant Chair	4
3	Understanding the Chair Position at Your University	7
4	Changing Relationships with Your Colleagues	10
5	The Power Paradox: Leading without Levers	13
6	The Slippery Slope of Accommodation	16
7	Chairing from a Beginner's Mindset	19
8	The Art of Information Management	22
9	Boundary Spanning (Betwixt and Between)	25
10	A Chair's Inbox	28
11	Department Meetings as More than Agenda Items	31
12	Creating an Agenda for a Department Meeting	34
13	Cultivating Constructive Dialogue in Department Meetings	37
14	Effectively Participating in College-Wide Chairs' Meetings	40
15	Setting Goals	43

16	The Power Paradox of an Academic Middle Manager	46
17	Big-Picture Budgeting	49
18	Your University's Budget Model and Where You Fit In	52
19	Budgeting Strategies and Tactics	55
20	Grade Appeals as Pedagogical Process	58
21	Becoming Privy to Department Drama	61
22	Informational Asymmetry, Confidentiality, and Managerial Trust	64
23	You Are Chair of Students, Not Just Faculty	67
24	Networking with Other Chairs	69
25	Agenda Interrupted	72
26	Advocacy and Influence from the Middle	75
27	Writing Memos for Resource Allocation Requests	78
28	Student Misconduct	81
29	Inappropriate Faculty Behavior	84
30	Unilateral Versus Multilateral Decision-Making	87
31	Focus on Where It Counts: The Pareto Principle and Demanding Faculty	89
32	Generous Leadership and the Power of Sharing Recognition	92
33	The Emotional Labor of Being Chair	95
34	The Visible Chair	98
35	When to Address Problems with Collective Policies	101
36	When to Address Problems with Private Conversations	104
37	Mentoring Junior Faculty	107
38	Working with Senior Faculty	110
39	Supporting Part-Time Faculty	113
40	The Art of Annual Reviews (The Big Picture)	116
41	Strategic Approaches to Annual Faculty Evaluations	119
42	Do Not Play Politics with Your Course Schedule	122
43	Course-Scheduling Strategies	125

44	The Summer Schedule	128
45	Your Department's Social Media Presence	131
46	Digital Dilemmas	134
47	Academic Bullies	137
48	Practical Advice for Handling Academic Bullies	140
49	Committee Assignments	143
50	Classroom Teaching Observations	146
51	Your Department's Approach to Online Education	149
52	Imposter Syndrome	152
53	Your Relationship with Your Dean	155
54	Your Relationship with Your Dean Continued	158
55	Your Relationship with Your Office Associate	161
56	Your Relationship with Your Provost	164
57	Supporting International Faculty	167
58	Assembling a Search Committee	170
59	Candidate Selection and Search Committee Processes	173
60	Your Increased Legal Liability	176
61	Strategies for Navigating the Legal Aspects of Being Chair	179
62	Hallway Diplomacy	183
63	Keys to Relationship Building in Your Department	186
64	Approaching Virtual Meetings	190
65	Effective Strategies for Virtual Meetings	193
66	Status-Based Inequality in Your Department	196
67	Fundraising and Interfacing with Donors	200
68	Departmental Culture	203
69	Your Blind Spots	206
70	Inclusivity, Diversity, and Departmental Culture	209
71	Enrollment Management	212

72	Recruiting New Students	215
73	Retention	218
74	Transfer Students	221
75	Students Switching Majors	224
76	Crisis Communication	227
77	Public-Facing Events and Public Speaking Anxiety	230
78	Your New Raise	233
79	Formal Discipline	236
80	One-on-One Meetings	239
81	Maintaining Your Scholarly Agenda	242
82	Higher Ed in Flux: Chairing through Uncertain Times	245
83	Your Department Website	248
84	Beyond Reluctance: Chairing toward Unexpected Opportunities and Growth	251
85	Contemplating the Pursuit of Upper Administration	254
86	Embracing Feedback: Learning to Listen and Adapt	257
87	The Value of Classroom Engagement	260
88	Leading Meaningful Assessment	263
89	Gossip, Trust, and Leadership	266
90	Chairing through the Tenure Process	269
91	Justifying Your Decisions	272
92	The Calculus of Change	275
93	Parent Complaints	278
94	Balancing Academic Leadership and Academic Management	281
95	The Academic Cycle	284
96	Performing as Chair	287
97	Summer and End-of-the-Year Planning	290
98	Authenticity and Pragmatism	293

99	Effective Communication	296
100	Lessons Learned and Paths Forward	299
Index		301
About the Author		313

Foreword

by Tony Adams

In 2014, when first approached about becoming chair of my department, I had just earned tenure and promotion to associate professor. Many academic friends advised me against taking the position. "You won't have time to write," some said. "You won't be compensated sufficiently," others remarked. "You'll become the enemy, a member of the despised administration," some advised. "Why assume the additional stress?" a few asked. "All you'll do is push papers and attend inane meetings all day, every day," others alleged. "You'll be disconnected from students and colleagues," cautioned some. "Don't you have better things to do with your talent and time?" Despite these well-intended concerns, I pursued the position. And except for two semester sabbaticals and a one-semester administrative reassignment, I have been a chair ever since, at two universities.

My friends were accurate: at times the position has been thankless and stressful. I don't write as much as I'd like; on most days I do only push papers and attend inane meetings; and I don't have much quality time with students and colleagues. I've had to seek legal counsel to protect myself and to deal with faculty who harm students and students who harm faculty. I have witnessed senior faculty bully junior faculty, and I've had to report, even fire, faculty for having sexual relations with students. I've had to work with several incompetent, unqualified, and unethical administrators who seem, at least within the academy, to continue to "fail up" and into top positions, often possible because competent, qualified, and ethical others do not want the increased headache of becoming higher (in) administration. Students have cursed at me, faculty have too, as have a few parents. I have to say "no" more than I get to say "yes," and I deliver more bad news than good. Yet, I can attest that *becoming chair has been one of the best professional decisions I have ever made.*

One of my best decisions?

Yes.

But how can such a thankless and stressful position be so rewarding? Read this book.

Using his extensive insider knowledge of being a chair at three universities, Ben offers one hundred "daily devotionals" that new and not-so-new chairs can use to understand what the role entails, brace for and embrace difficult times, and cherish and celebrate the finer moments of academic leadership. Sure, Ben describes the bad—the emotional labor and increased legal liability of being a chair; having to deal with tiring and entitled personalities; the impossibility of being fully transparent with decisions, especially those involving personnel matters. But he simultaneously highlights, even emphasizes, the good—establishing and enforcing equitable workloads; recruiting, retaining, and graduating students; the ability to engage in "quiet" advocacy; hiring, supporting, and mentoring part-time, international, and new faculty; cultivating meaningful camaraderie with colleagues, alums, and donors. Ben also offers critical advice for making chair life manageable and meaningful, for example, prioritizing tasks and time management; caring about self-care; conveying realistic expectations for ourselves and others; valuing the insights of office staff; recognizing the benefits of "hallway diplomacy"; understanding budgets; navigating imposter syndrome; and doing our best to recognize, and be open to learning about, our limitations and strengths.

Throughout, Ben shows how, if you pursue the chair role confidently, humbly, ethically, and earnestly, and if you can envision the good you can do and how you can contribute to improving staff, student, and faculty life, then you will likely do well in the role. But if you want to pursue the chair role only to seek power and status and to boss people around, you likely won't be an effective leader or last long as a chair.

In August 2024, I began my tenth year as a chair. I returned to the position after a one-year leave from it. Reading this manuscript has comforted and rejuvenated me; it reminds me about the potential and privilege of the role, and it even reframes my understanding of what it entails. As such, I am hopeful about my return. Yes, hopeful. There will be difficult times, especially at a university where administration just eliminated several academic programs and faculty, and while working in a national climate that challenges the purpose and importance of higher education. But as Ben beautifully shows, there's a lot of personal and professional good that can come from assuming the position.

Tony E. Adams
Caterpillar Professor and Chair
Department of Communication
Bradley University
June 2024

Acknowledgements

This book has been a joy to write. I have relished distilling what I have learned over the past eleven years as chair into the lessons that follow. It has been rewarding to think back on and find retrospective meaning in the challenges that seemed all consuming at the time. I have also enjoyed recounting the things that have worked in my time as chair. I am extremely grateful for all those who have contributed to this book coming to fruition. While I may have been the one putting figurative pen to paper, I could not have done it without my network of family, peers, colleagues, and friends. I owe a debt of gratitude to them.

First, I must thank my beautiful and supportive spouse, Tasha Dunn. She has been my brainstorming partner, informal editor, proofreader, and motivational life coach during the process. I am blessed that she is not only my spouse, but my colleague as well. She has been suggesting I write this book for several years, and her support has made the entire project possible. Beyond her help with this specific manuscript, she has helped me be a better chair by reminding me of the importance of bringing an emotional component to the job. She is good at things I am not, and I am a better chair when her strengths rub off on me. I truly cannot imagine this accomplishment (or any feat) without her by my side.

There have been several other people who have contributed directly to the success of this manuscript. My editor at Bloomsbury, Nathan Davidson, helped me think through layout and framing. Hollis Peterson and Tricia Currie-Knight helped with layout and copy editing. The support I have received from Bloomsbury has been exceptional.

I have also had many conversations with people about the themes in this book. Zach Walton was one of the first people I talked to about this project. We had a long conversation about how to frame the volume around a campfire with beers on a hiking trip to Hocking Hills, Ohio. Much of that framing stuck and shaped the volume. This volume would look different (and worse) if not for that and many subsequent conversations with him. I have also had very productive discussions about this volume with Tony Adams, Jay Brower, Keith Berry, Adam Tyma, Andrew Herrmann, Kathy Denker and Megan Wood. Each of those has shaped some component of this volume.

Some chapters required consultations with individuals who had expertise and perspectives in specific areas. I reached out to them hoping they could help me make the chapters better, and they delivered. An Chung Cheng provided insights for the chapter on international faculty. Karon Price assisted with the section on office associates. Melissa Gregory contributed to the discussion on Deans. Scott Molitor offered guidance for the chapter on Provosts. Thank you all for your generosity with your time and wisdom.

Lisa Johnson and Emily Kofoed invited me to deliver a workshop to chairs at USC Upstate. Developing that workshop was instrumental in helping me think through how to structure this volume. I am thankful that they provided me with a much-needed deadline, which was what I needed to jumpstart the project that Tasha had been encouraging me to write. The timing was serendipitous.

I am also thankful to all of those who have been a part of my journey as a department chair. These pages are filled with lessons I have learned from my experience. The role of chair can be isolating, but a strong support system is essential for success. I've been fortunate to work with numerous chairs who have mentored me and served as exemplary role models. Peter Caster, Jimm Cox, Ralph Hanson, Dwight Haas, Patrick Lawrence, Sara Lundquist, Barbara Miner, Lisa Johnson, Andrew Mattison, Ami Pflugrad-Jackish, Holly Monsos, Jason Stumbo, John Sarnecki and Sharon Barnes are all chairs who I have collaborated with over the years. Their guidance and the conversations we shared have profoundly influenced my approach and effectiveness as a chair.

I would like to extend my appreciation to the Deans I have worked with: Dirk Schlingmann, Bill Jurma, Peter Longo, Charlene Gilbert, and Melissa Gregory. Each of them has been instrumental in my professional journey and brought different perspectives that have enriched my understanding of academic leadership.

Additionally, the faculty and staff at each of the three institutions I have served at have been a core part of my support system. Trusting a chair is an act of faith. I appreciate that you all entrusted me with that responsibility. I have been fortunate to work with (mostly) incredibly supportive and brilliant colleagues.

I am grateful to the entire community that has supported me through both this book and my career as a department chair. It is a joy to be a storehouse of the collective wisdom you all have imparted on me that now shapes these pages. All the support, directly and indirectly, has enriched both this book and my career as an academic leader. I trust you all will see your influence in these pages. I am overwhelmed with gratitude.

Introduction

I was standing in front of my department, leading my first meeting as chair when I felt out of breath. My face got hot. My hands felt numb. My voice left me. I stood at the front of the room overcome by emotion, unable to speak. I looked down at the meeting agenda in my hand in an attempt to re-center on the job of leading my department through this meeting for the first time. We were on agenda item number two out of ten. I realized I had a long way to go before I was done with this meeting.

My focus shifted from the agenda I was struggling to get through, and I started to notice the faces of the twenty or so faculty and staff in attendance. I saw eyebrows being furrowed, lower lips being bitten, and faces scanning the floor in what I assumed was an attempt to avoid looking directly at the cause of the secondhand embarrassment they were all feeling from watching their new department chair suffer a communicative breakdown in his first meeting.

I found myself disassociating from my body as every cognitive function needed to lead a meeting was replaced with an intense anxiety that rendered me helpless. At this point, I abandoned all hope of being able to skillfully navigate through this department meeting and I froze. The assistant chair, a full professor who had been at the university for twenty years, stood and offered me a lifeline. She politely suggested that maybe I should take a few minutes to gather myself and that she could lead the meeting in my absence. I left and spent the next fifteen minutes in the bathroom giving myself a pep talk in the mirror.

It may sound dramatic, but it took me more than a year to fully emotionally recover from this failed first department meeting. I spent my first academic year as chair consumed by the same anxiety I experienced at that department meeting. I was overwhelmed by the responsibilities. I found any excuse possible to avoid participating in public-facing responsibilities. My blood pressure rose to the point where my doctor suggested medication. I lost weight. I couldn't sleep well. I started drinking more alcohol to alleviate the anxiety. I would have panic attacks before department meetings. Before an event where I was scheduled to provide an introduction, I got so nervous I faked a flat tire.

Since that department meeting, I have served as chair for eleven consecutive years. The ensuing decade of experience in the role of chair has provided me context for making sense of the anxiety suffered during that first department meeting and the subsequent year. Moving into the chair position was a pretty profound change from my role as a faculty member. Changes at work are more likely to lead to stress if the changes are central to an employee's sense of self (Wisse & Sleebos, 2016). The move from faculty member to department chair fits this bill. I was thirty-three years old and relatively early in my career as I had received my PhD and become a university professor only six years earlier. I moved into the position at the same time I received tenure. I found myself saddled with a litany of responsibilities that I was unprepared to handle. These responsibilities directly impacted the working life of the twenty or so full-time faculty/staff, twelve part-time faculty, and five hundred students in our department. This was a hard turn from my time as a faculty member when I was primarily responsible for myself and the dozens of students in my class.

My anxiety was compounded by the fact that not only was I not prepared to be chair, but leading up to that department meeting I was unaware of how unaware I was. Kruger and Dunning (1999) explain this phenomenon quite well in their astutely titled study "Unskilled and unaware of it: How difficulties in recognizing one's own incompetence lead to inflated self-assessments." My lack of knowledge about what being chair entailed led me to grossly overestimate my own readiness to take on the challenges of the position. I was a case study of the Kruger-Dunning effect in action.

This is unsurprising in retrospect. My preparation for the chair position consisted of a half-day workshop that focused solely on budget and course-scheduling software. The workshop didn't dedicate any time to covering the complexities of my new role as a department chair: managerial strategy, time management, conflict resolution, workload negotiation, emotional labor, and the numerous other responsibilities that are baked into the position. Leaving this workshop, I did not understand that these would be important parts of my new role. Standing in that first department meeting, I came face-to-face with the realization that I was now an academic leader and having a perfunctory knowledge of the budget software was going to be unhelpful in most settings.

I am not alone in feeling unprepared when stepping into the department chair position (Normore & Brooks, 2014; Aziz et al., 2005). Floyd (2016) reports that only one-third of academics who have moved into middle higher-ed management positions ever receive any formal training in leadership and management practices. Two-thirds of those who did receive training still reported feeling unprepared. I am not surprised at this given that my half-day workshop would technically fall under the formal training Floyd (2016) discusses. Based on my own anecdotal experience of talking with other department chairs, feeling unprepared for the chair position is a very common experience.

BECOMING CHAIR

Eleven years in, I am much less anxious than I was that first year. Like most things, the more you do it, the easier it gets. Maybe you are a less anxious person than I am, and your role as chair isn't as anxiety-producing as it was for me. I certainly hope so. Regardless of your emotional state, my experience as a new chair is instructive as to the kinds of topics we should pay attention to when people become chair.

Being a new chair is difficult. The move from faculty to a department chair requires a completely different orientation. Gmelch (2004) explains that much of the difficulty of the transition stems from the change in focus. Faculty generally become successful by becoming experts at something narrow. When faculty step into leadership positions they must instead become jacks-of-all-trades.

Most folks who find themselves in the position to become chair have probably been teaching and researching long enough to have some degree of comfort in those areas. You are usually promoted to the chair position because you are good at those things. But your skills in teaching and research do not directly translate to the job of being a chair. A different skill set and orientation are necessary for success as a department chair. In the classroom you enjoy a degree of authority (you assign the grades after all) that you don't have as chair. While there are exceptions, research often doesn't involve negotiating with multiple constituencies who are financially and professionally effected by the choices you make. There is a pretty steep learning curve in the move from faculty member to department chair.

To be a successful chair you must be able to be creative, diplomatic, persuasive, empathetic, adaptable, transparent, firm, improvisational, strategic, and charismatic. Different situations call for these competencies to be deployed in different measures. There is no operations manual that lays out a formula for sorting out how to calculate which situations call for which approach and in what degree.

THE SURVIVAL METAPHOR

On my first day as chair I entered the office to find a wrapped gift waiting for me on my desk. I checked the card. It was from my provost. Appreciative of the gesture, I opened it. Inside was the first edition of the book *The College Administrator's Survival Guide* (Gunsalus, 2006). The cover featured a frazzled-looking man in an ill-fitting suit staring apprehensively at a telephone as if he's dreading the call that's coming. I'd encourage you to go check out the image for yourself online (I only mention that I received the first edition because the revised edition has less of a jarring image on the front).

I was ready for increased responsibilities and paperwork. But as I stood in front of my department at that first meeting, I came to the realization that being a department chair involved more than that. The position was not only difficult in a "this is more work" way, but in a "this is a change in my identity" kind of way. I was coming to the realization that being a department chair was vulnerable. The increased visibility (Armstrong & Woloshyn, 2014), the change in relationships with my colleagues (Rambo, 2016), and the change in orientation (Czech & Forward, 2010) all became much less abstract as I stood in front of that room.

Given the way we frame department chairing, it is not surprising that my provost saw fit to gift me a book about surviving the position. The survival metaphor is prevalent in the ways we discuss department chairing. The *Chronicle of Higher Education* and *Inside Higher Ed* have published articles titled, respectively, "5 Tips on Surviving Your First Year as a Department Head" (Kramer & Mucha, 2018) and "How to Survive Your First Year as Department Chair" (Rockquemore, 2016). Type "survival" and "department chair" into a search engine and you'll find content such as: "Surviving and (Sometimes) Thriving as a Department Chair" (Mertz et al., 2021), "Department Chair Survival Guide" (McLure, 2022), "Surviving Chairdom: Observations of a Past Chair" (Ellis, 2008), and plenty of other similarly titled projects.

This is a metaphor worth investigating. To do this, let's briefly explore Lakoff and Johnson's (1980) influential (and impressively still relevant) book, *Metaphors We Live By*. They argue that metaphors are foundational to our understanding of the world. We often think of metaphors as rhetorical flourish, but they are far more important than that. Metaphorical understanding is so engrained in our language and sense-making that we often don't even realize the work metaphors are doing in sense-making.

The classic example Lakoff and Johnson provide is the metaphor of *war* to understand argumentation. We *win* or *lose* arguments. We *defend* positions. We *attack* our *opponent's* claims. This metaphorical framing highlights certain elements of argumentation while suppressing others. Arguments are an important part of relational maintenance, and as anyone who has ever been in a serious relationship knows, losing an argument is often beneficial to the relationship. But, the metaphor of *war* does not allow for that, as success in war is measured by victory or defeat. Lakoff and Johnson ask us to think about how we might understand argumentation differently if we use the metaphor of a *dance* to understand argumentation. Arguments could consist of partners engaged in a cooperative performance rather than opponents at odds with each other.

What elements of department chairing are emphasized and which are concealed in the metaphor of *survival* to understand department chairing? The metaphor frames one's success as chair as reactionary as survival is usually about responding to the elements around you. *Survival* also privileges an adversarial relationship to one's surroundings (there's an assumption that the elements are out to harm you). Additionally, *survival* often (but not always) involves prioritizing oneself over others. The *survival* metaphor brings to mind expressions like "Please be sure to secure your own air mask before helping those around you" or "I don't have to outrun the bear; I just have to outrun you."

The *survival* metaphor does not privilege a deliberate and thoughtful approach to being chair. It does not leave room for long-term planning, nor does it emphasize the rewards or the personal growth that can come from becoming a department chair. We lose a lot of positive ethos when we frame the chair position as something to be survived. Do we make our best decisions when we're in survival mode? The *survival* framing encourages department chairs to lead from the very bottom of Maslow's hierarchy of needs, far from the realm of self-actualization and esteem at the top. It is no wonder that the *Chronicle of Higher Education* (Zahneis, 2022) called the chair position "The Faculty Job (Almost) No One Wants."

Even if not explicitly invoked, this survival mentality is inherent in how our academic institutions and cultures often understand and prepare people for the department chair position. Rather than setting up chairs to succeed, they are set up not to fail—*to survive*. Chairs are given training on "the basics" and told to follow up with the dean if they have any problems. There's usually a monthly or biweekly chairs meeting with the dean where department chairs can touch base with other chairs. Otherwise, they are left alone in the rough department wilderness to practice their survival skills.

I posed a call to reframe this troublesome metaphor to a group of department chairs at a workshop I was leading. I gave them the phrase "Surviving Your Term as Department Chair" and asked them to provide a new metaphor that would move us up Maslow's hierarchy. They offered suggestions such as:

- Embracing Your Term as Department Chair
- Cultivating Your Term as Department Chair

- Elevating Your Term as Department Chair
- Steering Your Term as Department Chair
- Designing Your Term as Department Chair

These are all great, but my favorite is *designing*. It has a level of intentionality and agency to it. It is proactive and strategic. It has an artistic quality to it as well. It emphasizes building and optimizing. It is in stark contrast to the passive approach that the current chair training in higher education seems to operate on. If taken seriously, it should help you avoid feeling as if your term as department chair is happening *to you*.

Using new metaphors to help shift our orientation is clearly not the only way to help chairs learn to thrive, but it is an important starting point. In this book, I am operating under the metaphor of design as an approach to your time as chair. This book should help guide you design your time by providing opportunities for you to reflect on how to better incorporate a sense of intentionality in your department chair practice.

WHY THIS BOOK?

Being a department chair is hard. Being a new department chair is especially hard. The uncertainty, learning the new required skill set, the shift in orientation, and the list of responsibilities can feel overwhelming. The increased vulnerability and lack of preparation add even more layers to the difficulties.

There are two approaches, both important, by which to address the challenges of being a department chair. The first is institutional. Universities should put considerable effort into meaningful preparation and support for department chairs. The other is for chairs to learn how to approach the work with purpose, intentionality, and balance. This book is focused on the second approach. Both the structure and the content of this book should help you meaningfully design your first year as chair in ways that foster reflexivity, growth, and success.

The structure of this book resembles a daily devotional. I was raised in a very religious household. I attended a religious school, went to church several times a week, and was quite devout in my personal spiritual life. I am not currently religious (who knows, maybe someday, especially if my mom gets her way), but I still hold dear many of the values and practices I learned growing up religiously. One of the most important was the daily devotional. I started every morning by reading a short reflection about some element of religious/spiritual life. It allowed me to center myself at the beginning of the day. The ritualistic element was important. Doing it over and over created a rhythm of focus to start my day.

The style of a daily devotional is especially relevant to our framing metaphor. Effective design requires sustained engagement, attention, long-term strategic thinking, and self-awareness. These competencies can all be included under the umbrella of mindfulness—an open-minded and clear attention to and an awareness of what is being experienced and perceived in the present moment (Quaglia et al., 2015). Companies such as Google, Intel, Nike, and many others have invested in helping their employees learn how to be in the present moment. At this point, the promotion of mindfulness in organizational contexts has become so pervasive that a cottage industry has sprung up around helping businesses cultivate it (Ferguson, 2016). While it may be a corporate buzzword at this point, mindfulness is nonetheless a key element of the design process.

Your time as chair is experienced in moments. Mindful design is best characterized here as cultivating an awareness that allows you to fully focus on each moment while also contextualizing them enough to make connections between them so you can learn from them. Effective design does not just happen. Daily reflections can help facilitate this process. Each chapter will encourage you to develop a mindful approach to some element of being a department chair. Most will not specifically mention mindfulness or design, but the repeated practice of focusing on and learning from the experiences of being chair is the act of mindful design. By identifying these moments and providing reflection prompts, this book can help with that process.

This book is not the only one to appropriate the religious devotional style. There is an excellent series called The Intellectual Devotional with several devotional books about science, history, philosophy, and modern culture. A new department chair is in a prime position for benefitting from a devotional approach. So much of the training is "data dump." Also, many chairs are given a book to read (as I was) when they get the position. That always seemed odd to me as you just earned a position that will require much more time and effort and now you to must find time to read a book as well. Your time as chair is a marathon, not a sprint. Successful terms as chair are accomplished through daily conscientious engagement with your own needs and those of your department and institution. This book's structure will match your own experience by facilitating daily reflection over the course of an academic year. You do not need to overload yourself with everything all at once by trying to hold on to dozens of new ideas in one sitting.

This book is written to be consumed in small portions. Don't read more than one chapter per day. Do it whenever you like in the day, but I suggest starting your time in the office every morning by shutting your door and taking five minutes to read the day's chapter. You can, of course, find the time of day that works best for you. But I suggest the morning because it starts your day off with an intentionality that can frame the rest of your day. Also, we all know how the workday tends to get away from us. This daily short reflection will allow you to think through some element of being a department chair.

This book is meant to be read over one hundred days in your first academic year as chair. Read one a day until you have completed the entries. Each entry is based on what my eleven years of being chair has taught me is important. These entries are not long enough to be in-depth explorations of the nuances of the subjects covered. These are instead entry points intended to give you an opportunity to reflect on how your own practice as chair intersects with the subject matter. This reflection is the foundation for you designing your time as chair. After completing your one hundred days of reflection, you can treat this book as a reference guide, returning to chapters as specific situations arise.

These are not to be understood as rules or facts. They are simply reflections on what I've found to be true in my own experience as chair. Every university and department is different. Universities come with different sizes, structures, histories, organizational culture, contracts, and support systems. I've tried to stick to general principles that I believe most chairs will deal with. But not every word will be applicable to every chair. When you come across a chapter that seems like it was written for a university that is not yours, I'd encourage you to reflect on why. What are the assumptions I make that don't apply to your university? And what does that tell you about how your university operates differently from others?

I have been a department chair at three different universities for a total of eleven years as of this writing. One of these appointments was in a fine arts and communication department. I was responsible for chairing communication, music, theater, art, and art education. I only mention this to assure you that I have some context on how different universities, and different academic disciplines, approach the position. Additionally, I returned to the role of student and received my MBA while being chair. I did this to formally study management processes. I also teach classes such as business communication, communication theory, small group communication, and leadership communication. These daily reflections rely on my own academic training, my eleven years of experience as chair at three different universities, and informal conversations with other chairs. I also consult relevant literature when necessary.

Some entries are explicitly practical, others adapt management theory and apply them to your role as an academic manager, and others are more meditative about your own emotional responses to the challenges of your new chair position. The boundaries between these three categories are fuzzy, as they all intersect in a variety of ways in this role.

Discretion and confidentiality are important parts of being chair, so in the examples I use I often alter some details to protect the identity of those involved or to keep sensitive information private. When discussing sensitive examples, I refrain from identifying which university the example came from. Details have been changed to preserve confidentiality, but the spirit of the experiences are intact. Every story I share happened to me at some point in the last eleven years.

I hope you find this daily meditation approach helpful. It may feel as if spending a few minutes each day reading and reflecting is taking time away from other duties you could be doing. You are right, but please remember that cultivating your self-awareness will make you better equipped to serve your department and your university. Taking time to improve your own practice as chair benefits your colleagues, your students, and your institution. This is how you become a conscientious chair. Your conscientiousness will ultimately help you be more efficient.

While it is certainly not always easy, I am happy I took on the challenge of becoming a chair because I have had an opportunity to grow in ways I wouldn't have if I had stayed in my relatively comfortable faculty position. The vulnerability and challenges have necessitated growth. This book should help cultivate your own growth as you embark on this journey. So, let's get to designing your term as chair.

REFERENCES

Armstrong, D. E., & Woloshyn, V. E. (2017). Exploring the tensions and ambiguities of university department chairs. *Canadian Journal of Higher Education, 47*(1), 97–113.

Aziz, S., Mullins, M. E., Balzer, W. K., Grauer, E., Burnfield, J. L., Lodato, M. A., & Cohen- Powless, M. A. (2005). Understanding the training needs of department chairs. *Studies in Higher Education, 30*(5), 571–593.

Czech, K., & Forward, G. L. (2010). Leader communication: Faculty perceptions of the department chair. *Communication Quarterly, 58*(4), 431–457.

Ellis, S. (2008) *Surviving chairdom: Observations of a past chair.* UW ADVANCE. https://advance.washington.edu/resources/surviving-chairdom-observations-past-chair

Ferguson, M. (2016). Introduction to symposium: Mindfulness and politics. *New Political Science, 38*(2), 201–205.

Floyd, Alan (2016). Supporting academic middle managers in higher education: Do we care? *Higher Education Policy, 29*(2), 167–183.

Gmelch, W. H. (2004). The department chair's balancing acts. In W. H. Gmelch & J. H. Schuh (Eds.), *The life cycle of a department chair* (pp. 69–85). Wiley Publishing.

Gunsalus, C. K. (2006). *The college administrator's survival guide.* Harvard University Press.

Kramer, R., & Mucha, P. J. (2018, September 7). *5 tips on surviving your first year as a department head.* Chronicle of Higher Education. https://www.chronicle.com/article/5-tips-on-surviving-your-first-year-as-a-department-head/?cid2=gen_login_refresh&cid=gen_sign_in

Kruger, J., & Dunning, D. (1999). Unskilled and unaware of it: How difficulties in recognizing one's own incompetence lead to inflated self-assessments. *Journal of Personality and Social Psychology, 77*(6), 1121–1134.

Lakoff, G., & Johnson, M. (1980). *Metaphors we live by*. University of Chicago Press.

McLure, L. (2022) *Department chair survival guide*. Stat girl. https://statgirlblog.wordpress.com/2022/08/14/department-chair-survival-guide

Mertz, P., Baird, T., & Provost, J. (2021). *Surviving and (sometimes) thriving as a department chair*. American Society for Biochemistry and Molecular Biology. https://www.asbmb.org/asbmb-today/careers/090721/surviving-and-sometimes-thrivingasa-department-c

Normore, A., & Brooks, J. (2014). The department chair: A conundrum of educational leadership versus management. In A. H. Normore, K. Ḥamdān, & A. I. Lahera (Eds.), *Pathways to excellence: Developing and cultivating leaders for the classroom and beyond* (pp. 3–19). Advances in Educational Administration (vol. 21). Emerald.

Quaglia, J. T., Brown, K. W., Lindsay, E. K., Creswell, J. D., & Goodman, R. J. (2015). From conception to operationalization of mindfulness. In K. W. Brown, J. D. Creswell, & R. M. Ryan (Eds.), *Handbook of mindfulness: Theory, research, and practice* (pp. 151–170). Guilford.

Rambo, C. (2016). Strange accounts: Applying for the department chair position and writing threats and secrets "in play." *Journal of Contemporary Ethnography, 45*(1), 3–33.

Rockquemore, K. A. (2016, December 7). *How to survive your first year as department chair*. Inside Higher Ed. https://www.insidehighered.com/advice/2016/12/07/how-survive-your-first-year-department-chair-essay

Wisse, B., & Sleebos, E. (2016). When change causes stress: Effects of self-construal and change consequences. *Journal of Business Psychology, 31*(3), 249–264.

Zahneis, M. (2022, July 12). *The faculty job (almost) no one wants*. Chronicle of Higher Education. https://www.chronicle.com/article/thefaculty-job-almost-no-one-wants

Chapter 1

Your New Professional Identity

Think back to the moment when you realized that being a department chair was a real possibility. I'm not asking you to refer to the abstract "I might be chair someday," but instead "I could actually be chair in the 20XX academic year." Perhaps your previous chair announced they were stepping down at the end of their term. Maybe you heard a rumor that they got another job offer and a colleague told you that you should go for it. Or your dean summoned you to their office and told you a chair position was opening up and you were the right person for the job. At that first moment of possibility, what did you envision being a department chair would feel like? What images of department chairship colored your perception? What did you imagine your average day would consist of?

It is worth examining your expectations of what being a chair would be like because they frame your early experiences. It is also a good idea to reflect not only on what your assumptions were, but where they came from. Your predictions of what the chair life entails likely had roots in observing department chairs at your university. You may have had some conversations with the former chair of your department. You probably discussed the position with your dean. Odds are that those conversations and observations were primarily focused on the duties and tasks associated with the position.

It is unlikely that your observations and conversations adequately prepared you for the most jarring aspects of your new role. While the newly accumulated responsibilities such as budgeting, scheduling, and the like are overwhelming, the aspect many new chairs struggle with most is the shift in orientation that comes with being a new department chair. Your focus as a faculty member was likely pretty provincial. Of course, there are collaborative projects and university-wide committees that require faculty to think beyond themselves, but ultimately a faculty orientation is primarily focused inward. Faculty are rewarded for privileging their own personal successes (Kruse, 2020). In addition to the insular focus, universities are usually built so that success as a faculty member comes from narrowing focus and becoming an expert in niche areas (Gmelch, 2004). Faculty are encouraged to prioritize themselves and to be specialists. They aren't doing anything wrong; that's how institutions generally train and incentivize faculty.

The most challenging aspect of the transition from faculty member to chair is not simply the accumulation of and accounting for all the new tasks associated with this list of proficiencies (although that is overwhelming). The most difficult part of the new position is likely the radical repositioning in your organizational and professional identity. It is unsurprising that this shift can be anxiety producing. Those of us in academia often see our professional work as a pretty important component of our identity (Billot, 2010). Our intellectual and pedagogical identities are carefully cultivated, and they are an important currency within our profession. We often take a lot of pride in our faculty identity. A move to a management position creates an "academic identity schism" (Winter, 2009).

Many of the things that made you a good faculty member will not make you a good chair. Narrow expertise and an inward focus are recipes for an unsuccessful (and unrewarding) run at being chair. Instead, your success in the chair position depends on you being outwardly focused and a generalist. You need to be proficient in a variety of tenuously connected areas such as budgeting, conflict mediation, persuasion/advocacy, project management, marketing/promotions, scheduling, and many others. Being proficient in all these areas requires a broad knowledge base and deliberate and careful collaboration with multiple constituencies. This can be very overwhelming.

This shift was challenging for me, and it was likely the catalyst for the public speaking breakdown I shared in the introduction. There is no trick to "cure" the anxiety and tension you likely feel as you embody this new professional identity. The uneasiness should be expected, and it would be odd if such a big change did not produce some anxiety about your professional identity. It is more productive to embrace the tension. Rather than focusing on trying to eliminate the uneasiness you are feeling, focus on accepting it as a natural part of the transition. Think about how to lead for the first year while experiencing anxiety. One of the most rewarding parts of moving into academic management is the growth you will experience. New challenges will push you. The tensions you feel are a necessary part of that growing process. Lean in to the uneasiness of your new professional identity and examine it rather than trying to eliminate it. This approach will likely help you process and grow from these new experiences.

REFLECTIONS

1. What do you think will be the biggest change for you in the move from faculty to department chair?
2. Which of the "tenuously connected" areas a chair needs to be proficient in (budgeting, conflict mediation, persuasion/advocacy, project management, marketing/promotions, scheduling, etc.) do you feel most ready for? Which do you feel least ready for?

REFERENCES

Billot, J. (2010). The imagined and the real: Identifying the tensions for academic identity. *Higher Education Research & Development, 29*(6), 709–721. https://doi.org/10.1080/07294360.2010.487201

Gmelch, W. H. (2004). The department chair's balancing acts. *New Directions for Higher Education, 2004*(126), 69–84. https://doi.org/10.1002/he.149

Kruse, S. D. (2020). Department chair leadership: Exploring the role's demands and tensions. *Educational Management Administration & Leadership, 50*(5), 739–757. https://doi.org/10.1177/1741143220953601

Winter, R. (2009). Academic manager or managed academic? Academic identity schisms in higher education. *Journal of Higher Education Policy and Management, 31*(2), 121–131. https://doi.org/10.1080/13600800902825835

Chapter 2

You Don't Have to Be a Reluctant Chair

When I was elected to my first chair position, I received very different responses from those inside and those outside of academe. My parents told me how proud they were of me for moving up the ladder at my organization. Their oldest child was now in management. How exciting! The high school and college friends who I keep in touch with congratulated me on accomplishing such a prestigious position.

Those inside academia had a very different sentiment. None of my colleagues responded with unequivocal accolades. Their congratulations were usually qualified. Some jokingly offered condolences. Others expressed admiration at my willingness to take on the role while noting that they would never have any interest. A few colleagues asked me directly why I would take this position, and some even thanked me for my service as if I was a first responder.

The academic chair is not always regarded as the most prestigious of positions within academia. It is often viewed as a kind of community service that one performs for their department. Your colleagues are usually thankful someone was willing to take on the role. *The Chronicle of Higher Education* called the department chair position "The Faculty Job (Almost) No One Wants" (Zahneis, 2022). The Higher Education Executive Search Firm reports that "Department Chair searches has become the fastest growing aspect of our [firm]—and it's not even close. Internal searches on campuses continue to fail at an alarming rate across all colleges and disciplines" (Skinner, n.d.).

One of the reasons people do not want to be chair is how the job is positioned in relationship to faculty within their universities. Faculty often do not like to be managed. Autonomy is one of the reasons that people are attracted to the faculty life. Also, the notion that faculty have the right to govern their own affairs is an almost sacred concept in many institutions. But, even the most ardent faculty governance advocate knows that someone must oversee the budget and class schedules and such. Often the unspoken compromise is these faculty will accept a department chair as a necessity, but the chair is expected to engage in a performance of reluctance about the position.

Department chairs who express too much enthusiasm for the managerial aspects of the position may be viewed with suspicion. What kind of person wants that much power? The managerial responsibilities of the chair position should be assumed because someone must do them, not because someone wants them.

You can see this operationalized in various places. Once I heard a faculty member judgmentally mention that a fellow department chair had gone "full administration" because he enjoyed the position a bit too much. The offense seemed to be that they committed to the managerial identity too much. Chairs are expected to be competent and to address managerial issues (budget, enrollment, workloads, evaluations, etc.) but to perform reluctance while doing it.

In a meeting recently, I heard a chair preface a statement with "Don't hate me for wearing my administrative hat here, but. . . ." Feeling as if you must be good at your job but apologetic for having it in the first place is a recipe for a miserable and ineffective term as chair. A good portion of your professional identity is now managerial. Embrace it. Being a department chair is very important. Department chairs are responsible for 80 percent of administrative decisions on campuses (Gonaim, 2016). Additionally, chairs are the administrative group who interface most directly with faculty. This direct contact with faculty means that chairs are the ones most responsible for ensuring the health of their own academic unit (Bryman, 2007). Chairs are also the administrators on the "ground level" who implement the strategic mission of the university (Manning, 2018). Upper administrators may develop organizational strategic plans, but they cannot execute those plans on a day-to-day basis the ways chairs can.

Your influence as chair is also more widespread than it was as a faculty. In the classroom, an instructor effects the dozens of students in their class. But as a chair, your leadership and daily decisions effect all of the students in your department (and students with other majors who take classes in your department). One of the first times I really felt a shift in my organizational position was when a student came to me with a concern that she wouldn't be able to graduate on time because the class she needed wasn't offered in the term she needed it. When this kind of thing happened to me as a faculty member, I would approach the chair on behalf of the student and petition for a substitute. The first time this happened to me when I was chair, I realized that

I could approve these substitutions myself. I had the ability to help students on my own authority. This was an empowering moment.

As department chair, you hold a critical position with some institutional authority. Embrace this fact, and let it sink in because it has the potential to fuel your sense of fulfillment and to enhance your effectiveness. Savor the sense of purpose that comes with holding such an important role. When you fully embrace your position, you become a leader who can impact not only your department, but your entire university.

REFLECTIONS

1. How did people in your own institution respond to the news that you would be a chair? What does that response tell you about how chairs are viewed at your institution?
2. What benefits can come from embracing the role of department chair rather than feeling apologetic for it?

REFERENCES

Bryman, A. (2007). Effective leadership in higher education: A literature review. *Studies in Higher Education, 32*(6), 693–710. https://doi.org/10.1080/03075070701685114

Gonaim, F. (2016). A department chair: A life guard without a life jacket. *Higher Education Policy, 29*(2), 272–286. https://doi.org/10.1057/hep.2015.26

Manning, K. (2018). *Organizational theory in higher education.* Routledge.

Skinner, R. (n.d.). *Recruiting department chairs (when no one wants the job)—some modest advice.* Harris Search Associates. Retrieved December 7, 2022, from https://harrissearch.com/pub/publications/publications/recruiting-department-chairs-when-no-one-wants-the-job-some-modest-advice

Zahneis, M. (2022, February 4). *The faculty job (almost) no one wants: Chairing a department has never been easy. The pandemic has only made it tougher.* Chronicle of Higher Education. https://www.chronicle.com/article/the-faculty-job-almost-no-one-wants?cid=gen_sign_in

Chapter 3

Understanding the Chair Position at Your University

Position descriptions for chair contracts usually include some combination of the following duties: course scheduling, budgeting, faculty class assignments, conducting annual reviews, managing enrollment, and recruiting. The responsibilities of the position are disassociated from each other (Cipriano, 2011). For example, the granular focus required for successful budgeting is very different from the diplomatic touch necessary for advocating to your dean for a new staff position. This is true for many of the functions of being chair. There is often very little overlap between the various (and essential) skill sets that require competency if you are going to be a good chair.

Ambiguity is a key feature of being a department chair (Armstrong & Woloshyn, 2017). Along with the official duties in your position description, you are generally responsible for the day-to-day operations of the department, long-term strategy, maintaining academic standards, ensuring student and faculty satisfaction, *and* your faculty duties of teaching and maintaining an active research agenda.

Having been a chair at three different institutions, I can assure you that there is no universal understanding of what a chair is. Being chair has meant something very different at each of the three universities where I've done it. With a few exceptions, most of the official duties were similar. The most notable difference has been how department chairs have been positioned on the spectrum of faculty and administration. In my first position, the ethos of chair was that you were a faculty member who had taken on a temporary position where you had to do some administrative things. While I had many administrative responsibilities like scheduling and budgeting, there was never any doubt that I was clearly "team faculty." I was expected to side with the faculty in any dispute with upper administration. I did not hold any formal power to discipline. My departmental colleagues complained to me about administrators (with the safe assumption that I was not one to be counted among their ranks).

Things are very different at my current chair position, where being chair clearly puts me in the administrative camp. Chairs are characterized as management. It is not uncommon for faculty members to request union representation if I ask to have a meeting with them. Conversations about my position often center around issues such as "management rights." I do not have a vote at department meetings. I am on a management annual pay raise schedule rather than a faculty one. I am not a member of the faculty union.

These may seem like mostly symbolic differences. Some are, but they still matter. When I moved to my current position, I came to the position assuming a faculty member mentality. I noticed that the departmental constitution was outdated. I took it upon myself to push for a revision. I charged the department with modernizing it, appointed an ad hoc committee to do the initial lift, and placed myself on the committee. I took on this project assuming that everyone would be thrilled that the new chair was getting down to business right away and cleaning up this document that hadn't been revised in so long that it referenced CD-ROMs as an acceptable way to submit promotion materials.

This proved to be a colossal misread of the situation. Many in my department saw the department constitution as a document primarily related to faculty governance, and I was not faculty. By focusing my attention on updating this document, I positioned myself as a manager meddling in faculty affairs. I cannot overemphasize the amount of stress this caused. The president of the union got involved, I had several meetings with members in Faculty Labor Relations to discuss the situation, sides formed within the department with some faculty supporting me and others calling for me to be disciplined, and my dean had to call a special department meeting to help sort through the issue. This all happened four years ago, and as of this writing the constitution remains unrevised. The silver lining of all this is that I left the situation with a much better understanding of what it means to be a chair at this university.

At my old institution, the department would not only have been supportive of me being involved in revising a departmental constitution, but they would also have applauded my initiative. I would have been perceived as a fellow faculty member (who happened to have some administrative powers that I was using for good). If this is your first department chair position, you may be tempted to just assume that your experience is standard. But a realization that different institutions construct the chair position differently is crucial to fully comprehending your responsibilities and place within your academic community.

REFLECTIONS

1. Where would you place the role of department chair on the spectrum of faculty/manager at your university? Are you a faculty member who happens to occupy a temporary administrative position *or* are you primarily a manager with a faculty sensibility?
2. How does your answer to the above question affect your day-to-day decisions? How about your long-term or bigger projects? Are there any areas of departmental decision-making that are off-limits to you now that you are a department chair?

REFERENCES

Armstrong, D. E., & Woloshyn, V. E. (2017). Exploring the tensions and ambiguities of university department chairs. *Canadian Journal of Higher Education, 47*(1), 97–113. https://doi.org/10.47678/cjhe.v47i1.186470

Cipriano, R. E. (2011). *Facilitating a collegial department in higher education: Strategies for Success.* Jossey-Bass.

Chapter 4

Changing Relationships with Your Colleagues

I graduated from my PhD program and went immediately in to my first academic appointment as an assistant professor. After five years, I applied for tenure. In that review year, the current department chair's second term ended. Per university policy, no chair could serve more than two consecutive terms. A senior faculty member approached me in my office and informed me that all the senior faculty had met and had decided that I should be the next chair. Flattered, but also nervous, I informed the dean of intent to run. One other faculty member ran for the position, but I was voted in by my department and then appointed by my dean.

This is a very different appointment process than the other two times I served as chair. In both of those cases, I saw an open chair position advertised in the National Communication Association listserv. I applied, interviewed as a potential incoming chair, and then was appointed directly to the chair position.

The move from faculty rank to chair was much more awkward than when I came into the position as chair as an outside hire. Coming from the outside was much easier because my new colleagues only knew me as department chair. Making the transition from faculty to department chair involves a status shift. Coming in as an external chair hire did not.

New department chairs often struggle with the changes in relationship (Rambo, 2015; Deal, 2014). Faculty are often suspicious of administrators, and now you are "one of them." I had spent many hours in colleagues' offices discussing and scrutinizing the decisions our chair had made. When I became chair, I realized that I was now excluded from these discussions. I was the one being discussed. While I understood conceptually that this would be true, I was unprepared for how emotionally jarring this was. I felt lonely when at work. The fact that it is a sudden rather than gradual shift makes the transition even more difficult. Additionally, as chair you are now responsible for evaluating people who were your peers before. Writing the word "equals" here makes me squirm (even with the quotation marks).

The need to reassure my departmental cohort that I know we are all "equals" underscores much of the anxiety associated with this shift. As a chair, I have obviously never thought of any of my colleagues as anything other than equal. But I found myself worried that now they would think that I thought that I was better than them. And by reassuring them that I didn't, I found myself reaffirming the fact that I am now "other" to them.

Most chairs are promoted from within their own departments. Given this, most chairs must deal with the transition. The temporary nature of most chair positions adds a further wrinkle to the transition (Berdrow, 2010). Most chairs know that once their term(s) is complete, they will return to being faculty. And faculty know this too. This mutual knowledge makes the entire relational shift situation feel even more delicate. No one can fully commit to the status change.

Any discomfort you're feeling over the shift is a common experience shared by many chairs. There is no easy way around this. There exists no hack that can help you bypass the uncomfortable (and temporary) change from "one of us" to "one of them." Accepting (and maybe even embracing) the discomfort is more productive than fighting it or running from it. There is psychological research that suggests that suppressing negative feelings tends to amplify them (Hu et al., 2014; Masedo & Esteve, 2007). You'll likely make things worse if you try to avoid this natural part of the transition.

Consider the awkwardness an opportunity for personal growth and introspection. Emotional labor is part of the work of a chair (we'll discuss that in a future reflection). The chair position will likely put you in many situations that feel emotionally inconvenient. Doing good work while managing your emotional well-being in these circumstances is a key part to successfully navigating your term as chair. The discomfort in this transition offers you a chance to practice doing so. Also, be open about any relational discomfort. Strong relationships with your colleagues built on trust are key to your success as a department chair. Opening yourself up with this kind of relational vulnerability can go a long way to building the necessary connections with your department.

REFLECTIONS

1. Are you surprised that the transition from faculty to chair is difficult for most new chairs? Why or why not? Have you had any interactions with colleagues where things have felt different from before you were chair?

What feels different for you? Are there any commonalities across the experiences when you feel different?
2. Is there a current chair at your institution who you consider a mentor? If so, do you feel comfortable asking them if they felt any discomfort at this transition?

REFERENCES

Berdrow, I. (2010). King among kings: Understanding the role and responsibilities of the department chair in higher education. *Educational Management Administration & Leadership, 38*(4), 499–514. https://doi.org/10.1177/1741143210368146

Deal, J. (2014). From faculty member to department chair: Making the transition to administration. *College Music Symposium, 54.*

Hu, T., Zhang, D., Wang, J., Mistry, R., Ran, G., & Wang, X. (2014). Relation between emotion regulation and mental health: A meta-analysis review. *Psychological Reports, 114*(2), 341–362. https://doi.org/10.2466/03.20.pr0.114k22w4

Masedo, A. I., & Rosa Esteve, M. (2007). Effects of suppression, acceptance and spontaneous coping on pain tolerance, pain intensity and distress. *Behaviour Research and Therapy, 45*(2), 199–209. https://doi.org/10.1016/j.brat.2006.02.006

Rambo, C. (2015). Strange accounts. *Journal of Contemporary Ethnography, 45*(1), 3–33. https://doi.org/10.1177/0891241615611729

Chapter 5

The Power Paradox

Leading without Levers

After I was elected to the chair position, I had a frightening thought. "Why would anyone in my department listen to me when I ask them to do something?" Until I had actually been appointed to the position, this fear had never materialized in this way. As my start date approached, I found myself growing increasingly scared. I shared this fear with a friend in my department, and she responded by asking me, "Why do you do what Jim tells you to do?" I hadn't really questioned that before. I just did what the current chair (Jim) asked because he was the chair. After this interaction, I realized that the ways that power intersects with the chair position was more complicated that it initially appeared.

At the heart of my fear was the realization that chairs don't really have traditional managerial power. Power and influence are vital to a department chair's success. It is how a chair moves a department to make necessary changes as well as to keep the day-to-day operations afloat. A chair without any power is an ineffective administrator who cannot serve those who they have been tasked with leading.

In other industries, managers have levers to pull that academic department chairs simply do not have. French and Raven's (1959) description of power has maintained its relevancy for decades and is still regularly cited in work on managerial authority. They described five bases from which a leader can derive power. They are legitimate (having the formal position/title), reward (the ability to compensate), expert (high levels of knowledge), coercive (the ability to punish), and referent (charisma and likability).

Managers can generally draw from these bases of power in different degrees as situations dictate. While the authority of department chairs varies from institution to institution (Bozeman et al., 2013), most of these bases of power are unavailable to academic department chairs. You cannot rely on legitimate power, as many faculty do not necessarily hold the position of department chair in high esteem. You cannot reward or punish, as academic chairs generally cannot fire faculty or give raises. You cannot rely on expert power, as you are working with highly educated people. So, you are left with referent power—the power to motivate people (Brown & Moshavi, 2002). Your managerial "toolbox" is much emptier than your counterparts in other industries. All of this is made much more difficult by the fact that faculty generally don't like to be led. Most academics got into academia because they value autonomy.

The one base of power a chair is left with (referent power) is arguably the most difficult to utilize effectively, and it certainly requires the most energy. Referent power requires a leader to establish buy-in from those they lead. This stems from your performance rather than from institutional authority. It is based on earning the respect and admiration of others through your character and behavior. It requires steady and authentic effort aimed at maintaining relationships with others. Also, it is not something that can be built overnight. It takes time to build a reputation as a department chair who is reliable, is competent, cares for others, and is trustworthy.

Additionally, referent power must not only be acquired, but must also be maintained. This requires consistent self-awareness and regulation. Buy-in can be lost much more easily than it can be won. One wrong decision, one weak moment, or one breach of trust can significantly damage reputational capital that you've spent a long time building.

As a chair you are expected to deliver managerial results without having traditional managerial power. It is important that you realize the precarious nature of the power that you have as a department chair. Effectively practicing referent power while also trying to get results is a balancing act. I have seen many chairs fail because they try too hard to operate from coercive, legitimate, or expert bases of power. These are not advantageous positions to chair from. Many of our reflections in this volume will focus on building influence from a referent power base. This connection will most often not be explicitly stated because successfully leading with referent power involves others believing you to be a competent, caring, self-aware, and intentional leader is built through you establishing these qualities through repeated interactions and situations. There is no one trick you can employ that will establish you in this regard. It is not an easy road, but cultivating this power base effectively leads to a flourishing and healthy departmental culture.

REFLECTIONS

1. Do you agree with the assessment that department chairs are generally expected to deliver managerial results without having managerial power? Are there any areas in your department where this seems more or less true than others? How might this effect the day-to-day operations of a department?
2. How can you, in your role as department chair, work to build and cultivate your referent power? What are your strengths and weaknesses in this regard?

REFERENCES

Bozeman, B., Fay, D., & Gaughan, M. (2012). Power to do . . . what? Department heads' decision autonomy and strategic priorities. *Research in Higher Education, 54*(3), 303–328. https://doi.org/10.1007/s11162-012-9270-7

Brown, F. W., & Moshavi, D. (2002). Herding academic cats: Faculty reactions to transformational and contingent reward leadership by department chairs. *Journal of Leadership Studies, 8*(3), 79–93. https://doi.org/10.1177/107179190200800307

French Jr., J. R. P., & Raven, B. H. (1959). The bases of social power. In D. Cartwright (Ed.), *Studies in social power* (pp. 150–167). Institute for Social Research.

Chapter 6

The Slippery Slope of Accommodation

The demands were annoying, but not so out of bounds that they warranted pushback. I was brand-new to the chair position, and I wanted to be accommodating. At the student welcome event, one faculty member couldn't possibly keep her remarks to the time frame required. She couldn't attend the department meeting because she was working on a new project. I accommodated these requests, yet the demands grew. She *had* to have new software, even though the budget was strapped. She had to trade offices with someone she had seniority over because neighbor was loud. While these were starting to feel egregious, I gave in. Finally, the demands entered the realm of the truly absurd. The Netflix show *The Chair* did not yet exist, but the demands might as well have been inspiration for it. She needed her course schedule changed because her "enemy" taught on the other end of the hall, and they would have to pass each other when she walked back to her office after class. She required an escort from the parking lot to her office because she had a stalker (who she ended up marrying a few months later). She demanded that I fire two faculty (one part-time and one tenure-track) because they were unable to keep up with the intellectual demands of the program. When I refused to grant these more outrageous requests, she took her demands to the dean and informed him that she would quit if they were not granted (and I removed as chair). When our dean refused, she handed in her letter of resignation.

I have had few experiences as chair that felt more instructive than this one. There have been "difficult faculty" within all three departments I've chaired. It is a common phenomenon. Managing "problem faculty" is the task that most chairs say they like the least about this position (Lipscomb et al., 2021). If you don't believe that, just ask a chair and I'm sure they will verify it. This is what department chairs generally talk about when they see each other at conferences. Every chair has their own stories to share. "Difficult faculty" are generally those who believe they are more valuable to the department than their colleagues. They believe they deserve more resources than others, seek to find fault with their colleagues and publicly humiliate them, require constant praise, and think pushing back on administrative decisions or departmental progress is a virtue unto itself. The vast majority of faculty do not fall into this category, but it requires only a very few to make your time as chair miserable.

There are certainly difficult people to manage in any workplace, but the structure of academia seems to exacerbate these problems in ways that generally do not happen in other industries (we will cover working with difficult faculty in later chapters). Faculty are generally smart, talented, and high-achieving individuals. In some faculty, this breeds a sense of exceptionalism. Also, as faculty, we spend a good portion of the day standing in front of students as the center of attention and the sole authority. These factors do not breed egotism in the majority of people, but for those already wired with a narcissistic framework it exacerbates it. When you combine that with the fact that faculty are generally protected by academic freedom and faculty rights, they might feel less of an impulse to curb bad impulses. This assessment is evidenced by the fact that I've seen difficult faculty justify bad behavior through "academic freedom" or "healthy academic debate." This is why you very rarely hear about these same kinds of problems with staff. They are not protected in the same way. And finally, as we've discussed before, department chairs generally do not have a lot of traditional management tools to curb problematic behavior.

While the story I started this chapter with ended up resolving itself as well as it could have from my point of view (very rarely do "difficult faculty" just resign), the process itself was stressful, embarrassing, and painful. I know that I was not ultimately responsible for the bad behavior, but with some distance I came to realize that I needed to claim some ownership over how the situation escalated. I made the situation much worse than it should have been by doing what chairs often do with difficult faculty (Hubbell & Homer, 1997). I gave in on the smaller demands when I knew they were wrong. My gut was telling me I was wrong to accommodate these demands, but I did it anyway. I wanted to avoid conflict. I assumed that if I granted these demands, it might make her feel valued and thereby curb future demands. By doing so, I communicated to her that I agreed with her that she should be treated differently than other faculty. Why wouldn't she ask for more and more when I had legitimized those kinds of requests?

You need to be especially vigilant as you start your term as chair. Demands are more likely to surface when you are new. This is not an invitation to be a dictator or to be unwilling to see things from another person's perspective. You should listen to people, but you have to recognize when someone is demanding unfair treatment. If something feels wrong, or someone is demanding unfair treatment, do not give in—no matter how small the request. Respectfully and politely explain that it would be unfair to the rest of the department if you granted the request.

This may seem like I am giving highly principled ethical advice. It is that, but it is more. It is also deeply practical. The conflict you avoid today will have to be confronted at some point. Would you rather have that conflict over a minor private issue or a major public issue? It may feel uncomfortable in the moment, but you are making things better for your future self. It is nice when the ethical decision is also the pragmatic one.

REFLECTIONS

1. Do you agree with the claim that demands for unfair treatment are more likely to surface when someone is new to a leadership role? Why might this be? Are there ways to mitigate this?
2. As a chair, how do you balance the need to listen to others with your responsibility to avoid unfair treatment and to maintain a productive and positive workplace?

REFERENCES

Hubbell, L., & Homer, F. (1997). The academic department chair: The logic of appeasement. *PS: Political Science & Politics, 30*(2), 209–213. https://doi.org/10.2307/420497

Lipscomb, M. F., Bailey, D. N., Howell, L. P., Johnson, R., Joste, N., Leonard, D. G. B., Markwood, P., Pinn, V. W., Powell, D., Thornburg, M., & Zander, D. S. (2021). Women in academic pathology: Pathways to department chair. *Academic Pathology, 8*. https://doi.org/10.1177/23742895211010322

Chapter 7

Chairing from a Beginner's Mindset

The game Go has been heralded as the most difficult in the world to play as the number of possible positions on the board is greater than the number of atoms in the universe. It had long been thought of as far too complex for a computer to master. However, in a surprising turn of events, the AI entity known as AlphaGo emerged in 2016 to challenge the world's greatest Go player. AlphaGo was not trained to play by humans, but was instead simply taught the rules of the game and then given the opportunity to explore its depths through countless self-play iteration. The computer emerged victorious, forever altering the way we understand the game. Key to its victory was an unprecedented move that left its grandmaster opponent so bewildered he stood up and temporarily abandoned the game in disbelief (Metz, 2016). No one in the 2,500-year-old history of the game had ever made this move. But it worked.

Rick Rubin (2023) in his book *The Creative Act: A Way of Being* uses this story to explain the power of approaching tasks without preconceived ideas. What allowed the AI to play so imaginatively? "It wasn't necessarily intelligence, it was the fact that the machine learned the game from scratch with no coach, no human intervention, no lessons based on experts' past experience . . . it wasn't held back by limiting beliefs" (p. 117). He summarizes this dynamic through the rhetorical question, "Did the computer win because it knew more than the grandmaster, or because it knew less?" (p. 119).

Your lack of experience as chair has most likely been characterized as a liability up to this point. Your dean, your mentor, and senior faculty have most likely wanted to give you well-meaning advice on how to be chair. Often these are the same people who have been telling you that the systems at your university are broken and in need of reform.

In her book *The Philosophical Baby: What Children's Minds Tell Us about Truth, Love, and the Meaning of Life,* Alison Gopnik (2010) explains the difference between children and adult minds. We often think of children as miniature adults awaiting development. Gopnik, through a series of convincing experiments, makes the case that this framework is wrong. Children, she contends, run on a fundamentally different operating system: an *explore* mindset. In stark contrast, adults operate within in an *exploit* mindset as they drive to extract value from their surroundings. An *exploit* mindset assumes meaning that adults can then leverage. This mode works for collecting resources, but it limits possibility. Children, uninterested in exploitation, seek to unravel the mysteries of the world as they approach each experience with fresh eyes. It is all new to them. They are not confined by assumptions. Given that you are new at chair, you now possess the opportunity to approach the position through a similar lens of novelty.

You will never have another chance to be a novice at this. Soon enough being chair will be old hat and you'll be settled into your own chair style. Rather than trying to rush to that point as quickly as possible, lean in to not knowing. You may be tempted to try to learn as much about the "right" way to do things as possible, but there is a lot of value in approaching things with an openness to how things might be, rather than how they are. It will never be easier for you to approach the chair position with an *explore* mindset than it is right now.

When I was a new chair, I noticed there were a lot of problems with student advising in my department. Not all students were receiving the same level of advisement from faculty. Some faculty really cared. Others did not and it showed. When it came time for annual reviews, I realized I had no data by which to note these observations. I asked my dean why we didn't formally evaluate advising since it was such an important part of student success? The answer was that no one had ever thought to. So, I developed an evaluation tool where students rated faculty on their advising (similar to the kind students get at the end of a class). We then had a metric by which to evaluate faculty in the advising process. The advising opinion polls eventually became adopted by the entire college. This insight was possible because I was new to the position.

The first year as chair will be fraught with firsts—the inaugural budget, course scheduling, and annual reviews, among others. Each of these offer an opportunity for you to adopt an *explore* mindset. Approach them without preconceived notions. Do not simply accept that the way you are instructed to do them is "the way." Start from a childlike perspective of not knowing and being okay with it. Ask "Why?," "Why not?," and "What if?" And if you encounter a process as suboptimal, don't just accept it.

This is not an excuse to discard sage advice from those with expertise. There is no contradiction in being open to an exploratory mindset while also accepting mentorship. Listen to the advice of others, but don't let it be your only teacher. Do not rush through this process assuming that you will be a "better" chair once you know more. You have different tools at your disposal at different times in your career. Right now, the tool of inexperience can be a very valuable one as it opens up the possibility for you to lead through the lens of discovery rather than that of assumption.

REFLECTIONS

1. As a new chair, what unique opportunities does your position offer to embrace the unknown and approach tasks with an openness to possibilities? How can you resist the temptation to conform to preexisting norms because they are norms?
2. How do you think your approach to leadership may change as you gain more experience in the chair position? How can you work to retain the exploratory mindset and continue to approach challenges with fresh eyes?

REFERENCES

Gopnik, A. (2010). *The philosophical baby: What children's minds tell us about truth, love, and the meaning of life*. Picador.

Metz, C. (2016, March 14). *How Google's AI viewed the move no human could understand*. Wired. https://www.wired.com/2016/03/googles-ai-viewed-move-no-human-understand/

Rubin, R. (2023). *The creative act: A way of being*. Penguin Books.

Chapter 8

The Art of Information Management

My colleague stormed into my office, her anger visibly displayed through her posture. "How could you keep me in the dark about the potential closure of this search?" she demanded. "I've invested hours reviewing the candidates." Without saying goodbye, she abruptly turned and left. The dean had warned me about tight budgets and the possibility of the candidate search being canceled. In his desperate attempt to salvage it, he had requested I withhold this information from the department. Fearful that setting the rumor mill in motion would further justify canceling the search, I made a conscious choice to heed his request and did not even inform the chair of the search committee. It was the wrong decision.

"I should have looped you in on that" is a phrase that you should be prepared to utter frequently. Regulating the flow of information, determining who should (and should not) know certain information, is an integral part of being a department chair.

Now that you hold the position of chair, the list of constituents you are accountable to has grown considerably. You are now responsible for interfacing with students, upper administration, your faculty, students, departmental staff, admissions, donors, the registrar, marketing and communication, alumni, facilities, IT, and many others. Much of your new job involves making sure that these various and tenuously connected people know what they need to know and don't know what they don't need to know. When I first became chair, I remarked to a colleague that I felt like a big part of the job was being a telephone operator between various departmental stakeholders. In hindsight, this analogy fell short. It assumes the chair is a mere conduit through which information flows, a passive entity in the process.

In reality, a department chair is more like a diplomat. Rather than a conduit through which informational content flows unaffected, a department chair navigates the landscape of different stakeholders by negotiating and mediating conflicts, translating people's points of views and needs to others, and representing the interests of various groups simultaneously. In this way, you are an active facilitator rather than a passive medium of information.

Many new chairs fall into the trap of promising transparency as a cornerstone of their leadership. However, commitments to transparency often oversimplify the complex reality of a department chair's relationship to information. Transparency is a symbolic construct rather than a pragmatic leadership style (Gawley, 2008). Rather than striving for transparency, chairs should intentionally employ strategic disclosure. Hancock and Hellawell (2003) believe that strategic disclosure is such a fundamental part of the job that they describe department chairing as a game of "hide-and-seek."

You simply cannot (and should not) be transparent about everything. Everyone does not need to know everything, and part of your job is determining who needs to know what and how they need to have the message delivered. I've seen chairs who pass along almost every bit of news in an effort to maintain transparency. This approach does not take into account the substantial organizational cost of information overload (Eppler & Mengis, 2004). When you, as chair, share information with your department, you implicitly ask them to invest time reflecting on it and potentially to act.

This is simultaneously the most high-level and low-level function of being a chair. It is high level because of its importance and the difficulty in mastering it. Yet it is low level since, at its core, you have been doing this since you were a child. We all absorb copious amounts of information daily and selectively relay fragments of it based on diverse filters such as whether someone will find it interesting or if your relationship warrants sharing such knowledge. You may debrief with your significant other at the end of the day, but you do not share everything that happened in your day. You know how to choose which information is relevant.

As chair, you consume information, filter it, and curate an experience for others. There are various filters you can use to determine who needs what information: Who requires this information to excel at their job? Who possesses valuable insights to help you make decisions based on this information? Who will use discretion if they know this information? Who will be affected by the information? Who will exacerbate the problems associated with this information? Who might feel excluded if they are left uninformed? Who can you genuinely trust? Sorting through which filter is appropriate for each unique situation falls squarely on your shoulders.

This is much more an art than a science. Every stakeholder to whom you serve as a link harbors countless connections of their own. When you share any information, an intricate web of variables come into play. Every time you share any information, there are a wide array of variables that you cannot possibly account for. Instead of seeking a formula, try to approach this facet of the job with intentionality and humble self-awareness. Despite your best efforts, you will never perfect this art.

REFLECTIONS

1. What are some strategies or techniques you can use to improve your ability to navigate the complexity of information sharing in your new role?
2. What are the long-term consequences of excessive information sharing? What are some situations where transparency might be more important than strategic disclosure?

REFERENCES

Eppler, M. J., & Mengis, J. (2004). The concept of information overload: A review of literature from organization science, accounting, marketing, MIS, and related disciplines. *Information Society, 20*(5), 325–344. https://doi.org/10.1080/01972240490507974

Gawley, T. (2008). University administrators as information tacticians: Understanding transparency as selective concealment and instrumental disclosure. *Symbolic Interaction, 31*(2), 183–204. https://doi.org/10.1525/si.2008.31.2.183

Hancock, N., & Hellawell, D. E. (2003). Academic middle management in higher education: A game of hide and seek? *Journal of Higher Education Policy and Management, 25*(1), 5–12. https://doi.org/10.1080/13600800305739

Chapter 9

Boundary Spanning (Betwixt and Between)

The concept of *liminality*, as introduced by ethnographer Arnold van Gennep (1961) in his book *Rites of Passage*, explains the transformative nature of rituals marking life transitions. During such ceremonies, individuals undergo significant changes in their identities. *Liminality* refers to the transitional period between the commencement and culmination of the rite. At this stage, individuals have not yet attained the status associated with the completion of the ritual, but they also have not completely shed their previous identity from before entering the ritual state. Individuals in *liminality* can be described as existing "betwixt and between" fixed states.

The anthropologist Victor Turner (1969) popularized the concept of *liminality* by highlighting its presence not only in these rites of passage, but in various aspects of society, such as theatrical performances, social conflicts, pilgrimages, and festivals. Turner argued that *liminality* tends to be characterized by ambiguous power relations, a sense of in-betweenness, temporality, and symbolic expressions. As a result, *liminality* has since become a popular theory for analyzing organizational and managerial behavior (Söderlund & Borg, 2017).

Liminality is an especially relevant theoretical construct for understanding the professional identity of a department chair. The qualities of *liminality* are most apparent in the multifaceted roles chairs must assume as intermediaries between faculty and administrators. Department chairs straddle the boundaries of organizational identity categories. While technically both faculty and administrators, they do not possess the authority of administrators or the autonomy of faculty. Rather, they occupy an ambiguous middle ground where they are both and neither.

This in-betweenness is necessary, as one of the primary responsibilities of a department chair is to act as a boundary spanner (Berdrow, 2010) bridging the gap between faculty and administrators. A department chair is organizationally located "betwixt and between" faculty and administration. Turner (1967) described the *liminal* identity as "neither this or that and yet both" (p. 99). This is essentially the calling of a chair to traverse between the categorical borders within the university structure. This is possible only because of the *liminal* nature of the department chair position.

Effectively practicing this *liminal* identity is demanding. It requires not only conveying but also understanding and embodying the needs and limitations of both faculty and administration as they work toward their respective aims. Department chairs must straddle both professional identities and articulate faculty needs to administrators while effectively communicating administrative constraints to faculty.

I have witnessed chairs who, as a matter of principle, always align with faculty whenever a conflict arises. Unfortunately, such chairs often lose political capital with administrators, which can impact future advocacy efforts. Similarly, some chairs cannot muster the courage to push back on unreasonable administrative demands, resulting in a loss of trust from the faculty they represent.

Effective chairs maintain a sense of dual loyalty. They stand up to administrators when it is necessary, effectively communicate the constraints faced by administrators to faculty, and know when to pick their battles. They cultivate trust among faculty and administrators, ensuring that their positions are communicated honestly, thoroughly, and impartially to both parties.

The betwixt and betweenness of the chair position can be stressful. But it is also a space of possibility. Turner (1967) explained that liminal space is "a realm of pure possibility whence novel configurations of ideas and relations may arise" (p. 97). Allow the ambiguity of the position to free you to make the position yours. Embrace the uncertainty and possibility of your job, using it as an opportunity for creative problem-solving and fostering positive relationships. Ultimately, your success as chair lies in your ability to bridge boundaries, to build trust, and to foster a sense of unity both within your department and between your department and upper administration. Embrace this unique role to position your department to be successful.

REFLECTIONS

1. What are areas or subjects where faculty and administration are likely to be at odds in your university? In these areas, how can you effectively communicate and advocate for faculty needs to administrators while simultaneously conveying administrative constraints to faculty?

2. How can you embrace the learning opportunities and professional transformations that arise from navigating diverse perspectives as chair? How might this help you grow as a leader?

REFERENCES

Berdrow, I. (2010). King among kings: Understanding the role and responsibilities of the department chair in higher education. *Educational Management Administration & Leadership*, *38*(4), 499–514. https://doi.org/10.1177/1741143210368146

Söderlund, J., & Borg, E. (2017). Liminality in management and organization studies: Process, position and place. *International Journal of Management Reviews*, *20*(4), 880–902. https://doi.org/10.1111/ijmr.12168

Turner, V. (1967). *The forest of symbols: Aspects of the Ndembu ritual.* Cornell University Press.

Turner, V. (1969). *The ritual process: Structure and anti-structure.* Aldine Publishing.

van Gennep, A. (1961). *Rites of passage.* University of Chicago Press.

Chapter 10

A Chair's Inbox

The sudden deluge of emails that coincided with my becoming chair not only surprised me but also created a heightened sense of obligation to respond swiftly. Seemingly overnight, the number of emails I received increased fivefold. It was jarring and sudden. Additionally, many of the emails seemed to contain an increased sense of urgency. I was obligated to respond quickly because people were often waiting on me (and sometimes approval) to move forward items and tasks that were on their to-do list. At first this all made me feel more important. I was more networked to the functions of the university, and people who didn't even know me before now emailed me asking for approval.

I took pride in responding thoroughly and promptly to all emails, considering it a reflection of my dedication to the job. I was tethered to my inbox, answering emails as they came in and often maintaining a "zero unread email" status. My inbox essentially functioned as my daily "to-do" list. After about one year in the chair position, an unexpected set of circumstances led me to rethink my relationship with my inbox. Out of nowhere, I received a notification that my email digital storage was over the university approved limit. I didn't even know such a limit existed. I called the IT department, and they informed me that I had reached capacity a few weeks ago and some messages hadn't been sent. I was confused and asked for clarification, and they explained that emails don't send when an inbox hits storage capacity. They are instead sent to the draft folder to wait for more digital space to become available. Horrified, I clicked on the draft folder to try to make sense of the situation. I saw every email I had sent for the past three weeks. While I was still receiving emails, there were hundreds of them sitting in my draft folder—unsent!

I was mortified and embarrassed. I had been electronically incommunicado with everyone for several weeks. After a few days of playing catch-up, I came to realize that experience warranted some reflection on my relationship to my inbox. How was it possible that I had gone for three weeks without knowing that no one was receiving my emails? Why didn't anyone say anything? Where were the angry phone calls and complaints to the dean about my unresponsiveness? In retrospect, a few conversations over the past weeks made a bit more sense now. There were a few times I thought to myself, "Didn't we already handle this via email?" But overall, the impact of this seemed to be close to absolutely nothing. The department kept functioning just fine. Perhaps my emails were not as essential to the core mission of the university as I had imagined. I spent hours each day checking and answering emails, and maybe it was low-value work.

The drag of email in organizational life is well documented. The average professional spends 28 percent of their workday on it. Email has a direct impact on efficiency, particularly by how it affects leaders' capacities to achieve organizational goals (Rosen et al., 2019). Email has a tendency to turn leaders into managers. In his book *A World without Email*, Cal Newport (2021) explains that the efficiency drag caused by email is not simply due to the amount of time it takes. Instead, email structures much of our daily professional life. Frictionless messaging has created a workplace that is full of anxious back-and-forth chatter that overloads us. Our inbox comes to set our daily professional priorities. Rather than engaging in meaningful work directly tied to organizational values, we embody a productivity that is measured by our ability to successfully play email ping-pong about issues that others have decided should be important to us that day. Burkeman (2021) points out the irony of email is that being responsive to it only results in you getting more emails. It increases rather than decreases the size of your inbox.

There is no "one size fits all" solution to the amount of emails you receive as department chair. There is plenty of conflicting advice on how to handle email effectively. I would encourage you to peruse some of this advice as you figure out how to find a balance that optimizes productivity and minimizes the negative impact of email on your daily work life. This is not an invitation to ignore email, but instead to have a healthy relationship to it. By understanding the true value of email and its limitations, you can better allocate your attention and focus as chair to tasks that contribute to the success of your department and make you feel professionally fulfilled. Devote your precious chair energy to higher-value work that truly drives departmental success and your own well-being.

REFLECTIONS

1. Have you noticed an increase in emails since becoming department chair? Do you feel more pressure to be tethered to your inbox than you did before? What is your ideal relationship with your inbox as a department chair?
2. Considering the negative effects of email as well as its centrality in university life, how can you strike a balance between effectively managing email and also focusing on high-value tasks that contribute to the success of your department?

REFERENCES

Burkeman, O. (2021). *Four thousand weeks: Time management for mortals.* Farrar, Straus and Giroux.

Newport, C. (2021). *A world without email: Reimagining work in an age of communication overload.* Portfolio Publishing.

Rosen, C. C., Simon, L. S., Gajendran, R., Johnson, R. E., Lee, H. W., & Lin, S. H. (2019). Boxed in by your inbox. Implications of daily email demands for managers' leadership behaviors. *Journal of Applied Psychology, 104,* 19–33. https://doi.org/10.1037/apl0000343

Chapter 11

Department Meetings as More than Agenda Items

It has become almost cliché to complain about department meetings. Faculty assume they are going to be a waste of time. "This meeting could have been an email" became a meme for a reason. People generally approach departmental meetings as obligatory disruptions that interrupt the *real* work of being a faculty member. You are never more popular than when you cancel a scheduled department meeting. This kind of framing has negative psychological effects on employees and creates a productivity drag (Luong & Rogelberg, 2005). I don't necessarily blame faculty, as department meetings are often tedious, boring, inefficient, and driven by personalities rather than departmental values.

Meetings are significant organizational investments. We often think of them as costing two or so hours of the workday. The true organizational price is much higher considering the number of people in attendance. If you have twelve faculty members and three staff in attendance, the cost is thirty organizational hours (fifteen people at two hours each). That doesn't include the time spent preparing an agenda, scheduling a room, preparing visual aids, travel to campus, and so on.

If you are going to have departmental meetings (which I strongly believe you should), you need to have a clear vision of the return on your organizational investment. Much of the disdain for meetings seems to come from faculty and staff feeling as if not enough is accomplished to justify the organizational and personal cost. While I sympathize, I've found that this sentiment often stems from a narrow view of what it means to "accomplish" things at meetings (i.e., a policy revision, a vote on a particular issue, a committee report).

This view ignores the role that meetings play in organizational culture. Framing departmental meetings as an interruption of *real* work relies on an individualist assumption and ignores the important role that meetings play in shaping organizational culture. Their value lies in far more than the accomplishing of specific tasks on the agenda. Meetings are not simply places to get things done. Schwartzman (1989) explains meetings through an anthropological lens in her ethnographic study of the role of meetings in organizations. She explains that meetings are organizational sense-making events. Meetings "generate the appearance that reason and logical processes are guiding discussions and decisions . . . whereas they facilitate relationship negotiations, struggles and commentary" (p. 42). Department meetings provide cultural stages to enact shared values: committee reports act as reminders of the department's place in the larger university structure, voting enacts commitment to democratic norms, the small talk before the meeting is a performance of collegiality, taking turns speaking reinforces the principle that everyone's voice is valuable, the approval of minutes reminds us of the importance of being faithful to honoring past agreements, and so on. As chair, you hold power to redefine the value of departmental meetings in the eyes of faculty and staff.

Since departmental meetings (re)inscribe cultural norms and values, it is important that they be led in ways that are productive. Bad departmental meetings (re)inscribe bad cultural norms. You now lead the department and have the authority to set the cultural norms they contribute to. While it may be tempting (and certainly easier) to simply follow historical precedents, you should instead approach and plan departmental meetings through the lens of values and vision. You can use meetings to create opportunities to strengthen cultural bonds and to align actions with a shared vision of what the department should be.

To gain buy-in from the department and to make meetings more effective, take a proactive approach. Engage with faculty and staff individually to solicit feedback. Share your values-based approach and inquire about their thoughts on departmental meetings. Ask what they find most and least valuable and encourage them to express how they see these meetings contributing to departmental culture. Their specific suggestions will be helpful in shaping future meetings in productive ways.

As the leader of your department, you know that leading departmental meetings is a key function of your role. It may be challenging, but it is worth the effort to guide your department toward more engaging and purposeful meetings. Given the importance of this task, the next few chapters will focus on various angles to create departmental meetings that are sources of collaboration and meaningful progress rather than obligatory functions that faculty begrudgingly attend.

REFLECTIONS

1. What are some things that your previous chair did in department meetings that you want to carry forward? What are some things that you want to change? What are the cultural values you see enacted historically in your department meetings?
2. What are some potential challenges you might face when trying to lead departmental meetings from a place of values and vision? How can you overcome these challenges to ensure that your leadership positively impacts these meetings?

REFERENCES

Luong, A., & Rogelberg, S. G. (2005). Meetings and more meetings: The relationship between meeting load and the daily well-being of employees. *Group Dynamics: Theory, Research, and Practice*, 9(1), 58–67. https://doi.org/10.1037/1089-2699.9.1.58

Schwartzman, H. B. (1989). *The meeting: Gathering in organizations and communities*. Springer Publishing.

Chapter 12

Creating an Agenda for a Department Meeting

When I first became a department chair, I didn't initially grasp the importance of having a well-structured agenda for running effective meetings. Some of this was because the chair who immediately preceded me was a theater professor with a gift for performance. He had charisma, charm, and presence and always seemed to know what to say at the right moment. This set of characteristics was on full display at these meetings. After five years of watching him successfully navigate these meetings, I mistakenly assumed that persona and performance were the necessary ingredients for successfully leading a meeting.

If you're blessed with a magnetic personality, then maybe you can rely on your performance and communicative skills to effectively lead meetings. Most of us don't have that gift, and I soon came to realize that a well-thought-through meeting agenda was what I would have to rely on. This doesn't diminish the importance of presence. But even gifted actors put in significant "backstage" work, rehearsing and memorizing lines.

In the previous chapter we discussed the ways in which meetings are stages for cultural dramas, shaping and being shaped by organizational values. An agenda is more than simply a list of topics to discuss. An agenda serves as the script for your meeting, providing you the opportunity to carefully plan in ways that give departmental members opportunities to engage in cultural performances that are generative and positive. Drawing from my experience of crafting meeting agendas for eleven years, here are some suggestions, each justified by its connection to specific cultural values.

Some of these may already be happening in your department meetings. If they are, then this list can provide you an opportunity to reflect on why you do them and what kind of cultural knowledge they generate. Others may not work based on some department variables. If that is the case, consider why they won't work and what that might tell you about your departmental culture.

- *Request suggestions for agenda items in a departmental email at least a week before the meeting.* Ask people to provide those suggestions at least a week in advance of the meeting. After faculty members send in their suggestions, write the agenda and send it back to your faculty. When distributing the agenda, ask your faculty to review it. In a friendly tone, ask if you've forgotten anything important. This practice communicates to the department that the agenda belongs to the entire department, not simply to the chair.
- *The order of agenda items matters.* Save things that will likely generate a lot of conversation for later in the meeting. Also, stagger the order of who talks. If there are several items that will require you to do a lot of talking, make sure you put agenda items that have others doing most of the talking between them. This will ensure that the meeting has an ethos of conversation rather than a monologue.
- *Keep a running list of staff and faculty accomplishments in the department.* One of the first agenda items should be a congratulatory acknowledgment of these accomplishments. Be liberal with what you include in this section. It doesn't matter the size of the accomplishment. Visibility and public praise from peers go a long way in making people feel valued. This contributes to a departmental culture that appreciates the contributions of its members.
- *Include the time you anticipate spending on each agenda item.* Stay flexibile with how long you spend on any one item, but do so with the agenda as a guide. It also allows you to move on from items that are taking too much time. You can always say, "We're already five minutes over the time allotted for this item, so let's table the rest of our conversation for the next meeting." Allotting specific time frames for each agenda item communicates to participants that you've thoughtfully considered how much of everyone's time should be committed to each item and that you plan to move through the agenda in a linear and orderly fashion.
- *Include a section whereby those who serve on committees that extend beyond the department (faculty senate, college council, provost search committee, university budget committee, etc.) can report on the activities of those committees.* This keeps department members connected to the larger enterprise of the university and allows them to understand how the department operates as part of a university system. Unlike hallway conversations, discussing university business at department meetings allows all members to communally engage in sense-making efforts about how the department operates as part of the university system.

These five suggestions are ones that have worked for me. Do not accept these at face value and automatically adopt them; instead consider this an invitation to think strategically and conscientiously about how to develop an agenda that makes meetings productive while also allowing participants to embody a healthy departmental culture.

REFLECTIONS

1. Consider the idea that a meeting agenda serves as a script for a department meeting. How does this concept impact your approach to planning and conducting meetings?
2. Are there any variables in your department that may affect the implementation of any of the suggested strategies? How can you adapt or tailor these strategies to better suit your departmental culture?

Chapter 13

Cultivating Constructive Dialogue in Department Meetings

The approval of the minutes alone took forty-five minutes in the worst department meeting I have ever led as chair. That is not an exaggeration intended to make a point. A senior member of the department, known for causing obstructions, revealed that she had been secretly recording previous meetings and would continue to do so. She attempted to remove one of our colleagues from a committee chair position and informed us she would be taking over the position herself. She dominated the conversation by talking for long stretches and refused to leave space for others to speak. Finally, she accused the entire department of conspiring against her because we were all threatened by her brilliance. In retrospect, I wish I would have handled the meeting differently. I was taken off guard and did not do my job to keep the meeting on track. There were signs that this faculty member was becoming unhappy, but I was not expecting this kind of public meltdown. After the meeting, almost everyone in the entire department reached out to me to express how unhappy they were that one person derailed the meeting in this way. Several reached out to the dean, who called an emergency department meeting to discuss the incident with us.

The previous two chapters focused on the benefits of cultivating healthy organizational culture through how you approach department meetings. In the best of cases, things go according to plan and the meetings are where members collectively embody a vision of what an effective, efficient, and ethical department looks like. I can almost feel you roll your eyes while reading this. I promise that I am not an out-of-touch idealist about department meetings. I understand that they rarely go according to plan.

Most meetings are (thankfully) not as chaotic as the one I shared. But the story above is a testament to the fact that it is usually personalities that lead to unproductive meetings. You can craft a solid agenda and have the best of intentions, but department meetings involve people with various temperaments, motivations, goals, and quirks. In academia, some common personality traits that may derail these meetings include those who believe they know more than everyone else and feel the need to show it, those who want to provide a multigenerational oral history for every decision, faculty who want to dominate conversations, participants who want to play "devil's advocate" for every agenda item, and colleagues who believe they should be running the meeting.

The difficult meeting recounted above had one positive outcome; it forced my department to have an open conversation about future meetings. The experience was so unpleasant for everyone that we were compelled to engage in explicit conversation about what we wanted our department meetings to be in the future. This type of talk, known as metadiscourse, is when people or groups communicate about communication for a pragmatic purpose (Craig, 2005). This explicit talk about talk plays a key role in maintaining relational health. It allows for an intentionality in the communicative rules that govern relationships. Unspoken norms become spoken commitments.

After that dreadful meeting, my department decided we wanted more structure to our department meetings. This involved participants raising hands and being called on by the chair before speaking. Also, the group decided that the chair should have the freedom to ask people to yield the floor if they speak for too long and that the overriding ethos should be that everyone gets a chance to speak on a topic once before anyone can comment twice. We discussed and voted on these guidelines, and it has been successful. These are not groundbreaking protocols, but the point is that all the meeting norms were informal up to that point. The absence of collectively agreed-upon guidelines left a lot of room for personalities to dominate the meeting space.

Constant recommitment to the agreed-upon norms is key to ensuring they have the desired effect. At the beginning of most meetings, I remind everyone that we've pledged ourselves to having these standards guide our communication. That doesn't mean we enact these principles perfectly at every meeting, but it sets a benchmark and allows participants to make efforts to redirect counterproductive communication in meetings. Counteractive communication is talk that redirects communication to remind the group to re-commit to them when it seems things are getting out of hand.

Assessment of what is and is not working is equally important. After meetings, I informally request feedback on how departmental members feel we've done with the meeting. I've started several meetings with some disclaimer like, "After the last meeting, I heard from several people that they don't think we did a good job turn-taking at our last meeting. So let's be more conscientious of that today." At first I was worried this would seem infantilizing, but

I've always gotten very positive feedback when I've done this and it seems to work.

The process of setting intention through metadiscourse, assessing, and then recommitting can create a more structured and purposeful meeting environment with a commitment to providing everyone equal opportunities to contribute. By openly addressing the variable of personalities in department meetings, a department can embrace the dynamics of a diverse group while also working toward a common goal.

REFLECTIONS

1. How have you seen previous chairs handle unexpected or disruptive behavior from meeting attendees? Which strategies seemed to work and which did not?
2. How intentional has your department been about the communicative rules within department meetings? Will your department generally be open to being more explicit? How will you handle any pushback or resistance?

REFERENCE

Craig, R. T. (2005). How we talk about how we talk: Communication theory in the public interest. *Journal of Communication, 55*(4), 659–667. https://doi.org/10.1111/j.1460-2466.2005.tb03015.x

Chapter 14

Effectively Participating in College-Wide Chairs' Meetings

The last few chapters have focused on how to effectively lead department meetings. Now, let's turn our attention to another recurring meeting that likely holds a spot on your calendar: the all-college chair meeting with the dean. These gatherings, most likely happening either monthly or biweekly depending on your dean's preference, are valuable opportunities for you as a chair. They allow you to contextualize your department's activities within the broader college and university context.

During these meetings, you will gain insight into enrollment trends, college/university initiatives, donor activity, budget updates, and changes in policies and processes. Much of the information covered will later become agenda items for your department meetings. You will be responsible for figuring out how these updates apply to your department and effectively conveying them to your faculty.

Moreover, these meetings also have a performative element, providing you with a chance to represent both yourself and your department to the dean and to your fellow chairs. Departments have reputations, and your performance at these meetings plays a vital role in how others in the college perceive the energy and collaboration potential of your department.

Over the past decade, I've attended dozens of these meetings, and I have observed that certain behaviors do not leave a good impression with fellow chairs or deans. These actions not only annoy me personally but are also common complaints I have heard from other chairs and deans. To help you make the most of these gatherings and foster a positive image of your department, consider the following suggestions:

- *Avoid monopolizing the conversation.* In more than a decade of these meetings, I've never been in one that ended early because there wasn't enough participation. You do not need to say something to keep conversation going. Do not contribute unnecessarily. In every chair group there are a few who dominate conversation, and everyone else finds it off-putting. Contribute thoughtfully and be intentional with your input. Asking questions is encouraged as it shows active engagement and a concern for the input of others.
- *Stick to topics that affect everyone.* There are few things more grating in these meetings than when one chair wants to get into the minutia of their schedule or their budget and it is inapplicable to many in the room. It is a waste of everyone's time. These kinds of issues should be handled in one-on-one meetings with the dean.
- *Be conscious of the political landscape.* Different departments have different resource allocations and needs. Be conscientious about how other departments might be implicated when you share. For example, perhaps your department is running a search, and another department has recently lost a faculty line. You might flippantly complain that HR has not gotten back to you approving the candidate pool yet. This might seem innocuous, but it could create division with the department that lost a faculty line as well as put your dean in an awkward position.
- *Act interested and attentive.* This may seem basic, but I mention it only because I have seen plenty of chairs do the opposite. Maintain eye contact, actively listen, and refrain from using your phone and working on unrelated tasks (like answering email) during the meeting.
- *Avoid airing departmental grievances.* These meetings are not the time to complain to your dean about decisions they have made or things you feel are unfair. It puts everyone in an uncomfortable position. Remember that there might be context that you are unaware of that your dean cannot discuss in an open meeting. Those are conversations best had in one-on-one meetings with your dean. It preserves your relationship with the dean and is more likely to yield a sympathetic ear.
- *Participate in problem-solving.* If something is working in your department, do not be proprietary about it. Share it as it seems relevant. If another chair discusses a problem, share if your department has a solution that's been working. Be a team player.

I generally enjoy these meetings and have usually found them to be quite beneficial. As a chair, the role can sometimes feel isolating. These gatherings provide an opportunity to collaborate with others who understand the challenges. By following the above suggestions, you can make the most out of these meetings while also positioning your department and your leadership as positive influences within your college.

REFLECTIONS

1. What are your initial impressions of all-chairs meetings? What are you hoping to get out of them?
2. If you have already been to some, who do you perceive as positive and negative contributors in those meetings? What behaviors are guiding your judgment?

Chapter 15

Setting Goals

"Now that I've approved you hiring for this position, your number one goal needs to be enrollment. That is your priority. You have the hire, you don't have any excuses to not increase your number of majors." The urgency of my dean's directive certainly caught my attention. I had never had a dean so explicitly order my professional priorities.

The landscape for universities has changed significantly, and the role of a department chair has changed along with it. In decades past, a department chair's job was more akin to an academic gardener or an academic ambassador. They were there to preserve academic standards, to guide students, to be a thought leader, and to be collegial. This is hardly the case anymore, as the role of chair has increasingly become an executive function as chairs are now much more likely to be evaluated based on their ability to manage departmental productivity, to bring in donors, to stay in budget, and to hit enrollment benchmarks (De Boer et al., 2010). You might bemoan this shift, but it is the reality, and it is unlikely to change given many of the challenges that higher education is facing.

While the focus on these functions might not quite match with the idealistic version of the academic life that you had when you applied for graduate school, there is still a nobility to it. The landscape of higher education is not particularly pleasant at this moment, and by paying attention to these "executive" concerns you protect the faculty and staff in your department. Effectively embodying an executive mindset decreases the chances that your department suffers the loss of faculty or staff lines or a substantial cut to the operating budget. Being successful in these executive areas is important, especially since they are likely the criteria for how you will be formally evaluated.

Toward that end, it is worthwhile that you set ambitious but achievable goals for the academic year in these executive areas. These should be both in areas of personal growth and professional progress. Do not base these goals solely on outcome-based targets, which can be influenced by external variables beyond your control. For example, you could set a goal to increase the number of majors by 7 percent. There are so many variables outside of your control. Enrollment at your university might drop by 2 to 3 percent, so the goal you've set might be unattainable even if you do everything right.

It is instead beneficial to set goals that are based on productivity rather than outcomes. Instead of a goal to increase enrollment by a certain amount, you can set a goal to revamp your marketing material or your approach to recruiting events. Instead of deciding if you want to increase your department's grant money by a certain amount, you could set a goal to create a mentorship program for faculty who want to pursue grants. These are tangible, achievable, and measurable goals that are tied to factors you can more easily manage. While they are not outcome based, they increase the likelihood of outcome-based success in these areas. They are also tied to the executive functions of your chair position and thereby increase your chances of being evaluated as "successful" in your position.

These goals should stem from your values as well as your departmental strengths and weaknesses. What is your vision for what your department should be and how does that intersect with what your department does well and struggles with? Understanding your vision for the department and aligning it with its inherent capacities will yield the most significant returns.

Once you've determined what goals you want to focus on, you should communicate them to your department. Presenting these goals in a department meeting and inviting faculty feedback fosters collaboration and feedback. Ask your faculty if these goals seem attainable, if they believe they should be prioritized, and if they will support you. Not only does consulting faculty in setting executive-level goals enhance organizational effectiveness (Teo & Low, 2016), but faculty also appreciate a chair who prioritizes these areas, as it allows them to focus on their core teaching and research responsibilities.

Achieving these goals not only enhances organizational efficiency but also provides opportunities for you to tout notable accomplishments on your annual review. You can thus effectively respond to the evolving landscape of higher education, position yourself to have a successful term as chair, and serve your department.

REFLECTIONS

1. Do you notice a shift toward chairs having more executive roles? How does this shift intersect with your experience so far as chair? How can you turn this into measurable and achievable goals?
2. Reflect on your department's strengths and weaknesses. How does your vision align with them and how might you turn that reflection in to specific goals?

REFERENCES

De Boer, H., Goedegebuure, L., & Meek, V. L. (2010). The changing nature of academic middle management: A framework for analysis. In V. L. Meek, L. Goedegebuure, R. Santiago, & T. Carvalho (Eds.), *The changing dynamics of higher education middle management* (pp. 229–242). Springer.

Teo, T. C., & Low, K. C. P. (2016). The impact of goal setting on employee effectiveness to improve organizational effectiveness: Empirical study of high-tech company in Singapore. *Journal of Business & Economic Policy, 3*(1), 1–16. https://ssrn.com/abstract=3088132

Chapter 16

The Power Paradox of an Academic Middle Manager

When I first became chair, I noticed that people seemed to laugh at my jokes a bit louder than they had before. I doubt that my change in position had helped me unlock some hidden comedic skills. I will admit that at first my newfound status was a little intoxicating. I don't want to exaggerate the amount of power that comes from being a department chair. As we discussed in previous reflections, compared to a managerial position in other industries, an academic department chair's authority is constrained. I don't want you to think I have an unrealistic sense of ego. I'm aware that as chair I am in middle management. With that caveat in mind, it is still important to note that there is a degree of power associated with the position. Your power as chair is through your ability to affect others through unequal control over limited resources (Magee & Galinsky, 2008) such as the departmental budget, faculty teaching schedules, and annual reviews. Power is a ubiquitous and inescapable force woven into our social interactions, which explains why my colleagues might find me a bit funnier than I used to be.

One particularly interesting element of power is that it not only affects the interpersonal dynamics between people but also changes the person who wields it. Several research studies have made this connection. For example, individuals who are primed to feel powerful systematically underestimate the physical size of others (Yap, Mason, & Ames, 2013). Another study (Hogeveen et al., 2014) found that subjects induced to feel powerful experienced difficulty mirroring the actions of others. They effectively found it harder to identify with those whose behavior they were trying to model.

When people become managers, they are granted a degree of power, which by its nature changes them. Keltner (2017) explains this as the "power paradox." The paradox is that those who rise to management positions usually do so by being able to connect with others. People who can empathize with others are the kind of people who get promoted. Newly promoted managers then lose the very abilities that secured them a leadership position. It becomes harder to identify and empathize with the people you are now tasked to lead when you have power over them.

The larger the power divide between you and others, the more pronounced the power paradox. For this reason, you are probably most in danger of experiencing the power paradox with staff, students, and part-time faculty. It is easier to discount the effects of your decisions when the people affected are at a safe distance from you in the organizational chart. These are also the people who are least likely to complain to you about how your decisions affect them. I've found that adjuncts are far less likely to protest about when a class is scheduled. I imagine this is because it is much easier to fire them than full-time faculty (imagine assigning a MWF 8:00 a.m. class to a senior faculty member—I assume you'd very quickly be reminded of the inconvenience of teaching at that time). A hesitancy to object can exacerbate the power paradox as it becomes even easier to discount the effects of your decisions when you are not forced to confront them.

Recognizing the inherent power that comes from being a department chair (even if limited in scope) is crucial for avoiding the potential pitfalls of the power paradox. You must acknowledge that power can subtly alter your perceptions and behavior in ways that you are not aware of. To mitigate the effects of the power paradox, practice leading from self-awareness and humility. Understand that power can change your perspective and make it challenging to empathize with those you lead. Stay connected with your colleagues, particularly staff, students, and part-time faculty, who may not feel as if they have as much of a voice as others. Encourage open communication and create an environment where their feedback is valued. Remember that the power paradox affects everyone in a leadership position and acknowledging its influence is the first step toward leading with empathy and understanding.

REFLECTIONS

1. Have you noticed power dynamics influencing your relationships with colleagues since you've become chair?
2. Who is a leader in your university who you believe effectively navigates the power paradox? How do you see them doing that? How can you mirror those practices in your own leadership?

REFERENCES

Hogeveen, J., Inzlicht, M., & Obhi, S. S. (2014). Power changes how the brain responds to others. *Journal of Experimental Psychology: General, 143*(2), 755–762. https://doi.org/10.1037/a0033477

Keltner, D. K. (2017). *The power paradox: How we gain and lose influence.* Penguin Books.

Magee, J. C., & Galinsky, A. D. (2008, November 9). The self-reinforcing nature of social hierarchy: Origins and consequences of power and status. *IACM 21st Annual Conference Paper.* https://doi.org/10.2139/ssrn.1298493

Yap, A. J., Mason, M. F., & Ames, D. R. (2013). The powerful size others down: The link between power and estimates of others' size. *Journal of Experimental Social Psychology, 49*(3), 591–594. https://doi.org/10.1016/j.jesp.2012.10.003

Chapter 17

Big-Picture Budgeting

In my department chair orientation, a seasoned department chair shared his approach to budgeting. He delegated the responsibility to the office secretary because he found it too complex and he "wasn't good with numbers." I had been a department chair for only a week, but even then, I was almost offended by this suggestion. It didn't seem fair to offload one of the most important responsibilities of the position on to someone with a lower salary and far less organizational protection. Managing the departmental budget effectively is your responsibility as chair and it is one of the most important functions of your job. Despite the significance of the task, chairs are often "thrown in the deep end" and expected to figure the budget out. Training often consists of being shown how to log in and navigate the software (information that is forgotten almost immediately upon leaving the training).

Given its critical role in your success, the next few reflections will focus on your responsibility in relationship to budget management. While the next two chapters cover budget structures and specific suggestions, this chapter focuses on how to philosophically approach your new budgetary responsibilities.

Budgeting can be daunting to new department chairs, as they may feel more comfortable when focusing on the aspects of the position associated with soft skills (e.g., negotiating, hiring, leading meetings). Managing a departmental budget is instead often framed as an intimidating encounter with math, finance, and new software, especially for chairs without backgrounds in these areas. The stakes feel high when money is involved, and the fear of making mistakes can be overwhelming.

Nonetheless, managing a departmental budget doesn't have to be overly complicated. You do not need to have an MBA, a CPA license, or even experience managing an organizational budget to do this well. A departmental budget does not involve any high-level financial knowledge. If you can manage your own personal budget, then you can certainly handle a departmental budget. Common sense, attentiveness, and transparency are all the tools you need to do this part of the job well.

The key is to reframe this responsibility. Approach budget management with a conscientious understanding of where the money for the budget comes from—primarily student tuition. While there are other sources of funds (donors, government, grants, etc.), the primary source of your departmental budget is money that students have entrusted you with to allocate toward their education. Your primary job is not departmental accountant, but instead steward of the tuition money that comes from loans, scholarships, jobs students work on the weekends, and accounts that parents have been contributing to for years.

Managing the budget is an opportunity to determine departmental priorities based on how to best use the resources you've been entrusted with. Since you cannot fund everything, decisions must be made. Faculty development funds or new marketing materials? New equipment or renovating space? Serving pizza at the student event or a new computer for a faculty member? These kinds of choices are about more than dollars and cents (although they are about that too). They come from a deliberative process about how to best allocate precious resources. Managing a departmental budget is fundamentally about managing departmental priorities.

As such, it is best to use budget management processes to embody and showcase the leadership principles that are most important to you. Accept the budgeting process as an opportunity to lead with proactiveness, integrity, and clarity. Do not get overwhelmed by feeling you need to remember every budget line index number or software shortcut. Those things will come to you with time. Instead, focus on how your approach to managing the budget can align with your leadership principles and values.

Lastly, be open in your budget decision-making process. Be prepared and willing to explain why you approved or disapproved budget items. While you do not need to consult everyone on every decision, seeking advice from trusted individuals when a budget decision intersects with their expertise or responsibilities is wise. This can instill a sense of departmental ownership and provide valuable perspectives for your decisions.

By keeping the big picture front and center, you can transform one of the most anxiety-producing aspects of the job into a powerful opportunity to showcase the type of leader you aspire to be for your department.

REFLECTIONS

1. How have you approached your budget responsibilities thus far? Have you found the process overwhelming? What are the specific aspects of the budget that cause the most uncertainty?
2. How will you approach budget management and what steps will you take to ensure you are a responsible financial steward of your department? How do you see your leadership values intersecting with the budget management process?

Chapter 18

Your University's Budget Model and Where You Fit In

To successfully navigate your budgetary responsibilities as chair, a clear understanding of your role within the university's budget structure is essential. I did not realize this was something to consider until I had a second chair appointment at a new university. Initially I assumed that university budget processes were standard. But I have since come to realize this is not the case as each university where I have served as chair had a distinct budget model. Each of these budget models had different assumptions about the chair's role in the budget process.

In my first term as chair, I operated in a **zero-based budget model**. In this model, every department started the annual budget process with $0 in all their indexes. My job was to build the annual budget from the bottom up, accounting for everything the department might need in the upcoming fiscal year. I then presented a proposed budget to the dean. We then negotiated the budget line items ("Do you really need $$$ for office supplies?"). The back-and-forth would go on for a few weeks. A chair had to be aware of all (potential) activities. You had to know your budget forward and backward, because if you forgot to include something in your projections, you wouldn't be able to fund it. Being a strong advocate and a negotiator was necessary for successfully navigating this budget model.

In my second term as chair, I operated in an **incremental budget model**. In this model the annual budget is based on the previous year's budget with small tweaks. The budget was loaded in without any input from the chair. There was usually a slight adjustment to account for increasing salaries or inflation, but this increase was standard for all departments. It usually amounted to a 2 percent increase from the previous year. The amount of money was fixed. There was no petitioning for more. It was a chair's job to ensure that all departmental activities stayed within the allocated amount. Successful budget management amounted to controlling costs and setting priorities. If you wanted to fund something not included in the budget, then you had to pull it from money allocated elsewhere.

My current university utilizes a **responsibility-centered budget model**. This is an incentive-based model where units are rewarded for performance. The college absorbs much of the annual variability of this model, so we're a bit protected as a department from large swings in the short term. I'll spare all the details, but generally the more revenue a unit brings in through full-time equivalents (FTEs) and majors, the more funds you have. The overriding principle is that units get to keep a portion of what they bring to the university. Successful budget management relies on generating revenue. This involves careful attention to recruiting, retention, and marketing the department. This model tends to lead departments to find ways to "game" the reimbursement model.

Centralized budgeting and **activity-based budgeting** are other popular models (Lees et al., 2019). Given my lack of experience with them, I cannot offer much insight about the experience of chairs using these models. There is much more that can be said about each of these budget models, but our purpose here is not to go in-depth on the pros and cons of each. It is instead to reflect on how much a university's budget model affects what it means to be a good budget manager. If you want to be good at this part of the job, then it is vital that you understand how the university budget process necessitates certain competencies.

Navigating budgetary responsibilities as a chair requires adaptability and an understanding of the budget models in place at your university. Based on my experience with different models, I have come to appreciate the diverse skills needed to successfully navigate the budget process at different universities. As you step into the role of budget manager, take the initiative to understand the budget process at your university and your place within that process. Seek advice from fellow chairs about how to adapt to the unique challenges and opportunities that different budget models offer.

REFLECTIONS

1. What is your university budget model? What do you see as the strengths and weaknesses of this model? What specific skill sets are valuable in this model?

2. What steps will you take to adapt to the unique challenges and opportunities presented by your university's budget model? Who are some people you can seek advice and insights from to enhance your budget management skills?

REFERENCE

Lees, N. D., Malik, D. J., & Williams, J. R. (2019). *Budgeting basics for new academic chairpersons*. Academic Chairpersons Conference Proceedings. https://newprairiepress.org/accp/2019/keynote/1

Chapter 19

Budgeting Strategies and Tactics

We have covered budgeting a bit more globally in the last two reflections. Here we will instead get a bit more granular and focus on specific practices that are applicable regardless of the budget model your university uses. Below are suggestions based on what I have learned from managing a departmental budget for the past ten years.

- *Stay informed and proactive.* It is essential to periodically review an up-to-date budget. Once a week, our departmental office associate sends me an updated budget. Reviewing it is the first thing I do on Monday mornings. This ensures that when unanticipated budget questions come up in conversations, my information is never more than six days old. It also keeps the budget in the forefront of my mind.
- *Understand budget lines and restrictions.* Budgets consist of various lines, each designated for specific purposes. It is crucial to understand what each budget line entails and the restrictions associated with it. Distinguishing between fixed budget lines (e.g., salary, fringe benefits, contracts) and variable budget lines (e.g., operating budget, travel account) helps you allocate resources more strategically and responsibly.
- *Have responsible spending and surplus.* Budgeting should not be an exercise in simply spending for the sake of utilizing the entire budget. Instead, focus on responsible spending that aligns with the department's objectives and priorities. Even if there is no carryover across fiscal years, do not go on a spending spree just to draw down your budget to $0. I heard a dean call this the "golden paper clip" problem. Some department chairs will spend money on anything if they think they will lose it. Buying gold paper clips is not being a good steward of your university's resources. Remember that ultimately your budget consists of student tuition money.

- *Manage the timing of your spending.* It generally makes sense that at a quarter through the fiscal year, you should have spent about 25 percent of your budget, at halfway through you should have spent 50 percent of your budget, and so on.
- *Embrace transparency and integrity.* Maintaining integrity and transparency throughout the budget process is vital. Be clear with people in your department who have spending privileges about what role you want to play in their purchasing process. Establish guidelines for when you should be consulted and when they have the freedom to spend within certain limits. This transparent approach fosters trust and ensures that everyone is aligned with the department's financial goals.
- *Wait for funds to come in before spending them.* I have only overspent my budget once. This happened because of an administrative office promising they would cover the expenses for an unanticipated opportunity. I then approved the medium-sized expense based on their pledge to offset it. After we had spent the money, the office reversed its decision. The lesson learned from this is not to spend departmental funds based on promises. Wait until the money hits your account.
- *Ask for faculty development fund request estimates at the beginning of the fiscal year.* If your department has a fund for faculty development (e.g., conference travel), at the beginning of the year ask all faculty to provide an estimate for how much of this money they might request. This will allow you to have a rough plan for how to disburse that money over the course of the year. This will ensure fairness while also allowing you to maximize the impact of those funds.
- *Ask questions.* Do not be embarrassed to admit you do not know something. Embrace an ethos of humility and a willingness to learn rather than feeling the need to showcase your competence.

Use these suggestions to develop the necessary budget management skills to contribute to the overall financial health of your department and university. Effective budget management necessitates not only understanding your global budget philosophy but also implementing it in your daily decision-making process. Balancing these dual foci will enable you to keep the focus on efficiently and effectively managing the budget while also practicing responsible stewardship of departmental resources.

REFLECTIONS

1. How do you think of the budgeting process after exploring these principles and suggestions? How will you approach budget management

and what steps will you take to ensure you are a responsible financial steward of your department?
2. What are the biggest unanswered questions you have about how the university budget works and how that effects your departmental budget? Who can you ask who might be able to help you better understand?

Chapter 20

Grade Appeals as Pedagogical Process

When I assumed the role of department chair, I was taken aback by the considerable time and energy devoted to grade appeals. I had assumed they would constitute a form of clerical labor that would pop up from time to time. I soon came to realize that this was simply not the case. Student grade appeals can be complex and emotionally charged, requiring a nuanced approach. They are often a tangle of variables such as faculty expertise, student rights, academic freedom, the consumer model of university education, institutional policies, scholarly rigor, organizational hierarchy, and faculty ego.

It took me several years to realize that the best way to approach student grade appeals is to understand them as a part of the pedagogical process. They are not simply mechanisms to adjudicate the grading process of a particular instructor. The grade appeal is itself an extension of that educational experience. With that framework in mind, as chair you should treat them as opportunities for learning and growth.

When a student reaches out to me to dispute a grade, I arrange a one-on-one meeting (preferably in person). In this, I first provide space for the student to explain their side of the story and how they understand the shortcomings in the grading process. Once they have shared, I ask if they have spoken to their instructor about the matter. Often, they have not. They have come directly to the chair because they are intimidated, or they do not know how to have the conversation.

This is where the grade appeal intersects with the learning process. Student reticence to initiating these kinds of conversations is unsurprising. Social anxiety among college students is prevalent and its growth over the past twelve years has outpaced all other mental health concerns measured by the Center for Collegiate Mental Health (2023). Social anxiety can make it difficult for students to initiate conversations with their peers, let alone an instructor with an advanced degree and the power to fail them in a class.

While these conversations might induce discomfort in students, having them requires the same kind of communication skills that are quite helpful in building careers (Priyadarshini, 2022). Rather than directly intervening in the grade dispute at this point, I try to use this as an opportunity to coach the student in self-advocacy. Proficiency in self-advocacy often correlates to increased confidence and academic performance (Cano-Daly et al., 2015), resulting in higher grade point averages and graduation rates (Pfeifer et al., 2021).

I explain to the student that it is premature for me to get involved, as the initial step is to speak with their instructor. I then spend time explaining how to do this. I help them figure out how to diplomatically and respectfully share their concern with their instructor. We talk through how to do this in a clear, friendly, and respectful way. I frame the conversations as good "practice," reminding them that in their careers they may regularly have disagreements about assessment with authority figures. I may assist them in writing an email to the instructor asking to have a conversation. I will also rehearse the conversations with students if they want. To provide a degree of safety, I assure them that I will be there to help them sort through the next steps if this conversation does not yield the results they are hoping for.

This pedagogical approach is dually beneficial. First, it helps students learn valuable skills. Secondly, it tends to resolve students' concerns. Around 90 percent of these complaints get resolved following this approach.

I recommend informing the faculty member whose student you met with that you have spoken with the student and they should expect a conversation. You do not need to get into specifics, but you want to avoid the appearance that you are talking about faculty behind their backs to students.

By recognizing grade appeals as intrinsic to the pedagogical process, you can harness a valuable opportunity to nurture student self-advocacy skills. Guiding students through constructive dialogue with instructors and fostering a supportive environment for communication allows you to not only empower students to address their concerns but also equips them with essential life skills. This pedagogical response not only benefits individual students by resolving issues but also contributes to the student's academic success while simultaneously fostering a culture of open communication and growth within the department.

REFLECTIONS

1. Have you noticed increases in social anxiety among college students in recent years? What are other areas of your job as chair that may be affected by increased social anxiety among students?

2. How can the suggestion of addressing grade appeals as learning opportunities transfer to an overall approach to handling academic challenges and conflicts?

REFERENCES

Cano-Daly, M., Vaccaro, A., & Newman, B. (2015). College student narratives about learning and using self-advocacy skills. *Journal of Postsecondary Education and Disability, 28*(2), 213–227. https://files.eric.ed.gov/fulltext/EJ1074673.pdf

Center for Collegiate Mental Health. (2023, January). *2022 Annual Report* (Publication No. STA 23-168). https://ccmh.psu.edu/assets/docs/2022%20Annual%20Report.pdf

Marijolovic, K. (2023, January 25). *Trauma and social anxiety are growing mental-health concerns for college students.* https://www.chronicle.com/article/trauma-and-social-anxiety-are-growing-mental-health-concerns-for-college-students?sra=true

Pfeifer, M. A., Reiter, E. M., Cordero, J. J., & Stanton, J. D. (2021). Inside and out: Factors that support and hinder the self-advocacy of undergraduates with ADHD and/or specific learning disabilities in STEM. *CBE—Life Sciences Education, 20*(2). https://doi.org/10.1187/cbe.20-06-0107

Priyadarshini, S. (2022). It's nice to be nice at work: Role of interpersonal skills for career success. *Strategic HR Review, 21*(3), 92–95. https://doi.org/10.1108/shr-03-2022-0013

Chapter 21

Becoming Privy to Department Drama

Before I decided to run for my first chair position, I met with the outgoing chair to learn about the job. I asked him what I should expect if I assumed the position. His answer was to "get ready to learn a lot about everyone's drama." I laughed it off in the moment, but I came to realize that he was spot-on. I was surprised at how much conflict was bubbling under the veneer of professional civility that I was completely unaware of. In retrospect, I think my ignorance of much of the interpersonal friction was a testament to having a good chair. The conflict was being managed and not leaking to those of us in the department who were not directly involved.

The most common way that I found myself becoming privy to conflicts was when faculty would tell me directly. They would come to my office, ask if I had a moment, then close the door to tell me something that "you need to know now that you're chair." What followed was usually a list of grievances and concerns the faculty member had about others in the department. In my experience, this has included complaints about colleagues being unqualified to teach certain classes, talking too much in meetings, not holding appropriate office hours, not being in the office enough, and not offering condolences when a family member passed away. This ritual has happened all three times I have taken a new chair position, so I'm inclined to believe that it is a common part of being a new chair.

I am not implying that these concerns are always unwarranted. Some are serious and things that you probably should know now that you are chair (bullying, discrimination, safety issues, etc.) Others are simply personality conflicts. Adjudicating which claims fall in which category is part of your responsibility, and a key one as you figure out how to approach them. Here are a few guiding principles to remember when you have these conversations:

- *It is not your responsibility as chair to make people get along.* I am embarrassed at how long it took me to understand and accept this. I labored under the illusion that a key function of my job was preserving interpersonal harmony among faculty members. This expectation came from my general disdain for conflict as well as the assumption by some faculty that I had the ability to enforce camaraderie. This is not only impossible, but it is an unfair expectation (interpersonal conflict is different from bullying or discrimination—both of which you do need to address and we cover in this volume). Your job as chair is to do your best to mitigate the role interpersonal conflict plays in departmental operations and deliberations, not to make people be friends.
- *Be noncommittal in these early conversations.* Listen more than you speak. Communicate, verbally and nonverbally, that you are listening. Do not give the appearance that you are taking sides. You are not hearing the whole context in these conversations. Other people have different perspectives. Until you hear from various stakeholders, you are in no position to decide how to proceed. Be warned that nonverbal warmth or cooperative overlap will likely be interpreted as agreement (Carmichael & Mizrahi, 2023). That is not an invitation to be cold or standoffish, but instead to have an awareness of how you are being read. It is probably helpful at the end of the discussion to assure the faculty member you are chatting with that you are going to think about the conversation and gather more information. This kind of transparency goes a long way to mitigating any misunderstandings.
- *Ask questions rather than make statements.* Your job in these conversations is to get information, not to litigate. You do not want to be in a situation where you offer support and then must walk it back when you get more information.
- *End the conversation if it turns into gossip.* You are only inviting trouble by having conversations about colleagues' private lives with people who they do not get along with. Gossip builds social solidarity between speakers (Jolly & Chang, 2021), which can contribute to a misperception that you are taking a side, even if you're just listening.
- *Ask the faculty member what they expect you to do about the situation.* Putting the onus on them to come up with an appropriate response encourages faculty to be mindful of the limitations that you are operating under. The most common response to this question is something like, "I don't expect you to do anything, I just want you to be aware." This helps reset any unrealistic expectations.

These kinds of conversations play a pivotal role in how faculty perceive you. Use these conversations to show yourself as judicious, fair, transparent, and a good listener. Interpersonal conflict in your department is inevitable. You do not need to feel an outsized burden of solving it. Do not make it worse, make sure faculty and staff are safe, and do your best to ensure that interpersonal conflict does not drive the decision-making in your department. Do not waste precious energy that can be better spent elsewhere on the Sisyphean effort of forcing camaraderie between your colleagues.

REFLECTIONS

1. What interpersonal conflicts in your department have you become privy to now that you are chair? What do you think the faculty involved in these interpersonal conflicts expect from you?
2. Do you agree that mitigating interpersonal conflict is outside of a department chair's responsibility? Why or why not?

REFERENCES

Carmichael, C. L., & Mizrahi, M. (2023). Connecting cues: The role of nonverbal cues in perceived responsiveness. *Current Opinion in Psychology, 53*, 101663. https://doi.org/10.1016/j.copsyc.2023.101663

Jolly, E., & Chang, L. J. (2021). Gossip drives vicarious learning and facilitates social connection. *Current Biology, 31*, 2539–2549. https://doi.org/10.1016/j.cub.2021.03.090

Chapter 22

Informational Asymmetry, Confidentiality, and Managerial Trust

I was staring at a computer screen in an office in the IT department with the head of Human Resources, the vice provost of Academic Affairs, an IT specialist, and a police officer. We were going through the internet history of a member of my department. On a large screen in the front of the room, the IT staff member clicked us through the browsing history from the past several weeks of this departmental member's university-provided computer. The police officer would occasionally ask the IT staff member to pause or go back and linger on something while he examined it.

This meeting was happening because of some internet chat rooms that my departmental colleague had accessed during the workday on her university computer. IT reached out with an alert that some troubling material had been accessed, and it was concerning enough that the local police were called in. It was a surreal experience. While law enforcement ultimately determined that criminal charges were unwarranted, Human Resources still felt an unpaid two-week leave was appropriate. I agreed with this decision and was tasked with relaying this information to my direct report.

This led to one of the more uncomfortable situations I have faced in relationship to my department. Without warning, this departmental member vanished without explanation about why or how long this absence would last. I was unable to give information about why she was gone and when she would be back, even when asked directly. She was generally well liked and had allies in the department. Given the nature of the suspension, she was certainly not inclined to share the details with the rest of the department. Several faculty assumed something shady was afoot. The rumor mill started, and everyone was wondering why. Some of her friends in the department assumed I was somehow responsible because I would not share details. Some directly accused me of being sexist and not standing up for a female faculty member. My continued silence on the issue further stoked suspicion.

Holding my tongue during all of this was very difficult. I desperately wanted to explain to my colleagues how misguided their efforts were. If they knew what I knew, not a single one of them would defend her. I was unable to offer any context or to even hint about the nature of her absence. To do so would be a violation of her privacy and open myself and the university to liability.

Informational asymmetry is well established as a prime driver of much of what happens within an organization (Bergh et al., 2018). People have access to different information in a department, and we aren't always even aware of where our knowledge does and does not overlap. The story above is an extreme example of managing informational asymmetry, but it is emblematic of much of being chair. You are constantly operating within an informational asymmetry.

Managing the informational asymmetry can be emotionally taxing. It can feel isolating to know more about certain things than your colleagues. Communication privacy management theory explains that informational boundary maintenance is a key part of organizational life (Smith & Brunner, 2017). Despite the emotional toll, maintaining confidentiality about such matters is essential. It can be especially hard because much of what you know would make for some pretty good gossip.

Despite the emotional challenges it poses, you must prioritize confidentiality and privacy in all matters related to personnel issues, performance reviews, health, human resources inquiries, student complaints, and disciplinary procedures. Whatever perceived benefit you gain by sharing context (or just good gossip) with people, you stand to lose much more by inviting this kind of informational boundary turbulence (Smith & Brunner, 2017) into your managerial practice. Not only do you open yourself up to a host of legal and ethical liabilities when you share, but it is also bad managerial practice. Upon sharing, you have relinquished your ability to control who learns the information and what they do with it (Petronio & Child, 2020). The value of cultivating a managerial identity as someone your department can trust with sensitive information far outweighs whatever short-term gain comes from sharing something you probably should not have.

REFLECTIONS

1. If faced with similar suspicions from faculty members, how would you handle the challenge of holding your tongue and maintaining confidentiality, even when the desire to explain or clarify is wrong?

2. Who is a leader in your institution who you would trust with sensitive information? What does that person do to cultivate a sense of trust and what can you learn from them in regards to building a reputation of trust?

REFERENCES

Bergh, D. D., Ketchen, D. J., Orlandi, I., Heugens, P. P. M. A. R., & Boyd, B. K. (2018). Information asymmetry in management research: Past accomplishments and future opportunities. *Journal of Management, 45*(1), 122–158. https://doi.org/10.1177/0149206318798026

Petronio, S., & Child, J. T. (2020). Conceptualization and operationalization: Utility of communication privacy management theory. *Current Opinion in Psychology, 31*, 76–82. https://doi.org/10.1016/j.copsyc.2019.08.009

Smith, S. A., & Brunner, S. R. (2017). To reveal or conceal: Using communication privacy management theory to understand disclosures in the workplace. *Management Communication Quarterly, 31*(3), 429–446. https://doi.org/10.1177/0893318917692896

Chapter 23

You Are Chair of Students, Not Just Faculty

A student was sitting in my office across from me pleading her case. "I turned the assignment in on time. Here's the syllabus. It says to email the professor and attach the assignment by midnight." She handed me a paper copy of the syllabus, pulled out her laptop, faced the screen toward me, opened her inbox, and clicked on the sent folder. "Here's the email, and you can see it is sent at 10:30 p.m." Tears started to form as she finished with "Dr. _____ is saying that the email didn't come through until 4:00 a.m. I worked really hard on this."

I asked the student to send me the email, with the time stamp, and assured her that I would look into the situation. When I approached the instructor, he was indignant and insisted that the student was lying to me. Displaying the email with its time stamp, I offered him the opportunity to save face, suggesting, "maybe it got delayed in cyberspace." The instructor became defensive, telling me that the student had manipulated the time stamp and that I was "falling for the oldest trick in the book." He explained that he knew how these "sorority girls" operated, and he was not going to be a sucker. I tried to explain that for a student to manipulate the time stamp, they would have to get IT involved in the scam, which was obviously highly unlikely. The professor still refused to budge. At this point I realized this was a fruitless conversation and explained that if he did not accept the assignment, I would encourage the student to file a grade appeal and I would write a letter of support along with it. My colleague lashed out and yelled (loud enough that others in the office heard), "You goddamn administrators think you know more than us faculty. It is my class, and you are not going to tell me how to run it."

Eventually, the professor relented and begrudgingly accepted the assignment. A version of this scene, thankfully with less dramatic tension, plays out a few times every semester. Faculty sometimes think that your job as chair is to back them in every student disagreement. This became clear to me when I was in the faculty Q&A section of my first chair interview. A faculty member asked, "How would you support faculty members in grade disputes?" The assumption in that question is clear. Your default position as chair is not to be an impartial decider in these matters, but instead to be a faculty advocate. Not all faculty assume this, but I have found that many do.

You must remember that you are chair to the students in your department as well. Students need advocates too. They have rights and are usually the less powerful person in the disagreement. Faculty can be wrong in these matters. This is often an unpopular opinion. I have heard many faculty talk about the classroom as if the space and time is theirs to do with as they please. They are the expert, and questioning classroom decisions is the same as questioning their self-worth or expertise. They expect a chair to be their "ride or die" in these situations.

Remember that your obligation is not automatically to faculty members. Your obligation is to what is right and sensible in each unique situation. Do not merely hold this position but hold it loudly. When faculty know this is a guiding principle, they are less likely to be upset when abiding by it results in you taking the side of the student.

Usually when these situations arise, I do end up taking the side of faculty. But that is a matter of pragmatics rather than policy. Faculty usually have more life experience and knowledge about the university and are subject matter experts. They tend to be the more reasonable party. Just because faculty are usually right does not mean you should approach the matter with that expectation. Go in with an open mind ready to listen and understand all parties. Then use your best judgment.

It is wise to clarify this approach to all faculty as a matter of policy rather than simply enacting it on a case-by-case basis. Faculty will likely be less hostile and take these matters less personally if they know this is how you operate. Also, when you do side with faculty, they will know it is because you think they are right rather than because of their status.

REFLECTIONS

1. Given your new role, how do you anticipate navigating situations where faculty expectations clash with your responsibility as an impartial decision-maker, and how would you address such conflicts?
2. In what ways can you actively promote an environment where faculty feel supported even when decisions may favor students, emphasizing the overarching importance of justice and fairness?

Chapter 24

Networking with Other Chairs

Several of our daily reflections thus far have focused on various ways in which being a new academic department chair can feel isolating and lonely. The change in relationships and the feeling that you're now on the outside can create a sense of "otherness." You are also now responsible for evaluating the work of your colleagues, which inherently creates social distance from the rest of your faculty. Research has established that loneliness is often correlated with a promotion to a leadership position, as the number of peers you have shrinks every time you advance (Rokach, 2014). In higher education that is compounded as the people who are your most direct peers (other chairs) are most likely scattered across the university. This kind of loneliness can have health effects and can lead to burnout (De Oliveira et al., 2011). Managing burnout is not only good for you personally but also an important part of ensuring that you maintain the ability to be a good chair.

One of the most effective ways that you can safeguard against this kind of loneliness is to find ways to connect with those who are your direct peers (Detmer-Goebel, 2015). You need to find ways to informally connect with other chairs across your university. You should have a few chairs who you regularly have lunch, coffee, or a happy hour drink with. If you do not yet have that kind of relationship with other chairs, ask your dean for advice. They will likely provide you with a few suggestions for chairs who might have overlap in the kinds of challenges they face. They may even set up a meeting time for you. I think it is beneficial to build informal relationships with at least one newer chair and one who has been at it for a while. The different perspectives will be valuable.

The benefits of these informal get-togethers with your peer leaders are immense. You will learn about how other departments run. Maybe they handle internships differently, or have more frequent department meetings, or handle the summer schedule in a unique way. Hearing about these differences is good, as it adds context to how your own department runs and might generate some ideas. Building these kinds of relationships also has the added benefit of fostering interdepartmental collaboration. Having an interpersonal connection with other chairs helps when you bring proposals or need help moving things through university committees.

The most substantial benefit from developing these interpersonal connections lies in the emotional support you receive from discussing the challenges of your position with someone who understands the intricacies of being chair. You can discuss frustrations and difficulties with other department chairs in a way you cannot with those in your department and your dean. Other chairs have the managerial experience to empathize but also the necessary critical distance from your department to be objective. Your decisions do not affect them directly. Unlike your dean, their professional success does not rely on solving your problems, so they can simply listen and offer advice. Swapping stories with other chairs is also a great way to get validation that the challenges you face are common.

Do not think about these informal get-togethers as ancillary to your administrative duties. They are instead an essential part of you building networks across campus, fostering a collaborative interdepartmental environment, leaning into mentorship opportunities, and attending to your own emotional well-being. Establishing interpersonal relationships makes you a better chair. Feel free to have these get-togethers on the clock—because yes, they are a part of your job, contributing not only to your personal well-being but also to the foundation of a resilient academic community. The ripple effects of these connections go beyond personal benefits and contribute to a more interconnected and supportive academic environment that thrives on shared wisdom and mutual assistance.

REFLECTIONS

1. How do you plan to actively seek out and foster connections with other chairs at your university? Which chairs would you like to build deeper connections with?
2. Consider the suggestion of having regular informal meetings with other chairs for lunch, coffee, or happy hour. How do you envision incorporating such gatherings into your schedule and what do you hope to get from such meetings?

REFERENCES

Detmer-Goebel, E. (2015). Informal support groups for chairs. *Department Chair, 26*, 8–9. https://doi.org/10.1002/dch.30045

De Oliveira, G. S., Ahmad, S., Stock, M. C., Harter, R. L., Almeida, M. D., Fitzgerald, P. C., & McCarthy, R. J. (2011). High incidence of burnout in academic chairpersons of anesthesiology: Should we be taking better care of our leaders? *Anesthesiology, 2011*(114), 181–193. https://doi.org/10.1097/ALN.0b013e318201cf6c

Rokach, A. (2014). Leadership and loneliness. *International Journal of Leadership and Change, 2*(1), article 6. https://digitalcommons.wku.edu/ijlc/vol2/iss1/6

Chapter 25

Agenda Interrupted

One of the most predictable cycles of being a chair goes like this: You've set your agenda for the day. You have a to-do list pulled up. You're thrilled that there is not much on your schedule today; you have several free hours where you can get your PowerPoint presentation done for class tomorrow, work on that annual evaluation you are a few days behind on, and then hopefully you can get an hour of writing done.

When you get to the office, the administrative assistant reminds you that the annual assessment data needs to be input by the end of the day. Also, she reminds you that there is a recruiting event this weekend that you need to have an activity planned for. Annoyed that you did not account for these tasks, you sit down to get started on them so you can quickly get through them and on to the items you had planned on getting done. A colleague comes to your office and wants to chitchat about the weekend. When they leave twenty minutes later, you finally get to it. Then the phone rings, and it is Faculty Labor Relations informing you that a faculty member has reached out and might be going on medical leave for a few weeks. Now it is all hands on deck, as you start scrambling to figure out how you are going to cover these classes. You must get ahold of the faculty member and your dean. You need to check the budget to see if you can hire an adjunct and then get on the phone with people to see if anyone has any ideas for who can take over the class on short notice. In the middle of this scramble, a student knocks on your door to ask if they can discuss an issue they are having with an instructor.

Before you have had time to really process it, the workday is almost over, and you have not even started any of the important things that you had on your to-do list at the start of the day. Department chairs report that the loss of control of their daily agenda is one of more frustrating aspects of the job (Hancock & Hellawell, 2003; Hecht, 1999).

While faculty members experience interruptions, the chair's role involves a different level of necessary responsiveness to urgent matters that were unforeseen at the beginning of the day. Much of your job can feel like it is taking care of urgent matters that you did not know existed when you woke up that morning. This can lead to feeling like you are being primarily reactive in your management. You may feel like you are responding to other people's emergencies rather than making progress on tasks that you are personally connected to. The unpredictable nature and the loss of autonomy is jarring. Many of us pursued careers in higher education because we value the freedom associated with it. Faculty generally have a lot of autonomy in how they approach the projects that interest them.

The loss of autonomy can be hard for a new chair. The unpredictability of this loss of autonomy makes handling it even more difficult. It is not just as if you lost your ability to control your agenda, you have also lost the ability to control when you lose control of your agenda. Timely tasks show up when they show up.

Future reflections will focus on managing your schedule and agenda, but in this one I am going to encourage you to reframe this loss of autonomy. Losing control over what you must deal with on a daily basis is part of you doing your job well. You are not simply responsible for your own concerns, but you have people you need to care for as part of your job now. Other people's problems are also your problems. Embrace that ethos.

Drawing inspiration from Lauren Berlant's *On the Inconvenience of Other People* (2022), this embrace involves accepting inconvenience as an inherent part of relationships. Inconvenience is what makes relationships beautiful. Similarly, the inconvenience and complexities arising from the loss of autonomy in the chair's role should be embraced as fundamental to the job. The complexity of handling emergencies is part of the ethos of caring for others in your department. This acceptance does not mean deprioritizing personal projects or not drawing healthy boundaries, but rather acknowledging it as a trade-off that comes from being chair.

You accepted that complexity of being the person who is responsible for handling emergencies when you decided to become chair. While responding to urgent matters that arise unexpectedly may not feel as rewarding as crossing items off your to-do list, embracing inconvenience should be part of every chair's to-do list as it contributes to the overall success and functionality of your academic unit. I would encourage you to welcome the inconvenience of unexpected agenda items as part of your to-do list as they are essential for a well-functioning department.

REFLECTIONS

1. Have you noticed a loss of autonomy and increase of "inconvenience" with your new role as chair? Has it surprised you?
2. Consider the idea of embracing inconvenience as an inherent part of a chair's role. Do you think this is the right approach to framing unexpected tasks that interrupt your personal agenda? Why or why not?

REFERENCES

Berlant, L. (2022). *On the inconvenience of other people*. Duke University Press.

Hancock, N., & Hellawell, D. E. (2003). Academic middle management in higher education: A game of hide and seek? *Journal of Higher Education Policy and Management, 25*(1), 5–12. https://doi.org/10.1080/13600800305739

Hecht, I. W. D. (1999). Transitions: From faculty member to department chair. *Department Chair, 10*(2). https://college.emory.edu/faculty/documents/articles/transitions-from-faculty-member-to-department-chair.pdf

Chapter 26

Advocacy and Influence from the Middle

Academic department chairs have various roles they must play at different times. They are managers, schedulers, problem solvers, cheerleaders, and bureaucrats. Each of these are important, but they are the bare minimum of what is expected of those in the position. If you cannot do these things, then you probably are an ineffective chair. The trait that I have found that most often distinguishes a sufficient department chair from a good one is the ability to act as an advocate for their department. The other roles mentioned are primarily inward facing. But advocacy faces outward and requires engagement with the broader university community.

In chapter 9 we discussed your role as a boundary spanner, bridging the gap between upper administration and faculty. Often that requires you to serve as a diplomat or a translator between the two parties, but there are other times when translation is insufficient and proactive advocacy becomes imperative (Hinson-Hasty, 2019). Situations where advocacy is required can vary. Perhaps administration is demanding that classes be cancelled when students need them to graduate. Maybe a request to fill a necessary faculty position is denied. Or maybe you are pursing funding for a new initiative. It could involve another department proposing a class that is suspiciously close to one that your department offers.

The reason that great chairs are usually great advocates is because it involves being a leader rather than a manager. Moments of successful advocacy are when your department feels like they not only have a chair who can ensure things are running smoothly, but one who can protect and advance the mission of the department.

We often think of advocacy as loud and bold. There are probably some folks at your university who are gifted rhetoricians who speak with clarity in meetings and public forums. They always say the right thing at the right time in the right way to the right audience. This kind of advocacy is valuable and may be one you are good at. But other forms exist and are just as effective.

Some of your best advocacy work may be quiet and introspective rather than loud and bold. Much of it is accomplished through fostering trust by building meaningful connections across the university hierarchy (Branson et al., 2016). This involves more than simply being friendly to people in faculty senate. It means cultivating a reputation as the kind of chair who people want to work with. It means showing yourself to be reasonable, reliable, open-minded, thoughtful, careful, and mission centered. Your identity as chair is one of the most important rhetorical tools you have. You are the face of your department, and who others think you are goes a long way when you need to advocate. While speaking eloquently at meetings is important, much of what finds its way onto the meeting agenda in the first place is determined by a quiet advocacy that is rooted in relational dynamics.

Being reasonable and helpful is one such way to cultivate the necessary capital to practice this kind of quiet advocacy. Help other departments when you can. If another department is working on a project and you have some expertise, lend it. This makes it much easier to ask for help when you need it. Also, give in on battles you can afford to lose. This builds goodwill, as your colleagues can see you as reasonable and it lends gravitas when you do choose to actively advocate for an issue. Your colleagues know it is important, and you are not simply taking it on as a matter of principle. People generally avoid working with those who are unwilling to give an inch on every issue.

Quiet advocacy, however, is not synonymous with timidity. It requires a boldness. While it behooves you to cultivate an identity as helpful and reasonable, it is also essential that you keep a ledger and are willing to call it up when necessary. Part of quiet advocacy means leaning in on the goodwill you have cultivated. When it matters, remind your dean or provost that the last decision did not go your way and that you were supportive and reasonable. Be explicit when you need a favor to be repaid. You must do the work of leaning into the goodwill that you have cultivated. You are not helping your department when you store up goodwill and leave it unspent.

The ability to advocate effectively is a hallmark of exceptional department chairs. It involves a nuanced approach that encompasses both bold and quiet advocacy strategies. Balancing reasonableness with assertiveness and leveraging accumulated goodwill when necessary ensures that your advocacy efforts contribute significantly to the success and mission advancement of your department.

REFLECTIONS

1. In what specific situations do you anticipate the need for advocacy, and what strategies might you employ to navigate those scenarios successfully?
2. How do you plan to build, and leverage, your identity as a department chair, recognizing that it is a powerful rhetorical tool in influencing perceptions within and beyond your department?

REFERENCES

Branson, C. M., Franken, M., & Penney, D. (2016). Middle leadership in higher education: A relational analysis. *Educational Management Administration & Leadership*, *44*(1), 128–145. https://doi.org/10.1177/1741143214558575

Hinson-Hasty, E. (2019). Departmental chair as faculty advocate and middle manager. *Journal of Moral Theology*, *8*(1), 126–140. https://doi.org/file:///Users/wdunnmy/Downloads/Hinson-Hasty_Vol._8__Special_Issue_1--April_2019--Contingent_Faculty.pdf

Chapter 27

Writing Memos for Resource Allocation Requests

In a previous chapter we discussed quiet advocacy. One opportunity to practice the art of quiet advocacy is in memo writing toward the goal of requesting resources. In my experience, memos of this kind typically arise when I have approached my dean about a departmental need or opportunity that requires some funding. If my dean finds the case strong, these meetings result in a request to "write it up in a memo." Memos get a bad rap. We associate them with institutional bureaucracy straight from the movie *Office Space* ("Did you get that memo about the TPS reports?"). I doubt this chapter stood out to you when you skimmed the table of contents. Memos are not sexy.

While they are often framed as exactly the kind of task that makes department chairing tedious, they are important. And they don't have to be terrible. The department chair accomplishments I am most proud of started as memos. These include several successful faculty position requests during university hiring freezes, starting a new graduate program, getting administrative funding for a video recording studio, and a major curricular overhaul to a general education course that allowed my department to hire two new faculty. While a well-crafted memo alone does not guarantee success in project proposals, it serves as a door-opener and a framework for subsequent discussions. Leveraging my background in rhetoric and organizational communication, I have found that a memo, when strategically composed, can be a powerful tool.

Even when used in service of an argument, memos are primarily thought of as informational. The form requires you to strip away all unnecessary information and boil it down to "just the facts." The key to a successful memo in higher education is to use the form of the memo as part of your argument. Memos are rhetoric disguised as information. The bare-bones structure is not an impediment, if done well the form can make your argument stronger. The form tends to make people less suspicious since most folks read it as an FYI.

Writing Memos for Resource Allocation Requests 79

A successful memo for resource allocation requires attention to your audience. Usually you are writing a memo because your dean or associate dean wants to take it up the hierarchy, maybe to the provost, chancellor, finance officer, or president. Your dean likely sees value in the request and wants to be able to provide a summary and evidence to upper administration. Your primary audience is likely a decision-maker at the top of the university hierarchy. Upper administrators get requests all the time, so how can you make yours more likely to be looked at favorably?

Too often these requests are unsuccessful because of how they are framed. I often see chairs write memos requesting resources using a variety of rationales, such as: it is fair (this other department was allowed to hire), or it has precedent (we used to have this many faculty lines), or it was promised (your predecessor assured us that if we waited a year we could have this faculty line), or it ensures disciplinary integrity (students will not learn what they need to know without this hire). These kinds of framing will not work. Every single department can make these kinds of claims.

Put yourself in the shoes of the upper administrator who regularly receives these kinds of requests. They are at an arm's length from your department and are likely not familiar with intricacies of curricular needs and disciplinary standards. Tailor your memo to align with their priorities, such as cutting costs, boosting efficiency, maintaining accreditation, and gaining positive publicity. Ideally your request will align with more than one of these objectives.

Mere claims will not suffice; you need to back them up with solid evidence. Pull comps from other departments or universities, use Bureau of Labor statistics, show what your competitors are doing, provide multiyear enrollment/FTE trends, use accreditation standards, find market trends for careers, and so on. You must do this. Every department can claim that the requested resources will boost enrollment, but you must show it. No memo will be successful without this.

After you have provided statistical information, it is your time to turn that data into information. Link it directly to your claim. Show how refusing this request will either lead to problems that upper administration will eventually have to fix or create an obstacle that directly impacts the bottom line. Focus on the potential negative outcomes, as administrators are more inclined to approve requests that prevent crises than those that strive for optimization.

Make your case directly and without flourish. Memos are not the place for flowery prose. Your memo should be skimable. Make your case with confidence. Do not write as if you are asking for a favor. Write as if you are doing upper administration a favor by fixing a problem. This approach not only enhances readability but also positions your request as a solution rather than a burden.

REFLECTIONS

1. How might memo writing intersect with your own chair term? What value do you see in memos? Do you feel confident in your ability to do this part of your job well?
2. This chapter suggests writing memos as if you are doing upper administration a favor by fixing a problem. How might adopting this perspective influence the tone and context of your future memos?

Chapter 28

Student Misconduct

"Hey Ben, can I talk to you about something?" I looked up and saw Amanda, one of our part-time faculty. "Of course," I responded. "What's on your mind?" She reached in her bag, pulled out a folder, and put it on my desk. I opened it and saw a student paper from a class she was teaching. The author was a student in my class as well. "Turn to the last page," Amanda instructed. Halfway down the page, after the conclusion to the essay, was a handwritten note from the student: "Hello professor xxxxxx, there is something I want to share with you. I have a foot fetish. I love feet and am a part of several web communities dedicated to beautiful feet. You wore sandals last week, and I couldn't stop staring at your feet. They are beautiful. I just wanted to let you know. And I would love to go out with you and maybe buy you some shoes some time after I graduate next semester."

I was taken aback: such behavior was unexpected from this student. Amanda was sheepish and apologized for this becoming an issue before she started to make some suggestions. "It is almost the end of the semester," she offered, "maybe I can just hand back the graded paper and not address the comment. Maybe he will think I didn't see it." I understood her impulse. She was young and new to the department and her position was precarious as a part-time faculty member. She did not want to make waves.

As much as ignoring the comment was an easier solution, I knew it was the wrong one. This student had to know that what he did was inappropriate, and Amanda had to know that she had a chair who would protect her from this kind of behavior. My position as a chair who wanted to create a safe working environment demanded that I get involved. "Amanda, I cannot look the other way on this. I have to address it." She was worried that it would be awkward seeing him at the next class meeting. "Please do not worry about that," I assured her, "he won't be in your class anymore." I promised to follow up with her, and after she left, I immediately contacted my dean and Human Resources.

During my meeting with the student, I explained how inappropriate this behavior was. I asked him what made him feel this kind of note was acceptable and to reflect on how this likely made the instructor feel. He was genuinely remorseful and embarrassed. I then explained to him that he would be completing the last two weeks of the class as an independent study under my supervision.

While such egregious issues are fortunately rare, they do arise occasionally. In my experience, instances of student harassment, bullying, inappropriate comments, public challenges to authority, and undermining of teachers have all involved male students acting as aggressors toward women faculty. This is not all that surprising as this tends to be the norm (Lampman et al., 2016; Lampman, 2012).

It is your job as chair to address this kind of behavior. It may feel uncomfortable, but you must do it. Your position as chair requires you to do what is in your power to keep faculty, staff, and students safe. By addressing this kind of behavior directly, you not only deal with the situation in front of you pragmatically, but you communicate to your department that the chair's office is a place where they can come to feel protected.

Before talking directly to students, it is best to loop in your dean, Human Resources, and Student Services. These are important but delicate matters. You need institutional support. Also, the folks in these offices may have suggestions to handle these matters that you had not thought of. They can also provide you with a clear sense of what you have the ability and authority to do.

When you have these direct conversations with students who have exhibited bad behavior, set clear expectations from the beginning. Highlight that this will be a calm but direct conversation. Then express your concern over their behavior and encourage reflection. Ask them to consider and evaluate their actions. They will often handle much of the conversation for you at this point as they usually acknowledge what they did. After this reflection, reiterate what constitutes professional conduct and then discuss consequences. These kinds of cases are not generally opportunities for them to go and apologize or "work it out." You are the one who imposes the consequence, which can involve a change in class structure or schedule or the involvement of relevant university authorities. End your conversation by emphasizing accountability. Reinforce that the university community deserves a safe and respectful learning environment.

While these conversations may be uncomfortable, they are crucial for maintaining a healthy departmental environment. Your commitment to addressing these issues directly communicates to both faculty and the student body that as chair you prioritize the safety and well-being of everyone in your department.

REFLECTIONS

1. In the example provided, Amanda initially suggested pretending she didn't see the comment. Did I make the right decision in insisting that we address the inappropriate comment? How would you have responded?
2. Is your department one where people feel safe? Why or why not? What are ways that you can use your position as chair to contribute to a culture that privileges safety and well-being for everyone in your department?

REFERENCES

Lampman, C. (2012). Women faculty at risk: U.S. professors report on their experiences with student incivility, bullying, aggression, and sexual attention. *NASPA Journal about Women in Higher Education*, 5(2), 184–208. https://doi.org/10.1515/njawhe-2012-1108

Lampman, C., Crew, E. C., Lowery, S., Tompkins, K. A., & Mulder, M. (2016). Women faculty distressed: Descriptions and consequences of academic contrapower harassment. *Journal about Women in Higher Education*, 9(2), 169–189. https://doi.org/10.1080/19407882.2016.1199385

Chapter 29

Inappropriate Faculty Behavior

While seated at my desk, my train of thought was abruptly halted by the ringing phone. Seeing an unrecognizable number on the caller ID, I picked up the phone and answered professionally. On the other end of the line was a student (from another major). The student explained that they were enrolled in one of our classes as an elective, and something concerning had happened in class. The professor had assigned students certain identities (some racially insensitive and others sexually suggestive) and had encouraged them to role-play scenarios as these identities. I am not going to share the details here, but it was every bit as bad as you can imagine. To make matters worse, the student explained that they were transgender and had been misgendered in this activity when assigned one of the sexually suggestive identities.

The gravity of the situation left me both astonished and alarmed. I assured the student that I would be getting to the bottom of this immediately and be back in touch. Upon hanging up the phone, I called Faculty Labor Relations, then Human Resources, and then my dean. This became a collaborative effort to address the issue. After several meetings with the appropriate offices, a course of action was determined. A Human Resources representative and I met with the professor. He was formally reprimanded and given a plan of improvement (with some mandatory training). I met with his class and debriefed the activity, discussed why it was problematic, and informed students of what their options were if they felt they could not stay in the class and how to report any future incidences.

This situation stands as one of the most uncomfortable I have encountered as chair. It was concerning, awkward, and unsettling. The crucial lesson here is the imperative to involve external offices when dealing with predatory faculty behavior. When faculty behavior is predatory or inappropriate, it is essential that you loop in others. There are offices with experts in them at handling these kinds of issues. To be clear, I am not talking about difficult faculty or bullying here (although this volume addresses those kinds of behaviors elsewhere). I am instead referring to predatory or lascivious behavior.

Predatory behavior is not always as easily recognizable as the example above. In many ways, this was an easy case given its egregiousness. I had no choice but to act. But often this is not the case. Less egregious examples are more difficult, because you do not always know where the line is. As chair I have witnessed examples of professors being a bit too friendly with students, talking with students about borderline inappropriate topics, and one example of a faculty member having kids at a departmental summer camp sit on his lap. In all these situations, my gut was telling me something was wrong, and I reported the behavior. If you are ever in question, or ever get an uncomfortable feeling, discuss it with a relevant office immediately.

It may feel awkward to report or bring up a situation based solely on an uncomfortable feeling, but the risks of not reporting such a situation far outweigh the potential awkwardness that might come as a result of reporting it. These are matters that are simply too important to look the other way or for you to handle on your own. Do not conduct your own investigation. I have been in a situation when a faculty member had some suspicions about another faculty member and then decided to conduct their own investigation, which included informally interviewing students. This made the situation much worse and hindered the real investigation that eventually took place. The informal faculty investigation was a gift for the accused party's lawyers in the legal proceedings that eventually materialized.

Reporting suspicious or potentially problematic faculty behavior is not only the right thing to do to protect students, but also in your own best interests. If you try to handle the problem on your own or decide it is probably not worth reporting, you open yourself up to liability. Careers can be lost over mishandling these kinds of issues.

Addressing faculty behavior that veers into predatory or inappropriate behavior is a challenging but nonnegotiable responsibility as a chair. A safe community depends on people in leadership roles acting when necessary. The importance of promptly reaching out to external offices cannot be overstated. It is crucial to recognize that predatory behavior may not always be as overt as the incident cited earlier, making vigilance and reliance on institutional support paramount. In these matters, prioritizing the well-being of students and protecting the integrity of the university community is not only ethically sound, but a vital act of self-preservation for all involved.

REFLECTIONS

1. Consider the challenge of recognizing predatory behavior, especially when it may not be as overt as the example provided. How would you stay vigilant to potential red flags and ensure a proactive approach to maintaining a safe learning environment?
2. Reflect on the potential discomfort mentioned in reporting suspicious or uncomfortable feelings about faculty behavior. How would you overcome hesitations and prioritize the well-being of students, even when faced with potential awkwardness?

Chapter 30

Unilateral Versus Multilateral Decision-Making

As we have discussed in earlier chapters, the role of a department chair involves multiple balancing acts. One crucial aspect of these balancing acts is in the art of decision-making. Here I am not referring to the challenges of decision-making itself (although that is often complex), but rather on discerning the appropriate level of faculty input before making decisions.

Democratic values and collaborative decision-making are generally held in high esteem in academia. Faculty members prefer not to feel excluded from the decision-making process by their chair. However, the practicality of bringing every decision to your faculty is unrealistic. I served under a chair who habitually sought faculty feedback on nearly every decision, inundating the department with constant deliberative emails. While his intention was collaborative, this approach led to faculty frustration, gossip, and ultimately a sense of apathy toward the issues raised in the constant stream of emails.

While the impulse to include faculty aligns with effective academic leadership principles (Bryman, 2007), there is a delicate balance between openness and unilateral decision-making. Overreliance on either approach has organizational costs. Constant unilateral decisions may breed mistrust and apathy, while excessive collaboration can lead to inefficiency and complaints. Establishing clear leadership principles and guidelines can help in navigating this decision-making tightrope effectively and consistently. Recognizing that not all decisions are equal, consider important variables when determining the appropriate approach. Develop a set of guidelines so you do not have to figure this out from scratch every time.

It is generally best to practice unilateral decision-making on items where time is short and a decision must be made quickly. Perhaps your dean needs to have something on his/her desk by the end of the day. Also, unilateral decisions are generally better when there is a clear best solution or an issue does not require a high degree of creativity. Finally, consider the makeup of your faculty. Do they deliberate well together? Consider if opening the deliberative process is going to cause unhealthy disagreements or open a historical wound.

On the other hand, multilateral decision-making is advantageous when there are multiple acceptable solutions. Bringing in a group can create space for creativity and diversity of opinions. New ideas will likely be generated. You may have blind spots, and multilateral decision-making helps you identify and navigate around them. Also, if faculty buy-in on the decision is important, then it is beneficial to have included faculty in the deliberations. If your faculty will have to implement the decision, you probably want them to have input. Finally, have your finger on the political pulse of the department. What is the historical precedence set on decisions about the matter at hand? Will faculty feel you have overstepped your jurisdiction by making a unilateral decision?

In essence, one important component of effective decision-making in academic leadership lies in you finding the right equilibrium and promoting a dynamic and adaptive decision-making approach that aligns with your department's personnel, history, culture, and specific needs. While mistakes are inevitable, learning from them contributes to your growth. It is essential that you remember to be transparent. A unilateral decision should not be driven by a desire to conceal information. It should instead be driven by a judicious assessment of the situation and an honest attempt to promote the department's overall health. Be ready to explain your rationale to those who ask. Your ability to master the art of balance will not only contribute to the efficiency and culture of your department but also build a trust between you and your faculty.

REFLECTIONS

1. How do you plan to calculate the potential organizational costs associated with both unilateral and multilateral decision-making? What strategies should you employ to foster trust, buy-in, and engagement?
2. Consider the historical precedence within your department regarding decision-making. How might this historical context influence your choices when deciding whether to consult faculty or make a unilateral decision?

REFERENCE

Bryman, A. (2007). Effective leadership in higher education: A literature review. *Studies in Higher Education, 32*(6), 693–710. DOI: 10.1080/03075070701685114

Chapter 31

Focus on Where It Counts
The Pareto Principle and Demanding Faculty

The Pareto principle, commonly known as the 80/20 rule (Koch, 1999), is an often-cited maxim in leadership literature, advising on how to effectively utilize managerial energy for maximum productivity. The principle posits that 80 percent of effects come from 20 percent of causes. It offers a lens through which managers can assess their efforts and impact on significant outcomes.

While the Pareto principle can be applied to various aspects of running a department (resource allocation, administrative tasks, and professional development), I have found it most useful to apply it to personnel management. During my eleven-year tenure as chair, I can confidently attest to the truth that 80 percent of your managerial stress related to personnel is going to stem from the loudest and most demanding 20 percent of your faculty. This should not be surprising upon reflection. Your top performers and most reliable, reasonable, and team-oriented faculty are not the ones who keep you up at night. They are not the faculty who create problems. They are cruising, and it does not feel like you need to do too much. Often the best strategy is to just let them do their thing and stay out of the way. They rarely cause problems, and when they do, they are easy to work with to find a resolution.

On the other end of the spectrum there are faculty who seem to always be commandeering your attention. You will find yourself agonizing over how to handle the disruptive, bullying, lazy, and continuously grievance-oriented faculty who seem to be on a mission to make everyone's life miserable by making themselves the center of attention. Here I am not suggesting that faculty do not often have legitimate needs, but some faculty seem to have it as a professional goal to cause as much chaos as possible. These faculty are few, but they command a lot of attention and energy. The Pareto principle is apt here, as you are likely to spend 80 percent of your personnel-oriented energy focused on these few faculty.

As mentioned above, the Pareto principle holds that you are spending too much time on things that do not actually yield results proportional to the energy input. That 80 percent of energy you are spending on conflict mediation, damage control, negotiating, indulging, discussing, stressing, planning around, and pacifying is not contributing in a meaningful way toward results for your department, faculty, and ultimately, students. To take the Pareto principle as instructive, you should flip these. You should be spending 80 percent of your personnel-oriented energy focusing on your top 20 percent faculty. Instead of trying to address and eliminate the disruptions caused by the most egregious and demanding faculty, you could be finding ways to support your superstars. You could be helping them find grants, offering mentorship, helping them identify opportunities on campus, introducing them to collaborators, soliciting their advice, and building them up. It is not hard to see how much more productive and outcome-oriented focusing on those priorities would be.

Of course, this is all easier said than done. You cannot, and should not, simply ignore faculty determined to grind the departmental gears to a standstill. Keeping the department functioning is a part of your job, and problem faculty affect others in the department. So, you must spend some of your efforts mitigating their effect. But you are likely spending too much. This is wasted effort. The near-universal truth here is that spending 80 percent of your efforts on trying to mitigate chaos caused by these people is fruitless. It does not seem to diminish the chaos by anywhere close to 80 percent. Difficult faculty will cause chaos regardless of your efforts. So, do not overinvest your resources in managing their disruptions. Spend 20-ish percent.

The application of the Pareto principle in academic leadership, particularly in managing faculty, offers valuable insights for you optimizing your managerial energy and resources. Recognize that a significant amount of your managerial stress and energy likely stem from a minority of faculty. While addressing the needs of disruptive and demanding faculty is necessary to maintain departmental functionality, do not disproportionately allocate energy to these individuals. Instead, shift focus to the top-performing faculty members; supporting their endeavors and fostering a conducive environment for their success will yield more meaningful outcomes. By recalibrating your efforts to align with the Pareto principle, you can enhance productivity, promote excellence, and sleep better at night.

REFLECTIONS

1. Reflecting on your own experiences as chair thus far, what percentage of your managerial stress and energy is being consumed by the most

demanding 20 percent of faculty members? Conversely, how much energy is consumed by your top 20 percent?
2. How effectively are you currently managing your energy and resources as chair, particularly in relationship to faculty management?

REFERENCE

Koch, R. (1999). *The 80/20 principle: The secret to achieving more with less*. Crown Currency.

Chapter 32

Generous Leadership and the Power of Sharing Recognition

I was working on a large project that involved putting together a rather intricate proposal. It took several weeks to complete. During that time, I worked closely with our office associate researching, brainstorming, drafting, and revising the proposal. She was new to the position and brought fresh enthusiasm and invaluable support to the table. While I assumed the role of the lead, her contributions were indispensable. The proposal's enthusiastic reception and subsequent approval garnered positive attention and press, directed toward myself.

A conversation at the office the following day highlighted an unanticipated interpersonal problem. Our office associate politely expressed hurt at her omission from the recognition. She told me that she had confided in her mom about her hurt feelings and her mom had told her that she needed to accept that she was not going to be acknowledged because "it is your job to make Ben look good." Our office associate shared her mom's advice with me in an attempt to demonstrate that she now understood that it was unreasonable of her to have hurt feelings. The comment, meant to alleviate my guilt, had the opposite effect. It made me feel much worse. It made me realize that my lack of attention to this issue was sexist, hierarchical, and generally selfish. This experience caused some internal reflection about how I approach issues of receiving and giving credit for work done. It was a tough pill to swallow when I realized that I had acted in a way that led to the assumption that I was the kind of person who expected office staff to operate as if it was their job to make me look good.

I have since tried to be conscientious about how credit for accomplishments is shared. I am not referring to not taking credit for other people's work. Not stealing credit is baseline being a good person. In the example above, I did not steal credit. I was just so oblivious to the fact that other people also deserved it that it did not even cross my mind to make sure they were included.

Credit and recognition matter to employees (Brun & Dugas, 2008). Your job should be to distribute credit rather than consolidate it. Make it a wide tent. There is much more to be gained from sharing credit than there is by taking it for yourself. Being perceived as the kind of academic leader who recognizes the efforts of others will make them much more likely to want to work with you in the future. It also builds morale.

While there are practical benefits, the best way to approach this generosity of acknowledgment is from a deep recognition that as chair you operate in an ecosystem and many people contribute to the success of a project. Go out of your way to generously include people in the acknowledgment. When you send out proposals, requests, and updates, always think in advance of those who collaborated. If someone's help was essential, include them and use "we." If someone's help was significant, but ancillary, give them a shout out. Earlier we discussed how important it is to cultivate referent power (French & Raven, 1959) since most of the usual managerial bases of power are not available to you as an academic leader. Being generous with credit is a surefire way to help gain buy-in from your team.

Here I'm not suggesting that you should give people credit for things they did not do or that you should downplay your own accomplishments. Giving people credit for things they did not do is likely to breed resentment from the high-accomplishing members of your department. Also, you should take some pride in accomplishments that are truly yours. Instead, I am suggesting that you operate from an ethos of generosity when it comes to sharing credit. If you are going to err on one side, it is better to err on the side of expanding the number of folks who feel ownership of accomplishments.

Recognize the importance of actively acknowledging and appreciating the contributions of others. It is not just about avoiding hurt feelings, as in the example I provided earlier, but about fostering a culture of inclusivity and collaboration. By striving to acknowledge collective efforts, you will show that you are a department chair who values relationships, collective ownership, and pride in departmental contributions. It is a simple and powerful ethos that not only benefits individuals but also contributes to the overall success and cohesion of your academic community.

REFLECTIONS

1. Who is an academic leader in your institution who operates from an ethos of generosity in terms of sharing credit? What can you learn from that person?
2. In what ways do you envision implementing a philosophy of generosity in credit-sharing as a part of your managerial practice?

REFERENCES

Brun, J. P., & Dugas, N. (2008). An analysis of employee recognition: Perspectives on human resources practices. *International Journal of Human Resource Management, 19*(4), 716–730. DOI: 10.1080/09585190801953723

French Jr., J. R. P., & Raven, B. H. (1959). The bases of social power. In D. Cartwright (Ed.), *Studies in social power* (pp. 150–167). Institute for Social Research.

Chapter 33

The Emotional Labor of Being Chair

Before assuming the role of department chair, I imagined that success primarily involved mastering specific tasks such as budgeting, strategic planning, course scheduling, and personnel management. However, I have since discovered that while these skills are important, one's proficiency in handling emotional challenges plays an equally decisive role in determining success or failure in the position. I am not alone in this realization. Gonzales and Ricones (2013) report that there is a notable absence of academic literature addressing the emotional aspect of academic administrative leadership. The academic literature on academic leadership often discusses challenges and frustrations, but the solutions offered tend to be pragmatic. Cowley's subsequent study (2019) delves into the the emotional lives of academic department chairs, revealing the extensive emotional labor involved, from maintaining positivity in the face of adversity to staying neutral during conflicts and remaining calm amidst chaos. Despite the importance of emotional regulation, department chairs often lack institutional guidance on managing their emotions, necessitating self-navigation.

Many of the mistakes I have made stemmed from my failure to regulate my emotions effectively. The job-related emotions you felt as a faculty are likely to be magnified now that you are a department chair. You know more, you are involved in more conflicts, you have to manage conflicting demands, and you have to make decisions that will sometimes lead to one or more parties being unhappy. More responsibility likely means you will be more stressed, which will tax your abilities to regulate your emotions. Keeping information confidential can feel lonely. Feeling the need to cheerlead when things get bleak can be emotionally exhausting.

Compounded by the unique vulnerability of the position (characterized by a lack of traditional managerial authority), department chairs must walk an emotional tightrope, all while still being expected to carry out the necessary tasks of being chair. All of this is a recipe for emotional intensity. The ways in which I have failed at emotional regulation have most often been when confronted with selfish behavior from faculty members that compromised the department's best interests. When I have reacted impulsively without considering the broader outcome, it usually exacerbates the underlying issues. I have learned a lot from such mistakes and make them much less frequently now.

What I am not going to do here is to urge you to be more rationale in your approach to being a department chair. Emotions are important; embrace them. They provide us important information and connect us to our colleagues. You should feel empathy when a colleague gets a rejection letter, anger when a faculty member treats a student unfairly, and joy when an initiative you have been working on gets approved. Emotional regulation does not mean emotional avoidance. It instead means having a healthy relationship with your emotions. Emotions should inform your decision-making but should not dictate it.

There are lots of ways to practice having a healthy relationship with your emotions. I am not a therapist, so I certainly do not want to prescribe any. For me, learning to meditate and practice the Buddhist principles of detachment has been invaluable. This concept promotes observing your emotions in an effort to allow them to inform but not dictate your actions. I try to spend a few minutes during each workday practicing some meditation based on these values. There are multiple other healthy practices as well. Talk to your therapist, exercise, spend time with people you love, identify emotional triggers, draw boundaries, learn not to take work matters personally, spend time focused on your hobbies, and so on. Find what works for you and invest in it.

While it is important to tend to your emotional health for the benefit of your own well-being, it is also integral to effective academic leadership. The inability to handle the emotional elements of being a department chair can impair your ability to lead effectively. The emotional component of being a department chair cannot be overstated. You will have many emotions about things that happen on your watch. By harnessing your emotions productively and healthily, you can ensure you bring your best self to the role, which ultimately benefits your department. So this is well worth you investing in. Do not feel guilty about doing things that protect your emotional well-being.

REFLECTIONS

1. How much thought did you put into the emotional labor of being a department chair before your term started? Do you agree that the

position is more emotional than it might seem? What kind of emotions have you experienced thus far as a result of being chair?
2. Do you agree that the unique vulnerabilities associated with being a department chair complicate the emotional landscape of the position? Why or why not?

REFERENCES

Cowley, S. (2019). Emotional labour in the role of university department chair. *SFU Educational Review, 12*(2), 9–26. https://doi.org/10.21810/sfuer.v12i2.766

Gonzales, L. D., & Rincones, R. (2013). Using participatory action research and photo methods to explore higher education administration as an emotional endeavor. *Qualitative Report, 18*(32), 1–17. https://doi.org/10.46743/2160-3715/2013.1481

Chapter 34

The Visible Chair

In my appointment as chair, a fellow newcomer to the position shared a story with me that I found rather disconcerting. After several months in the position, she came back to her office one day to find a crudely crafted chart slid under her office door. The chart tracked the number of times over the past week that the anonymous author had come by the chair's office only to find no one there. The chart also included a reference to the chair's new salary increase. The message was clear—"You are not in your office enough and people are noticing." Thankfully I have never been the recipient of this kind of passive-aggressive strategy, but even in hearing her tell the story I realized the implication. To be clear, while I think this is a very bad conflict resolution strategy (bordering on bullying), there is still a clear lesson here. Faculty will likely now have a sense of ownership of your time, decisions, and actions.

Several chapters thus far have focused on the differences between being a department chair and a faculty member. There are many great things about the faculty life, and as I have marked a few times thus far, two notable ones are autonomy and freedom. There is certainly accountability, but it generally tends to be punctuated in an annual review. When you are faculty, you can, for the most part, come and go as you please so long as there are no complaints about your unavailability. Becoming chair changes all of that. We discussed your changing relationship to your colleagues in an earlier chapter. There, we primarily focused on the ways in which your managerial identity and your evaluative responsibilities create distance. The distance is a result of your upward movement on the organizational hierarchy chart, altering power dynamics. But there is another significant change: now you are accountable to your department in ways you were not before. The power dynamics change in more than one way.

This new feeling of being under a microscope is one of the characteristics of the job that new chairs find most daunting (Armstrong & Woloshyn, 2017). In my experience, this is one of the things that new chairs complain about quite a bit. It is a foundational shift in one's experience at work, and even sense of self. While it may be tempting to think of this change as an annoying and unfortunate aspect of your new position, I would urge you to move beyond framing this shift as an unfortunate side effect of being chair. These changes are instead fundamental to what it means to be an effective chair. This shift reflects a newfound sense of connection between your faculty/staff and yourself.

We have previously discussed that one near-universal chair experience is a decrease in control over your agenda. You are now the person charged with taking care of things. Your success as chair is measured not by what you accomplish but by your ability to make your department and its members better (Hess, 2013). Increased availability, visibility, and accountability are all essential elements of being responsive and handling issues as they arise. It is often said in sports that "availability is your best ability." Being there to handle unexpected problems is the key to actually being able to handle unexpected problems. Your department is likely willing to overlook many faults if you are the kind of chair who prioritizes being accessible, available, and open to feedback.

You are now connected to your department in new ways. The members of your department have become invested in your performance in ways they were not when you were a faculty member. Accept that this increased investment means you need to make yourself available and open to feedback from others. Additionally, being around and visible communicates to the people in your department that you are in fact available. It is not enough simply to be available; you must perform availability in the form of visibility.

Like many chapters in this volume discuss, this requires a balancing act. Many previous chapters have covered the difficulties and emotional stress associated with the department chair position. You will still have to draw boundaries. Being open and available does not mean you always need to deprioritize your needs or be at the office from sunup to sundown. It also does not mean you need to justify every decision you make. In fact, I think you probably shouldn't feel the need to justify bad faith demands to do so (we will address this in a later chapter). Instead, it means that there should be a conscientiousness associated with these matters. Read the proverbial room to get a sense of what the right amount of availability, openness, and accessibility is. Do not become the chair who feels far away and detached. I have seen plenty of those kinds of chairs, and they tend not to last long in the position. Appreciate that your department is invested in your performance as chair. It is more welcoming and enjoyable, and you position yourself for long-term success.

REFLECTIONS

1. Consider the balance between autonomy and accountability. How will you maintain a sense of freedom and accountability for yourself?
2. How did your predecessor handle the demands of increased availability, accountability, and visibility? What are the expectations of your department, and how do you plan on accounting for them?

REFERENCES

Armstrong, D. E., & Woloshyn, V. E. (2017). Exploring the tensions and ambiguities of university department chairs. *Canadian Journal of Higher Education, 47*(1), 97–113. https://doi.org/10.47678/cjhe.v47i1.186470

Hess, Jon A. (2013). The risks and rewards of serving as a department chair. *Communication Faculty Publications*. Paper 13. http://ecommons.udayton.edu/cmm_fac_pub/13

Chapter 35

When to Address Problems with Collective Policies

When I came in as an external hire to one of my department chair appointments, I quickly realized that department meetings had long been an issue for a variety of reasons. While there were several possible areas of concern, I found one very odd. A senior faculty member would regularly arrive to meetings late, nonchalantly get a seat, and pull out a grooming kit from her purse. She would then file her nails during the department meeting. This happened almost every meeting. Other departmental members found the practice disgusting and distracting (I did too). I received numerous complaints from various faculty and staff.

Addressing the issue of the faculty member's grooming habit presented a unique challenge, particularly due to her seniority and popularity within the department. Knowing her well (and liking her), I knew this was not the kind of conversation she would take in stride. She would likely be upset. While I was hesitant to confront her directly, the persistent complaints from other department members made it clear that action needed to be taken to address the disruptive behavior in department meetings.

In situations like these, where individual conversations may be potentially confrontational and create division, implementing collective policies that apply to everyone can be a useful course of action. By establishing clear expectations and standards of conduct for all department members, collective policies can create a framework for behavior that applies uniformly to everyone. Developing collective policies can also have the added benefit of addressing ancillary matters. Here, I used the opportunity to address a wide range of disruptive behaviors at department meetings (tardiness, turn-taking in talking, voting procedures, etc.). This not only avoided singling out the specific nail-filing faculty member but also promoted a culture of accountability and professionalism within the department as a whole.

In this case, I decided to address the issue during a department meeting where I could introduce a new policy regarding professional conduct during meetings. I framed the conversation positively, gently including language that would cover personal grooming. The conversation happened within the context of the greater good of the department, and we all maintained a respectful and focused atmosphere. I emphasized the need for all departmental members to be mindful of their behavior and to refrain from all activities that could detract from the meeting's purpose.

By addressing the issue collectively, we avoided placing undue scrutiny on the individual faculty member while still addressing the problem at hand. The new policy served as a clear message to all departmental members that certain behaviors were not conducive to a productive meeting environment. We set expectations that addressed not only the issue at hand (i.e., personal grooming in a departmental meeting) but also a range of suboptimal behaviors.

Implementing collective policies can be best when:

- *Consistency is needed.* Collective policies ensure that all department members are subject to the same standards of behavior. This helps you navigate claims that you are unfairly targeting someone. As counterintuitive as it may seem, the person whose behavior prompted the collective policy often feels less targeted when a policy is implemented. This is because you have shown that you are willing to apply the same standards across the board.
- *Numerous concerns have been voiced.* I had received several complaints about the personal grooming situation. While the complaints were made behind closed doors, I knew there was a lot of chatter about it in the department. A few snide remarks had been made by different people. A public response was warranted. It was important for the department to know that their concerns had been taken seriously. A private conversation with the faculty member would have left people wondering if any action had been taken.
- *You are worried about the issue recurring.* Having a clear policy to point to is very helpful if issues resurface. Rather than having your opinion about best practices, you have a policy (that has been publicly discussed) to rely on for future violations.
- *The person who prompted the conversation is reasonable and can read the room.* It is key that the person whose behavior is being addressed must be generally agreeable and reflexive enough to understand that they are implicated in the policy and will need to change. The reason for this will become clear in the next chapter.
- *There are ancillary issues that can be addressed.* In this situation, there were other departmental meeting issues that I thought needed to be addressed. The nail-filing incident represented an opportunity to initiate a

public conversation about what we wanted meetings to be in the future. See these moments as opportunities to initiate larger conversations.

The introduction of the new policy had a positive impact on department meetings. While the faculty member initially pushed back a bit, she ultimately complied with the new expectations and the personal grooming stopped. A host of other less-than-ideal behaviors were addressed as well. The collective approach allowed for a resolution without causing friction or tension. In fact, it was a positive experience.

Overall, the experience highlighted the importance of balancing individual concerns with the broader needs of the department. To be clear, collective policies are not always the best course of action. Sometimes addressing the problem with one person is a better course of action. We will address that in the next chapter. Be judicious in determining when a collective policy is appropriate and when a conversation with an individual is the right decision.

REFLECTIONS

1. Do you agree that the nail-filing incident was best handled via collective policy? How would you have handled the situation and why?
2. What are the general criteria that you feel most necessitate collective policies as a response? Do you feel comfortable generating policies in these situations?

Chapter 36

When to Address Problems with Private Conversations

A call from the head of our Human Resources office alerted me to a concerning situation involving a faculty member. The faculty member had not personally violated a policy or harassed anyone, but had instead inserted himself into an ongoing investigation of another faculty member by doing his own mini-investigation. Without consultation or warning, he had reached out to students and faculty directly to interrogate them about the incident that was being investigated. This had unnecessarily complicated and compromised the ongoing investigation. It risked opening the university to liability and to allowing the perpetrator to avoid discipline based on a procedural violation.

Human Resources thought it might be a good idea to offer a workshop at our next department meeting. Why not gather everyone together to have an open and frank conversation about students' rights, our faculty relationship to those rights, and how we as a department should act when there are ongoing investigations? The faculty member whose behavior prompted the visit was a notorious meddler, seemingly always asserting himself in other people's business. Human Resources thought it a good idea to get us all on board so as not to single him out and to get us all collectively working together. At the subsequent department meeting, we all listened to the presentation that clearly covered the behavior of this faculty member. The entire department sat through the presentation that only one of us really needed.

A few days later, I had a disagreement over email with this faculty member about something unrelated (disagreements with this faculty member were common). In our email exchange, with multiple people cc'd, he emphatically referenced the meeting and informed the cc'd folks that Human Resources had come to our department meeting to tell him (and other faculty) about their rights in relationship to managerial oversight.

"After the presentation from Human Resources, I now realize you have violated my rights," he added. The meeting had the opposite of its intended effect. It had been called to address his behavior, but he believed that it was called to protect him.

I realized that the situation was not handled well. In the previous chapter we discussed when developing collective polices are best for addressing problems. While there are certainly advantages, there are times when the best course of action is not a public conversation with the goal of a formal policy. A private, direct, and personal conversation is best when:

- *Someone is likely unable to read the room or be reflexive.* Some people may not possess the necessary reflexivity to see their own behavior implicated in a larger conversation or policy. Some believe that other people are always the problem. If someone is unlikely to realize that their behavior is problematic, then a direct conversation that specifically and clearly identifies the problematic behavior is likely to be more effective.
- *The subject matter is sufficiently serious that you cannot risk misunderstanding.* Sometimes the issue is serious enough that acknowledgment and directness are paramount. The example above is one such situation. Human Resources investigations are serious business. In retrospect, I should have pushed for a direct conversation that acknowledged the seriousness of tampering in such an investigation.
- *There are not ancillary matters, and the intended audience is truly one person.* Some conversations truly benefit everyone, even if one person's behavior was the impetus (like in the last chapter with the nail-filing). But other times, there is really just one person who needs the message. Roping everyone in unnecessarily risks making your department resentful. Respect everyone's time by handling these kinds of issues in private.
- *You want to avoid misinterpretation and rumors.* Private conversations minimize the risk of misinterpretation and the spread of rumors in the department. When issues are addressed publicly, people often start to wonder and discuss where the problem originated. This can lead to unnecessary anxiety, speculation, and gossip. By dealing with sensitive issues in a one-on-one setting, you ensure that the intended message is clear and direct, reducing the likelihood of misinformation spreading.
- *You want to facilitate immediate and direct feedback.* A private conversation allows for immediate and direct feedback and error-correcting in real time. This can be valuable in clarifying misunderstandings and identifying immediate concerns. The immediacy of the feedback loop ensures that both you and the faculty member understand each other's perspectives and can work together. This can lead to quicker resolutions and effective strategies without the delays that can come from more formal or public interventions.

It is your job as chair to decide which approach is appropriate for various issues as they arise. Be judicious and use the criteria in this and the previous chapter to help you sort through if a collective policy or a direct conversation is more likely to yield the results you are hoping for. Ask for advice from your dean or a fellow chair with more experience.

REFLECTIONS

1. How would you evaluate your ability to read the dynamics of your department and in identifying when a private conversation versus a public discussion is the more appropriate course of action?
2. Do you generally feel more comfortable with having public discussions about collective policy or private conversations? Which do you think lends itself more to your communicative style and why?

Chapter 37

Mentoring Junior Faculty

Junior faculty are the burgeoning scholars, educators, and future leaders of your department. They represent both the present vitality and the future legacy of it. As chair, your support is vital in nurturing their potential, guarding their professional trajectory, and safe-guarding their well-being. Junior faculty are at a critical juncture in their careers, and the foundations for their success or failure are being built. The trajectories they set in these early years can determine their career longevity and impact. Your insight and guidance as chair can help them navigate the academic landscape and institutional politics. While the onus is on them, as chair you should play a key role in fostering their growth and helping them avoid pitfalls. When you invest in junior faculty, you are contributing to the stability of your department for years to come. This is worth the effort, as mentorship of junior faculty significantly decreases attrition rates in higher education (Tenorio-Lopes, 2023).

I'll offer some specific suggestions below, but your overarching ethos should be to develop meaningful relationships with your junior faculty. Your role is not to direct, but to empower. This involves a careful balance between providing guidance and fostering autonomy, encouraging junior faculty to align their efforts with both their personal aspirations and the department's strategic goals. Do this by embodying a spirit of collaboration and demonstrating your investment and interest in them. It is not enough to be interested and invested in their success, you must outwardly perform and demonstrate that you are interested and invested. Make sure they feel it. Be interpersonally warm, available, and open. Be the first place junior faculty want to turn to when they have questions and concerns.

One of the pitfalls that junior faculty often fall into is overcommitment. Junior faculty are often eager to prove themselves. They are also in a vulnerable position and sometimes worry that saying "no" to a request will adversely affect their chances at promotion or tenure. They are often viewed as the "new shiny object" on campus, so invitations to participate in various clubs, committees, and projects abound. You need to protect junior faculty from overcommitment by actively guiding them in prioritizing their responsibilities. Ensure that their efforts are aligned with their goals and best interests. And offer to be the bad guy on their behalf. Saying "no" to an invitation from a senior faculty member or administrator can be nerve-wracking. Tell them that they can respond to invitations with something like, "My chair does not think it is a good idea for me to undertake this responsibility." You can also offer to decline the invitation on their behalf.

I would also encourage you to engage in anticipatory guidance (Schor et al., 2011). Junior faculty often do not know what they do not know. Do not always wait for them to come to you with problems; instead, offer guidance on potential challenges and milestones that they may not see. You know the landscape of your department, institution, and academic discipline better than they do. Be proactive in your guidance. This includes helping junior faculty understand the unwritten rules and cultural nuances of the institution.

Help your junior faculty network. They may feel siloed in your department. Your institutional/disciplinary network likely extends further than theirs. Introduce them to people in your network. This can provide them with additional mentors and collaborators and broader perspectives. It also crowdsources the support, so it does not all fall on you. If junior faculty feel connected, they are much more likely to feel satisfied.

Your guidance should not be only pragmatically related to professional tasks. Also provide emotional and psychological support. Remember how vulnerable you felt as a junior faculty member. Try to alleviate anxiety. Do this not simply because it is the kind thing to do, but also because emotional health helps alleviate burnout and creates institutional buy-in. Secure and safe department members generally make better teachers and colleagues. Encourage open dialogue about stress, burnout, and work–life integration and provide resources to address these issues. Do not shy away from these kinds of conversations.

Finally, celebrate their successes. Find ways to show that you notice and value their accomplishments. This means a lot. But also find ways to be encouraging and offer support during setbacks. Do your best to make sure that junior faculty know they can share failures with you. They should not feel like they need to "front" or perform for you. You need to be a mentor when they succeed and when they fail. This can take the form of pragmatic advice, but also emotional support. Let them know that their value to the department is not contingent on the outcome of their latest grant proposal or article submission.

Take your mentorship role seriously as it is essential but often undervalued. At the heart of this practice lies the principle of fostering professional growth through genuine connection, strategic guidance, and emotional support. Your job is not only to steer junior faculty toward professional milestones but also to cultivate their abilities to thrive intellectually, emotionally, and socially. In doing so, you become more than a guide; you are a pivotal figure in shaping the legacy of your department through the success of its emerging scholars. The ripple effects will be felt for years to come.

REFLECTIONS

1. When you were a junior faculty member, who served as a mentor to you? What elements of that relationship were most helpful? How can you replicate them in your own mentorship relationship?
2. Reflect on the balance between guiding and empowering junior faculty. How can you foster autonomy while also ensuring you dispense practical advice when necessary? What does this look like in your leadership practice?

REFERENCES

Schor, N. F., Guillet, R., & McAnarney, E. R. (2011). Anticipatory guidance as a principle of faculty development: Managing transition and change. *Academic Medicine, 86*(10), 1235–1240. DOI: 10.1097/ACM.0b013e31822c1317

Tenorio-Lopes, L. (2023). Mentor-mentee relationships in academia: Insights toward a fulfilling career. *Frontiers in Education, 8*(1198094). https://doi.org/10.3389/feduc.2023.1198094

Chapter 38

Working with Senior Faculty

In the last chapter we covered your relationship with junior faculty. It is easy to understand your responsibility to provide mentorship for those early in their academic careers. They do not know all that you know, and it is clear how they benefit from guidance. But we often overlook the ways in which senior faculty also need mentorship (Stearns et al., 2013). We may assume that senior faculty have things figured out, so they do not need that relationship with their department chair. While senior faculty generally have more institutional and disciplinary knowledge than junior faculty, it is still worth cultivating a mentorship relationship with senior faculty. While junior faculty often look to you for guidance and instruction, the mentorship you offer to senior faculty must be approached differently, with a recognition of their experience and existing contributions to the department.

Different faculty are at different stages in their academic careers, but do not fall into the trap of assuming that your senior faculty are a finished product. It may be tempting to assume that senior faculty have it made due to their years of accumulated accomplishments, institutional investment, and professional advancement. While there are certainly some advantages, senior faculty still face challenges that you need to help with. Research has demonstrated that age has a negative correlation to student teaching evaluations (Stonebraker & Stone, 2015). Senior and midcareer faculty may face challenges that junior faculty do not in adapting to continued changes in online learning (Mansbach & Austin, 2018). Some senior faculty may be prone to professional burnout and academic disengagement (Cruz & Herzog, 2018).

There are often a host of formal resources at a university to help junior faculty in their professional development. They are well advertised and often a point of pride among administrators. That institutional investment generally does not extend to senior faculty. That makes your efforts to this end even more important. It is well worth investing in your senior faculty. Their journey of professional development continues, and you have a role in facilitating it. They are pillars of your department, possessing a wealth of knowledge and a legacy of contributions. There is much to be gained by fostering their continued professional development and departmental engagement. Your role is to honor their expertise while facilitating opportunities for professional growth, adaptation to the evolving demands of higher education, and continued engagement with the department.

The feeling of being left behind is one that sometimes can lead to withdrawal for senior faculty (Cruz & Herzog, 2018). The world of higher education is changing at a rapid pace. Online education, artificial intelligence, social media, and virtual reality are areas that are increasingly becoming more integrated into the college classroom. While there are plenty of exceptions, those who have recently graduated may have certain advantages when it comes to incorporating these technologies into their professional lives. Find ways to help guide and support the professional development of those senior faculty who need it. It is generally not a good idea to specifically single them out, but instead find ways to communicate to all your faculty that you value continued engagement in innovation in higher education. Celebrate those faculty who are engaging and learning new skills to help them stay up-to-date with disciplinary and academic trends. When your senior faculty engage in these professional development opportunities, take extra care to publicly praise their efforts. Mention these efforts in annual reviews. At a department meeting, ask them to report about what they have learned. When possible, offer extrinsic reward and financially support these efforts.

You should also find ways to keep your senior faculty engaged. Include senior faculty in decision-making processes by seeking their advice and considering their perspectives. This not only leverages their wealth of knowledge but also reinforces their value to the department. When innovating, balance the new with the traditional, showing respect for the foundations senior faculty helped build.

So often we hear about the importance of building mentorship opportunities for junior faculty. But do not let this overshadow the importance of caring for all your faculty. Your role as a department chair is not just to manage, but to work to cultivate an environment where every member, regardless of rank or seniority, feels empowered to contribute to the department's success.

REFLECTIONS

1. What does a mentorship relationship look like with senior faculty in your department? How does it differ from that of your junior faculty? Do you feel comfortable with this relationship?
2. What specific actions can you take to ensure that senior faculty feel engaged and invested in the department's future?

REFERENCES

Cruz, L., & Herzog, M. J. (2018). Setting the faculty on fire: Fostering vitality in late career faculty. *Journal of Faculty Development*, *32*(3), 25–34. https://www.researchgate.net/publication/327892040_Setting_the_Faculty_on_Fire_Fostering_Vitality_in_Late_Career_Faculty

Mansbach, J., & Austin, A. E. (2018). Nuanced perspectives about online teaching: Mid-career and senior faculty voices reflecting on academic work in the digital age. *Innovative Higher Education*, *43*, 257–272. https://doi.org/10.1007/s10755-018-9424-4

Stearns, J., Everard, K. M., Gjerde, C. L., Stearns, M., & Shore, W. (2013). Understanding the needs and concerns of senior faculty in academic medicine. *Academic Medicine*, *88*(12), 1927–1933. https://doi.org/10.1097/acm.0000000000000010

Stonebraker, R. J., & Stone, G. S. (2015). Too old to teach? The effect of age on college and university professors. *Research in Higher Education*, *56*, 793–812. https://doi.org/10.1007/s11162-015-9374-y

Chapter 39

Supporting Part-Time Faculty

When department chairs consider their constituents, they usually include students, faculty, and staff. Part-time faculty are often not included in that list. This is due to the fact that adjunct faculty are often considered more like academic gig workers rather than as full-fledged members of the academic communities they serve (Nelson et al., 2020). While adjunct faculty have a different role than full-time faculty at the university, it is an important one. The number of academics who are in part-time roles has been increasing steadily. Given that adjunct faculty (as of this writing) constitute nearly half of all the instructional workforce in universities (National Center for Education Statistics, 2023), their inclusion and support is imperative for the health and function of higher education. As department chair, you should actively foster a culture where part-time faculty are afforded the same respect, support, and sense of community that their full-time counterparts enjoy.

Your support should be rooted in an understanding of the challenges associated with being part-time faculty. They are not compensated at nearly the same rate as their full-time colleagues (Robinson, 2023), despite often teaching the same classes and possessing the same degrees. They lack job security as there is no long-term commitment from the institution for them (Nelson et al., 2020). They may feel isolated from the rest of the department as they are often not included in deliberations or curricular development (Dolan, 2011). I have found that adjunct faculty are often more concerned about student complaints and go out of their way to avoid any confrontations with full-time faculty or staff given their level of vulnerability. They generally are not protected by many of the labor/personnel policies or academic freedom principles that their colleagues take for granted. Furthermore, much of the institutional rhetoric about adjuncts I have been privy to in leadership meetings is centered around how detrimental the increased reliance on part-time faculty is for higher education.

Given the important role that part-time faculty play in providing instruction, it is your obligation to pay attention to their needs. Happy and invested teachers generally provide better instruction. Also, given their general lack of protection at the university, it is your responsibility to do what you can to safeguard them. It is the right thing to do. Sometimes your options for ensuring fair labor practices are limited by the institution (you often cannot pay more or offer increased job security), but you should do what you can.

The first step is to cultivate an inclusive environment where they see you as a resource. They should not be made to feel like second-class departmental citizens. When you have new adjuncts, enthusiastically introduce them to the department as part of the team. Let them know your door is open to them when they have issues in the classroom. When you speak about your part-time faculty with full-time faculty, do so in a way that does not position them as outsiders or "hired hands."

When deliberations or curricular questions arise that intersect with their areas of expertise, reach out and ask for suggestions. While you should not put pressure on them to do additional labor that they are not compensated for, I have found that part-time faculty are usually happy to offer suggestions. Their feedback has been valuable, which is unsurprising given that they often teach a wide array of courses and have a direct line to student feedback. This inclusive approach can communicate that you value them for more than their ability to fill a particular teaching assignment.

Invite adjunct faculty to attend department meetings but communicate that their presence is optional (they should not feel obligated given that they are not compensated for attending meetings). If possible, provide office space or at least a dedicated area where they can work and meet with students. This physical presence within the department can enhance their sense of belonging and professional identity. Add perks and additional incentives when you can. Include them on the department website. Advocate for conversion to full-time status when opportunities arise and they are a good fit. Some of the moments that have made me happiest as chair have been when I have been able to secure a more stable or permanent position for a hardworking adjunct.

Finally, be mindful of the emotional landscape of adjunct faculty. Many may have entered academia with aspirations of a tenure-track position. It is certainly not always the case, but for some, adjunct work may be a source of frustration and disappointment. Approach conversations with empathy and the recognition that they are professionals who have invested significantly in their academic careers. Be encouraging, but also manage expectations and avoid making any promises about job security that may not be fulfilled. One of the experiences I have found most difficult as chair has been informing a part-time faculty member that they did not get the full-time job they had applied for. These conversations are only made more painful if you have contributed to unrealized expectations.

When you can, address systemic issues. Advocate for fair labor practices and institutional protection. This advocacy may make a material difference in the lives of your adjuncts and it can be a strong statement about the values of your department. In fostering an environment of inclusivity, respect, and support for your adjunct faculty, you can not only enhance the quality of education that your students receive but also affirm the value and dignity of every member's contribution to the academic community.

REFLECTIONS

1. What has been your institution's general approach to part-time faculty? Are they treated equitably and fairly? How about in your department? What can you do as a new department chair to contribute to fair labor practices?
2. What measures can you take to acknowledge and address the emotional challenges that part-time faculty may face in their roles?

REFERENCES

Dolan, V. (2011). The isolation of online adjunct faculty and its impact on their performance. *International Review of Research in Open and Distributed Learning*, *12*(2), 62–77. https://doi.org/10.19173/irrodl.v12i2.793

National Center for Education Statistics. (2023). *Characteristics of postsecondary faculty. Condition of education*. U.S. Department of Education, Institution of Education Sciences. https://nces.ed.gov/programs/coe/indicator/csc.

Nelson, G., Monson, M. J., Adibifar, K., & Tinoca, L. (Reviewing editor). (2020). The gig economy comes to academia: Job satisfaction among adjunct faculty. *Cogent Education*, *7*(1). DOI: 10.1080/2331186X.2020.1786338

Robinson, M. A. (2023). Caring for yourself as an adjunct faculty member. In M. A. Robinson (Ed.), *Becoming and supporting online adjunct faculty in a gig economy* (pp. 98–118). IGI Global. https://doi.org/10.4018/978-1-6684-7776-2.ch006

Chapter 40

The Art of Annual Reviews (The Big Picture)

The ritual of the annual evaluation is one of the most daunting aspects of becoming a new department chair. Most chairs do not enjoy doing evaluations as they are time intensive, they are politically and relationally delicate, and they can have profound impacts on the careers of colleagues and the culture of the department. As we have explored in previous chapters, the precarious nature of a chair's managerial authority and the discomfort stemming from your changing relationship with your colleagues can feel particularly palpable during the evaluation process. Writing evaluations underscores your transformation from peer to boss, marking a moment where your authority is formalized, yet the boundaries of your power are also evident through the procedural checks and balances of responses, opportunities for formal challenges, and oversight from other committees and upper administrators. This is all especially daunting when you are new and still acclimating to your position. Having been a chair for eleven years now, I have written around 150 annual reviews. I still find it challenging and one of the least pleasant parts of the job.

While they may not be fun, they are very important. The annual review is a responsibility that comes with the chair position, and you need to just accept that and commit to doing it right. It helps steer faculty growth and shape the department's future. It is your opportunity to motivate, identify and resolve problems, and celebrate accomplishments. While it very important that you approach every annual evaluation season carefully, your first cycle of annual reviews requires a very high level of intentionality. You are setting precedent for your future annual reviews. Comparing this year's annual review to last year's is common, so I would suggest you do so (especially when deficiencies or areas of improvement are marked). Faculty may interpret any changes in approach as disciplinary (even if you assure them otherwise).

Annual reviews really do matter, as they serve as a mirror reflecting both the accomplishments and challenges of a faculty member. Assessments can move careers forward or signal a need for redirection. You must balance your role as both assessor and mentor and recognize the weight that your words carry in these reviews. Some faculty are very sensitive with reviews and are likely to take your words very seriously. Others are very litigious and are likely to challenge the suggestion that there are any areas where they could improve. Your words will likely be parsed for nuance with both sensitive and litigious faculty, so choose them carefully.

The most important piece of advice I can give is to approach the task with humility and a readiness to learn. We all have opinions and individual assessments of our colleagues. There are likely some faculty you respect more than others based on what you have seen of their contributions. As much as possible, try to set your previous assumptions about your colleagues aside and approach each annual review with an open mind. See it as an opportunity to learn more about your colleagues, to understand their motivations, achievements, and challenges. Sometimes you will be surprised by the things that your colleagues have accomplished in the previous year. The reverse also happens; a colleague whose achievements seemed very impressive might not be so under further review. Resist forming conclusions before you have reviewed the evidence. Be willing to have your mind changed. Develop a mindset for objectivity. The goal is to create a space where faculty are evaluated based on their accomplishments (or lack thereof) rather than their reputation. This open-minded approach is important not only because it is fair, but because it establishes your credibility and the trustworthiness of the process.

Disentangling your professional judgments from your personal relationships is also essential. This is easier said than done, as departments are often close-knit units. Divorce your professional assessment from your personal relationships. Given this challenge, it can be tempting to approach annual reviews as opportunities to offer rhetorical support. Remember that evaluations are meant to assess, not cheerlead. This sometimes means identifying areas where growth is necessary. Faculty often do not appreciate this, but evaluations become meaningless if you are unwilling to identify gaps and ways faculty can improve. You do not do faculty members any favors by being too afraid to identify areas where they can grow. Unwillingness to provide honest assessment creates a far too common scenario where faculty become surprised by more thorough reviews later (Perlmutter, 2012). Additionally, not identifying clear gaps reflects poorly on you as chair. When you sign an evaluation, your reputation is on the line. Failing to address obvious improvement areas is not a good look.

Do not approach annual faculty evaluations as merely an administrative exercise. Instead, recognize them as an opportunity to make a statement on the value and direction of academic work. While they make feel daunting, remember that it is labor that is worth approaching mindfully. When executed with thoughtfulness and care, the annual evaluation can contribute to an environment where excellence is recognized, mediocrity is challenged, and potential is nurtured. Approach this task with the gravity and dedication it deserves as it is one of the most significant contributions you can make to your department and university.

REFLECTIONS

1. How do you feel about conducting annual reviews? What challenges do you foresee? Is there anyone whose annual review you are particularly anxious to conduct? Why?
2. Have annual reviews in your department generally been productive? What precedent do you want to set in your first cycle of annual reviews? How do you plan on setting it?

REFERENCE

Perlmutter, D. D. (2012, January 9). You are never a sure thing. *Chronicle of Higher Education*. https://www.chronicle.com/article/you-are-never-a-sure-thing

Chapter 41

Strategic Approaches to Annual Faculty Evaluations

The previous chapter offered a broad overview of how you should approach the annual review process. This chapter gets in the weeds a bit more, outlining some strategic methods for writing annual reviews so that they foster growth, ensure accountability, and reward excellence within your department. The overarching thing to remember is that annual evaluations should be approached as a road map for faculty, helping them identify what is and what is not working and providing options for future paths. The following suggestions offer some guidance on how you might operationalize that ethos.

Understand policy and precedent. You must be well versed in your university's policies regarding evaluation. They exist to ensure that evaluations align with the institution's broader goals and adhere to standards of equity and fairness. Review those policies carefully. If you are in a unionized environment, find the relevant sections in your collective bargaining agreement. There are often explicit instructions. You must follow protocol to the letter of the law. If there are any disagreements over the content of the review, they become much more complicated if the formal processes are not adhered to. Equally important is the consideration of precedent. You are new to doing this, and that is important. Review the past few annual evaluations of each faculty member before you write yours. There will be things you did not know in them. This can inform you of the faculty's historical performance and departmental expectations. It also allows you to recognize and address persistent challenges and ongoing successes.

Have clarity, consistency, and directness. Your evaluations must be clear, leaving no room for ambiguity or misinterpretation. They should be straightforward, stating clearly what has been done well and what needs improvement. This allows your evaluations to be legible to your faculty and other administrators or committees who might participate in the evaluation process

(Rogers, 2021). Direct statements such as, "Your recent article titled xxxx is exemplary; I encourage you to continue this line of research" is far more clear than vague praise about a faculty member's overall research agenda. When there are deficiencies, stick to direct language that identifies the problems but does not place blame. "You were the faculty adviser to xxxx club. This past year the club only met once. I would encourage you to find ways to engage students to be more involved" is less volatile than "You only held one meeting last year for xxxx student club. Please hold more meetings." Consistency is also key. It is best to have a basic format that you follow for these annual evaluations. This not only ensures fairness, but also helps you maintain an objective stance. A standardized approach allows for equitable assessment and can protect you against claims of bias. It also streamlines the labor. Finally, directness should not be confused with harshness. The tone of your evaluation should be professional and respectful, offering specific guidance.

Encourage transparency. You should verify claims of faculty achievements. It has happened several times in my own experience as chair that an accomplishment or presentation has been significantly exaggerated in a faculty member's annual review of accomplishments. I have had faculty claim that a classification given to all the members of an academic division was a prestigious award, that a blog post was a peer-reviewed research article, that a query letter sent to a book editor was a book contract, and that a conference presentation was a keynote address. I now check all accomplishments. This is much easier in the digital age than previously. When a faculty member lists an award or a conference presentation, due diligence from you not only validates these claims but it expresses a genuine interest in the faculty's work. If there are discrepancies in the records, it is prudent to seek clarification without presumption or accusation. Just bring the confusion to the faculty member. Asking for context can lead to a more accurate understanding of their accomplishments. This practice also reinforces the expectation of transparency and honesty in the department.

Manage reactions. Faculty will have various reactions to their evaluations. Some may be receptive, while others may be resistant or emotional. Do not let your evaluation be dictated by your anticipation of a faculty member's potential reaction. You should be prepared to respond to these reactions with grace and openness. Always be willing to meet with faculty members to discuss the annual review. Offer a meeting when you submit the review. If faculty want to meet, listen to them with an open mind. When you meet, focus on setting clear goals and how you can support them. Use these meetings as an opportunity to build relationships with your colleagues and to emphasize that you understand the evaluation process as a dialogue rather than a monologue. Work to make faculty feel understood and valued. These meetings also provide an opportunity to discuss the long-term vision of the department and how faculty members see themselves contributing.

Evaluations are not anyone's favorite part of the job. But, approaching them strategically and with a clear sense of what you want to accomplish will help you feel like you are getting the most out of them. Clear, fair, and transparent evaluations can go a long way toward not only serving your university's needs, but also supporting the professional journey of each of your faculty members.

REFLECTIONS

1. Reflecting on the suggestion to standardize your approach to evaluations, how do you envision creating an evaluative process that is fair, objective, and respectful while also tailored to individual faculty members?
2. Do you agree with the suggestion to verify faculty accomplishments? Why or why not? What are the drawbacks of each approach? How would you handle a situation where an accomplishment was exaggerated in a faculty member's report?

REFERENCE

Rogers, G. (2021, October 21). *Too much information: Candor and the department chair.* Chronicle of Higher Education. https://www.chronicle.com/article/too-much-information-candor-and-the-department-chair

Chapter 42

Do Not Play Politics with Your Course Schedule

A colleague (a senior faculty member and former chair) pleaded with me. "You do not want people reading into the political implications of the schedule. You are opening a can of worms here." I knew that he was right, but it was a frustrating realization. This conversation had been prompted by an escalating conflict with another faculty member who often refused to participate in departmental events. He taught two days a week, scheduled his office hours (which he left his door closed for) immediately after class, and then left. When departmental obligations would fall outside of these few hours, he would not participate. He made it a policy to not answer emails outside of office hours. As a chair, I certainly understand and respect reasonable boundaries, but this withdrawal was impacting the department too much. This professor did not run a lab, have an additional institutional responsibility, or an aggressive research agenda that warranted this kind of unavailability. Complaints about his inaccessibility were frequent among students, and his colleagues were increasingly frustrated by the scheduling constraints his absence imposed.

My breaking point surfaced when we had a job candidate on campus. The widely accepted departmental practice was that all faculty attend teaching and research demonstrations for job candidates. Despite prior reminders of this expectation, the absentee faculty member was nowhere to be found when our prospective hire was on campus. When I queried about his absence, he replied by explaining, "As you know, I only teach on Tuesday and Thursday, so those are the only days I am on campus." In an earlier chapter, we focused on the emotional labor of being chair, which involves emotional regulation. In this situation I failed and unwisely let my emotions do all the heavy lifting in the decision-making process. I fired off an email that said, "As you know, I am currently in the process of building next semester's course schedule.

Since you can only be on campus on days you teach, and we often have things that require attendance on other days, I will be scheduling you for classes Monday–Friday."

The faculty member cried "foul" to me and then reported the interaction with the senior colleague mentioned at the opening of this chapter. His urging confirmed what I already knew was true. This was an ill-advised decision on my part. It was reactive, was rash, and would lead to downstream consequences that I did not want.

I include the story above because it crystallizes a few overarching lessons that are paramount as you approach the course schedule. While there are a variety of tasks that you are responsible for as a department chair, few are as essential as building a schedule—it is a core duty. My mistake in the example above was in weaponizing the schedule. I should not have played office politics with something central to the functioning of the department and essential for student success.

So many of the tasks we do as chair are inherently connected to the politics of academic life. Committee assignments, annual reviews, department meeting agendas, the budget, who gets featured on the department's social media page, and many of the other responsibilities of the chair—these all have ways of becoming political (often in unanticipated ways). The course schedule is the backbone of the department though. It is ultimately the product your department offers—the thing that keeps the lights on. You should do your best to avoid making it political, as it is how students engage with your department directly and one of the primary keys of student satisfaction and success.

Building a course schedule is already political enough without intentionally making it so. When course-scheduling season comes around, you are likely to hear from faculty about a host of requests. Faculty will relay which times do not work for them, what classrooms they prefer, why they are more qualified than another faculty member to teach a certain subject, why their classes should be back-to-back, and so on. Some of these rationales are perfectly reasonable and appropriate. But you will most likely not be able to create the optimal schedule based on student need while accommodating all of the faculty requests you field.

As chair, you need to be able to communicate to faculty that the course schedule is based on student needs. You are trying to ensure that students have the courses they need to graduate on time. You need courses to fill and you need to ensure that students have access to the courses that they want. Faculty preferences/needs come second. Faculty will be much more forgiving when their requests are not honored if they believe that you made the decision in the interest of students.

This is why my senior colleague wisely talked me out of using the course schedule to modify faculty behavior. It is not enough to simply tell your faculty that the singular criteria for building the schedule is student need—they have to believe it. By politicizing the schedule in this way, I was undermining my credibility and invited other departmental members to question the schedule. The error was not in my desire to fix the absent faculty member's behavior, but instead using the course schedule as the tool to do so. Some things are too important to be made more political than they already are.

REFLECTIONS

1. Do you agree that using the schedule in this way to communicate to a faculty member about availability was problematic? How would you have handled the situation?
2. Which other responsibilities of a department chair should be safeguarded against becoming unnecessarily politicized?

Chapter 43

Course-Scheduling Strategies

In the last chapter we discussed the importance of not weaponizing course scheduling. Here we will discuss some specific strategies to consider when you build your first course schedule. While I recognize the importance of building an optimized schedule, it is not something I particularly enjoy. I think this feeling is motivated by the stakes. Your faculty's work life is immediately affected by the decisions you make when building the schedule. Also, there is not a lot of grace in building the schedule. When you screw something up, it is visible for everyone to see and often has material consequences (i.e., classes getting cancelled). Unlike some other decisions you make as chair, it is not easy to pivot once the schedule is in place. It can be stressful and high pressure, especially doing it for the first time. Below are a few suggestions that can help you avoid missteps in the process.

Leverage experienced resources. Your first experience as a schedule creator should not be a solitary endeavor. Draw on the wisdom and experience of those who have built course schedules in the past. This is invaluable, as there are histories, tendencies, and idiosyncrasies that you will not know. Work with the former chair, your office associate, and the dean's office carefully. It is also advantageous to meet with someone in the registrar's office, as they often have bird's-eye insight. If your university is large enough to have one, meeting with someone in the advising office about student need is wise as well. These folks can offer practical advice and solutions to problems that a first-time course scheduler may not even foresee.

Limit faculty input. This suggestion seemingly contradicts the last one, but it stands. While it may seem beneficial to gather as much input as possible from your faculty, this approach can quickly become counterproductive. Faculty members are experts in their respective fields, but generally not in course scheduling. They are myopic. That is not a judgment. Their view is just narrower than yours. Their advice is often (unintentionally) not aligned with the broader needs of the department and students. If you ask, then you may very well find yourself in a situation where you have to justify why you are not implementing their suggestion. Certainly, ask if you have a specific question about a particular class that a faculty member is equipped to answer, but generally I have found it much easier not to crowdsource the schedule.

Recognize obligations and opportunities. As chair, it is important to be aware of your own scheduling obligations and to avoid conflicts that could impede your ability to fulfill your chair duties. Be conscientious about standing meetings, and make sure you do not schedule your classes during them. One semester, very early in my career as chair, I scheduled my own class during the same time as our biweekly all-chairs meeting with the dean. I had to alternate between sending the assistant chair to the meetings and finding substitute teachers for my class. I never made that mistake again. This awareness should extend to fostering student success through thoughtful scheduling. Consider student needs, popular classes, and the benefits of block scheduling, where related courses are scheduled back-to-back to facilitate student enrollment and success.

Make data-driven decisions. Making informed scheduling decisions requires a data-driven approach. Your university may have software that helps with this. If so, familiarize yourself with it. Analyze patterns from previous semesters to get a sense of which classes filled quickly, which did not, which instructors are most popular, and how class time impacts enrollment. This analysis can guide your decision-making on which courses to offer, at what times and with which instructors to maximize student engagement and satisfaction. It also gives you a clear rationale to provide if anyone has questions about the schedule.

Manage new preparations and premium times. Avoid overburdening faculty with too many courses they have never taught before. This can affect the quality of instruction and decrease faculty satisfaction. Additionally, manage the allocation of premium class times (generally 10:00 a.m. to 2:00 p.m.) in a way that is fairly distributed among faculty. This can prevent resentment and burnout. Communicate openly about the impossibility of giving everyone their preferred times and emphasize the necessity of a rotation.

Avoid conflicts. Avoid double-scheduling classes that compete for the same pool of students. Coordinate with other departments to avoid scheduling conflicts, especially for upper-level specialty classes or classes popular with majors from other departments. This coordination can ensure that students have access to the courses they need without unnecessary scheduling conflicts.

Don't allow faculty and class ownership. Build the schedule remembering that the university owns classes, not individual faculty members. Some faculty act as if they have ownership of certain classes. This is unproductive and unfair. Instead, a more dynamic and equitable approach is to assign courses as if no one owns them. This does not mean that some faculty are not more qualified than others, but instead that faculty should not claim ownership of a class based on the sole fact that they have taught it before. Faculty ownership claims generally disadvantages junior faculty (and students who do not get to learn from the junior faculty). Instead, if more than one faculty are interested and qualified in a class, find ways to work them into a rotation.

Understand departmental peculiarities. Every department has unique characteristics that affect the schedule. It may be a high number of student-athletes, nontraditional students needing night classes, or specific requirements for online degree programs. Understanding these issues and accounting for them in the scheduling process is important.

Building a course schedule is difficult. No one expects you to be perfect your first time. Ask lots of questions, have someone check your work, and pay attention to what did and did not work. The ultimate goal is to make schedule building an ongoing process. It happens every semester, so you have lots of opportunities to get better. Be open to feedback, and in time you will be able to efficiently create a schedule that supports student success.

REFLECTIONS

1. How much do you know about how the schedule is developed in your department? What processes have been used in the past? How much input has the previous chair solicited? Are you happy with the current scheduling system? Are students?
2. Your first course schedule will not be perfect. How will you create systems for feedback and learning from the experience? How will you review the effectiveness of the schedule and adjustments in subsequent years?

Chapter 44

The Summer Schedule

In the last chapter I confessed that, despite understanding the necessity of doing it well, I find little joy in crafting the course schedule due to its immediate impact on faculty and students and my inability to give everyone what they want. This feeling is even more pronounced when it comes to creating the summer schedule, which I find particularly taxing. It stands as one of the least enjoyable and most stressful responsibilities of my role as chair. At each of the three universities where I have served as chair, organizing the summer schedule has been a significant source of stress for me and a cause of dissatisfaction among faculty members.

The stress associated with crafting the summer course schedule comes from various factors (many of which were covered in the last chapter). The loudest factor, and the one distinct to the summer, is faculty demand. Summer classes offer a chance to augment salary. The financial incentive varies from institution to institution, but it is usually desirable. The financial incentive can turn summer scheduling into an academic version of *The Hunger Games*. It is rare that every faculty member who wants a summer class can get one. Around the time that summer scheduling comes, you may notice some faculty members dropping hints about "necessary" summer courses that are coincidentally the one they happen to teach—what are the odds? You may have some faculty members randomly mentioning why another faculty member should not be teaching a particular class that is offered in the summer. Other times, the pretense is dropped, and some faculty will approach and explicitly appeal to you (based on fairness or monetary need). The jockeying can be overwhelming and uncomfortable.

The noise created by faculty posturing can get loud and can drown out the thing you should truly be focused on when building the schedule—student need. Summer represents a critical period for students to get ahead, catch up, or lighten the load for their upcoming academic year. Therefore, when putting together the schedule, view it as an extension of the fall and spring terms, ensuring a coherent and logical flow of course offerings (Lytle & Kops, 2021).

Developing a fair and transparent scheduling policy is key to managing the summer scheduling process effectively. When I first started as chair, I did not have a policy to rely on. I was tasked with developing and proposing a summer schedule based on what I thought was necessary. I now have a policy, and it makes all the difference in my stress level. When developing a summer schedule policy, start by seeking input from faculty, as their buy-in is essential for any policy to be successful. Ask faculty to clarify the values they want to see in a summer course policy. The more automated and clear the policy can be, the better.

If you are in a situation to do so, ask your faculty to develop the summer policy. Assemble an ad hoc committee and have them bring a proposal to the whole faculty. Be judicious about who is on the committee. Include both senior and junior faculty who vary in areas of expertise. Ask the committee to develop a policy that covers every likely situation, so you are not required to make any independent decisions. Be explicit about the scheduling process, including whose turn it is to teach in the summer, where the rotation starts, and how future opportunities will be distributed. Include scenarios where a faculty member is assigned a class that does not make the schedule or a faculty member is up in the rotation but they are not qualified to teach the class that needs to be offered. There should be little room for interpretation.

When charging the committee, be clear that while you want them to develop the policy on their own, you are willing to veto any policy that is not equitable. A policy that has the same people teaching every summer is not a fair policy and will breed contempt. Everyone, regardless of seniority, needs to be included in a rotation. I have always been bothered when senior faculty try to bogart these kinds of financial opportunities. A policy that places too much weight on seniority benefits those who are already among the highest earners. I have advocated for a system that favors junior faculty, who typically earn less, though this idea has generally not received wide support when I've suggested it.

Perhaps you already have a summer policy in your department. If so, this may not be the most relevant of chapters to you. Regardless, it is worth revisiting the policy periodically to ensure that it is working and represents the values of your department.

When you have a policy, your job in relationship to the summer schedule becomes about enforcing the policy rather than adjudicating the course schedule. Do not ever bend the policy. No good will come of it. I suggest repeatedly reminding your faculty when summer scheduling season comes around that your responsibility is to apply the policy rather than make decisions. There is no point in anyone appealing to you as you are bound to it. This should help alleviate concerns of unfairness and help mitigate some of the underlying stress associated with summer scheduling.

REFLECTIONS

1. How are summer schedules developed in your department? Is it fair? Are people generally happy with it? What can be done to improve the process?
2. Do you feel comfortable about your involvement in terms of the summer schedule? What obstacles do you foresee in relationship to the summer schedule?

REFERENCE

Lytle, L., & Kops, W. (2021). What every president and every chief academic officer should know about college and university summer sessions—redux. *Summer Academe: A Journal of Higher Education, 14.* https://doi.org/10.25894/sa.121

Chapter 45

Your Department's Social Media Presence

One of the things that you may not have been necessarily conscious of when signing up to be a department chair is that you now have some ownership of the department's social media presence. This may seem daunting, especially if digital communication is not your area of expertise. Social media is too important to ignore though. You being new to the position offers a precious opportunity to reassess and potentially revitalize how your department presents itself to the outside world through social media.

Effective social media strategy in an academic setting revolves around authenticity and engagement. Your department's social media presence is not only about broadcasting what you are doing but also about engaging platforms for interaction that showcase your unique departmental personality, achievements, and connections to the community.

To leverage social media effectively, it is essential to start with a clear plan, which leads to a strategy. Identify the platforms that best align with what you want to accomplish (Horvath & Romano, 2022). Are you trying to attract prospective students, engage alumni, create community among current students, solicit donations, promote events, or highlight faculty achievements? Every platform has its strengths and limitations. You likely cannot use them all without significant time investment, so choose strategically. I am not going to make any suggestions here about specific platforms, as that information is likely to be outdated by the time this goes to print. The digital landscape is always moving. Stay open and seek guidance from those who have knowledge about these trends, especially students.

One of the benefits of a departmental social media account is that you can infuse it with your departmental personality. It is divorced from the usually slick, sanitized, and packaged university website (Herrmann, 2015). Unlike the university's broader marketing efforts, your social media presence can be more personalized and informal. It can have more heart and character. It is not an invitation to completely depart from the university's messaging (as there should be some alignment), but rather a reminder to highlight what makes your department unique. While you may not be a social media expert, you are an expert in why your department stands out.

Given that you have a lot of things on your plate, and you are learning a whole new skill set as chair, it is unlikely that you have the bandwidth to manage your department's social media directly. Consider delegating this. Bring in an intern, perhaps a student in communications, business, or marketing. As a chair of a communications department, we regularly put students in these kinds of internship opportunities. This not only offloads much of the work, but it also puts your strategy in the hands of someone who is likely more informed about the kinds of things that make a social media presence attractive to many departmental stakeholders.

Make sure you meet with your intern to discuss and refine social media strategy. This collaboration should focus on setting goals, identifying target audiences, determining frequency of posts and how to increase engagement, and which content themes align with your department's identity. Also discuss what determines success and how you will measure it. Then monitor your feed and check in periodically. Also, set up preferred communication channels with your intern so you know you can get ahold of them quickly when something comes up unexpectedly that you want to feature.

Engaging in social media offers you an opportunity to showcase your department's vibrancy, diversity, and excellence. It provides an opportunity to have some control over your department's public image. The one thing you absolutely do not want to do is to have an inactive social media presence. An infrequently updated and out-of-date page is far worse than not having one at all. You do not want to cultivate the idea that your department is stagnant. If you do not think you can keep up, then do not try. If you find yourself unable to keep up, delete your accounts so people do not log on and find an account that has not been updated in a year. A sad and sorry social media presence can actively drive students and donors away.

One last thing to consider is who gets regularly featured in your department's social media presence. This can become more political than you might imagine. I say this from experience, as I have had faculty upset and complain that other faculty have been more prominently featured in social media posts. This is just a word of caution to be conscientious. You may not even consider who is being repeatedly featured as you simply highlight what is happening, and active faculty tend to do lots of things that you want to highlight. But it is worth making sure that a variety of faculty are represented at different times.

Cultivating an engaging departmental social media presence is a great way to show yourself as a proactive, forward-thinking, and engaged department chair. It allows you to connect with key stakeholders in meaningful ways. It helps you in both outward- and inward-facing ways. As a new chair, social media offers a powerful opportunity to directly influence perception and build connection. By thoughtfully engaging in this way, you can ensure that your department's digital presence is an active and accurate reflection of its vibrant academic community and values.

REFLECTIONS

1. How would you rate your department's current social media presence? What is the current social media strategy? What is and is not working?
2. Given your limited time and resources, how can you effectively manage and delegate social media responsibilities? How involved do you think you can and should be in the day-to-day management of your department's social media presence?

REFERENCES

Herrmann, R. (2015, August 31). *Why your department needs social media.* Chronicle of Higher Education. https://www.chronicle.com/article/why-your-department-needs-social-media

Horvath, M., & Romano, C. (2022, September 19). *Does every department need Insta?* Volt. https://voltedu.com/insights/does-every-department-need-insta

Chapter 46

Digital Dilemmas

STORY #1

"Maybe none of us in the department should be friends with each other on social media then," my colleague stated in raised voice as she stood from her seat in my office. "You don't have to be Facebook friends with anyone you don't want to, including me," I replied. She turned around and walked out without another word. Later that afternoon, in my dean's office recounting the series of events that led to that conversation, he reassured me that my response had been the correct one. "It seems like she abused your trust. My brother is an employment lawyer, and he was telling me just the other day how messy it is sorting through all the legal implications of social media in the workplace. I am still sorting all this out myself, but I think it is good that you explained to her that she does not have any kind of professional requirement to maintain a social media connection with you, or anyone in the department." As he was talking, a quick glance at my phone confirmed that she had made good on her threat. We were no longer Facebook friends.

This friction stemmed from a conversation we had a few weeks earlier. She explained that her father was ill, and she needed to help him transition to an assisted care facility. He lived overseas, so she had to travel, and she would be gone for about two weeks. She needed to take care of this urgent family matter, so could she move her classes online for a few weeks? As much as I hate mid-semester class modality pivots, I was understanding and supportive given the gravity of the situation. A few days into her trip, another faculty member came to my office and sheepishly explained that he didn't want to get anyone in trouble, but that I should check her social media page. Photos of fancy hotels, delicious-looking food, wildlife excursions, a sporting tournament that her daughter was participating in, and a spa day all seemed to contradict the gravity of the situation that she had presented to me. News of her Facebook posts spread among the department, and her colleagues grew increasingly unhappy. To make matters worse, she was Facebook friends with many of her students, who had been informed by the department about her classes moving online due to a family emergency. They could all see these photos as well.

STORY #2

"I understand your impulse to address this, Ben. But these things get tricky and you have to be careful. You do not want her accusing you of violating her right to free speech." My colleague in Human Resources continued with "let's work on a response to her email together." A department member was unhappy with some changes to the department that had been voted on democratically. This faculty member took her displeasure to social media and publicly contradicted departmental messaging about the changes. I had sent what I thought was a friendly request politely asking her if she would consider removing the post as it was bad public relations for us. She responded with a message cc'ing the dean, the provost, and a lawyer accusing me of silencing her.

Both stories can serve as cautionary tales as they highlight the pitfalls and the nuanced judgment required to manage such situations effectively. Social media has changed our relationships, and as a department chair it is likely that at some point you will have to address some issues related to social media. The first story highlights the complicated blurring of lines between personal and professional life on social media. When my colleague's online activity became public within the department, it not only raised questions about integrity but also exposed the department to public scrutiny. The takeaway here is that there should be clear communication about how personal activities can impact professional reputations. If my colleague wanted to have some fun while abroad, she should have considered the bind it put us all in when she broadcast it. I was left without a choice. I had to respond.

Connecting this to the second story, the theme of careful navigation around these issues becomes even more important. My attempt to mitigate the situation, and the subsequent accusation of free-speech violation, illustrates the complexity of addressing issues accounting for departmental best interest, institutional policy, and legal liability. Social media is a multiedged sword. While it can be a tool for camaraderie and connection with your colleagues, as a department chair you must remember that your role comes with the need to sometimes makes difficult decisions that can be complicated by the public nature of social media. The complication in both stories is the ways in which the lines between the personal and professional are blurred and made public.

There are often no easy answers as the politics, norms, and technology embedded in social media are constantly in flux and presenting new challenges. The best advice I can give is to be vigilant and not to sort through these matters on your own. Ask for advice and consult others who you trust, specifically in your dean's office, Human Resources, and your institution's legal office. Sorting through this ever-evolving landscape of social media requires you to seek guidance from those who can help you sort through the legal and ethical frameworks to best inform your actions on a case-by-case basis.

REFLECTIONS

1. What do you think constitutes ethical leadership in the face of the kinds of challenges that social media presents? How comfortable would you feel confronting a colleague about social media behavior that reflects poorly on your department?
2. Reflect on the two stories presented. How would you handle each one? What are the interests that a chair is required to balance in these kinds of situations? How do you prioritize them in any given situation?

Chapter 47

Academic Bullies

"I just feel like she is trying to get me fired," Richard explained, wiping away a tear. I stood and walked to my desk to grab a tissue for him. I knew his tears were warranted. Jen was, in fact, trying to get him fired. She had made that explicit to me the day before this conversation when she criticized his teaching qualifications, claiming that she was forced not only to teach her own classes now, but also to unteach all of the misconceptions he had put in students' heads. Richard was in his first year, which no doubt left him feeling vulnerable. When I challenged Jen wondering why she had given him such a strong endorsement when she chaired the search committee that selected him, she retorted that he had falsified his qualifications. This was a claim she could not substantiate, but she just "knew it was true."

What followed was a targeted campaign of harassment directed against Richard as Jen undermined him at every turn. She belittled him in front of students, insisted on overseeing his campus collaborations, encouraged students to secretly record conversations with him in hopes of finding material to use against him, lodged numerous complaints against him with Human Resources, and spread rumors to students. She even showed up unannounced to sit in on his class to observe his teaching. Sadly, this was not new territory for Jen. She had a history of targeting colleagues through public humiliation, leveraging the tenure review process for intimidation, spreading lies and conspiracy theories, and demanding special treatment. The outgoing department chair had warned me about her, suggesting I do my best not to "get on her bad side."

While bullying in the workplace is generally a pervasive issue that transcends sectors and job titles, it seems to be especially prevalent in higher education. Academic bullying is likely due to the unique structure and cultural factors inherent in academia. It tends to occur in situations where there is a power imbalance, where the victim has limited options for defense, and where there are opportunities for repetitive harassment (Berry, 2016). Higher education has a dispersed power structure, an emphasis on hierarchy, and protections offered by tenure and a peer-review tenure process. These all provide fertile ground for such behavior (Twale & De Luca, 2008). Academic bullying can manifest in a variety of forms, including disputes over resources, policies, colleagues' credentials, procedures, and academic appointments. These disputes often mask the true motive of the academic bully: asserting and maintaining power.

The culture of fear created by an academic bully often leads departmental members to alter their behavior preemptively to avoid triggering confrontations. I have had faculty confess to me that they get scared before sending emails to the department for fear of the response it will trigger in a bully. This ethos undermines the collegial and collaborative atmosphere that you want to cultivate as a chair.

One particularly insidious aspect of academic bullying is the pervasiveness of "victim bullies" (Gunsalus, 2006). This is the most common kind of bully that I have observed in higher education. These folks continually portray themselves as a wounded martyr facing persecution whenever they do not receive preferential treatment or their authority is questioned. They often leverage claims of academic freedom or faculty governance to justify their actions. Any attempt to push back or address their behavior is then framed as further proof of their victim status. The irony is that these individuals often enjoy significant protection and resources within the institution.

We have discussed difficult faculty elsewhere in the volume, but the distinction between problem faculty and bullies is crucial. The former may be challenging, but the latter actively exploits power imbalances to foster fear and assert dominance. This kind of behavior not only affects individual departmental members directly but also erodes departmental culture. It hinders collaboration, redirects attention, sows an ethos of mistrust, and harms the overall well-being of faculty, staff, and students alike. The modus operandi of the department can easily become "don't upset the bully or it is going to be a whole thing."

The role of a department chair is pivotal in addressing and mitigating the impact of academic bullying. You will likely become exposed to more of it now. Prior to being chair you might have had the luxury of distancing yourself from these issues. However, now that you are chair, confronting and managing bullying becomes a critical responsibility. Doing so is rewarding, but difficult. In my eleven years as chair, publicly confronting a bully is the thing I have received the most faculty "thank-you's" for. Successfully addressing a bully may not show up on your curriculum vitae or annual review, but it can be one of the most impactful achievements of your tenure as chair.

REFLECTIONS

1. Do you agree that bullying seems especially prevalent in higher education? What is it about higher education that invites this kind of behavior? What is a chair's role in addressing it?
2. Have you become privy to any bullying behavior since you assumed the role of chair? How have you initially addressed these issues?

REFERENCES

Berry, K. (2016). *Bullied: Tales of torment, identity and youth*. Taylor and Francis.

Gunsalus, C. K. (2006). *The college administrator's survival guide*. Harvard University Press.

Mahmoudi, M. (2019). Academic bullies leave no trace. *BioImpacts, 9*(3), 129–130. https://doi.org/10.15171/bi.2019.17

Twale, D. J., & De Luca, B. M. (2008). *Faculty incivility: The rise of the academic bully culture and what to do about it*. Jossey Bass.

Chapter 48

Practical Advice for Handling Academic Bullies

Handling academic bullies is not easy. I have more experience dealing with them than I wish. By my count, in my eleven years as chair, I have served as chair of four people who I would unequivocally label as academic bullies. As I explained in the last chapter, I am not referring to difficult faculty, but instead to people who seem to relish in harassing people as a way of preserving their own power and influence. My success with bullies has improved over the last eleven years, though it has been tough going at times.

Universities are not typically designed to combat bullies, especially when bullies are shielded by tenure and those with less power fear they will lose their jobs if they speak up. Disciplinary procedures can be ineffectual, giving bullies a lot of latitude for bad behavior. Institutional support tends to be lacking. You might find plenty of sympathetic ears in your dean's and Human Resource offices, but tangible support is often scarce. Academic bullies are clever (they usually have advanced degrees after all), knowing how to work within the system's gray areas to avoid official reprimand (Mahmoudi, 2019). They straddle the line of plausible deniability, making formal institutional intervention difficult. When they are reprimanded, it is usually just further proof of their victimhood. Additionally, bullying is rarely about a single egregious act. It is usually a series of smaller aggressive behaviors that take their toll over time. It is hard to explain patterns of behaviors to outsiders. To outsiders without context, it may not always be clear why certain bullying behaviors are problematic. Given these factors, the burden primarily falls on you as chair to handle at a departmental level.

The most important lesson when dealing with a bully is one that took me far too long to learn. You cannot stop the behavior. I labored under the illusion that I could communicate and persuade bullies to change their behavior. Most departmental members are reasonable people who are moved by appeals to the common good, but not bullies. I offer this advice as a chair of a communications department. I teach persuasion and organizational communication, so I believe in the power of communication. We often assume we can communicate our way to resolution in all conflicts. This assumes good faith and a common desire by all parties for best outcomes. Bullies do not share these objectives. Initially, give people the benefit of the doubt and attempt communication, but do not expend energy on those who do not reciprocate in good faith.

Your focus should then shift to mitigating the bully's impact and empowering your department. Direct your managerial efforts to the rest of the department, to those who are tired of being bullied. A bully's power rests on the fear they can instill. The best way to deal with a bully is to expose their threats as powerless. While you may not be able stop the bullying behavior, you can empower those in your department to respond to it in healthy ways. A bully's power relies on the fear they create. Your best strategy is to break the spell that the bully casts on your department. If you can make your department unafraid, then the bully loses their power.

This is certainly easier said than done, but I have found that the hardest part is initiating this plan. Once you begin to undermine the bully's perceived power, it can crumble quickly. The best way to do this is to model being unafraid for your department. Do your work without trembling. Do not let the bully drive your agenda or drain your energy. This often involves publicly labeling and identifying the behavior. Bullying thrives in environments where it is tacitly tolerated. People may roll their eyes or whisper in hallways, but the behavior itself is usually not confronted. The initial step is to confront these behaviors directly. When the bully sends out a departmental email attacking someone, you can send a simple reply that says, "We should all be keeping these conversations civil. Personal attacks are counterproductive and not in our best interest. We do not have to agree on everything, but we should be engaging each other with respect." Your response sets the tone for the department culture. Lead by example and show that you are not afraid and that you will not tolerate incivility.

It is also effective to work to "box in" the bully by gradually reducing their influence. This involves being firm and assertive in your decisions, especially when they go against the bully's wishes. When the bully loudly challenges you at a department meeting, thank them for their input and move on. Do not get into a tit-for-tat exchange. This favors the bully. George Orwell once said, "Never wrestle a pig in the mud. You will both get dirty, and the pig likes it." Bullies thrive on the fight. They enjoy it. Do not give it to them. You are under no obligation to get into a back-and-forth with a bully.

I have also found it effective to take a bully at their word. They often grossly overestimate their influence. When they threaten to go to the provost with a complaint about you, respond with "Let me know what they say." When they try to intimidate with promises to file a Title IX or human resources complaint against you, send them the link to the paperwork. When they threaten to quit if you do not do what they want, ask when you can expect their resignation letter. They will soon realize that they do not have the influence they thought they had.

There is a myriad of academic resources out there for dealing with academic bullies, and I cannot give it the full treatment here. But I would encourage you to explore them if you are dealing with a bully. I am reminded of the end of the movie *Training Day*, where Alonzo Harris (played by Denzel Washington) is exposed as a bully. He delivers an Oscar-winning rant when his kingdom crumbles, demanding that "I am the man up in here," as he beats on his chest comparing himself to King Kong. But the spell is broken. Those he once controlled are unfazed, ignore him, and move on. That is the ideal outcome when addressing a departmental bully. Render their threats powerless as you lead your department by example through focusing on the work at hand rather than fretting over the bully.

REFLECTIONS

1. Reflect on the George Orwell quote provided. Do you agree with it as a method to respond to bullying? How might you operationalize it?
2. Do you agree that it is unlikely that you will ever actually be able to stop bullying behavior and that you should instead focus on those who are impacted by the behavior? Why or why not?

REFERENCE

Mahmoudi, M. (2019). Academic bullies leave no trace. *BioImpacts, 9*(3), 129–130. https://doi.org/10.15171/bi.2019.17

Chapter 49

Committee Assignments

One of your new responsibilities is likely assigning faculty members to various committees. This task can often feel as delicate as assembling a complex jigsaw puzzle. You are required to balance issues of equitable labor distribution, interpersonal relationships, skill set utilization, and faculty schedules/preferences. Also, to echo a refrain that is becoming common in these chapters, this often becomes political. While it can be taxing to sort through and deliberate, thoughtful committee assignments are well worth the effort. Committees play an indispensable role in your department's ecosystem. They are where much of the deliberative processes and decision-making take shape. Assigning committees is no mere administrative task; it is instrumental in molding your departmental culture and ensuring effectiveness. Selfishly, smart committee decision assignments can go a long way toward making your job much easier.

Approach the task of committee assignments remembering that there are varying levels of eagerness among faculty. Some faculty members are happy to participate in this kind of formal departmental service, while others would rather allocate their efforts elsewhere. This is understandable as service helps faculty differently depending on their strengths and where they are in their career. For some, service will not be doing much heavy lifting in their career trajectory, but for others it will be paramount. Therefore, it is important to approach committee assignments with clear strategy and guiding principles that account for this variance.

First, resist the temptation to disproportionately allocate committee assignments to your most willing and capable faculty members. It is tempting to continue to rely on these individuals as they have likely proven themselves competent in the past and are happy to take on the additional service responsibilities. While this approach may alleviate some immediate challenges, it is likely to create long-term problems. It can reward service-slackers with less work (Dettmar, 2024), and you can bet that everyone else in your department notices the unfair labor imbalance. This can demotivate folks. More critically, such an approach often inadvertently disadvantages minority faculty members, which perpetuates inequality in your department (Fogg, 2003). The need for equitable distribution of committee responsibilities cannot be overstated.

It may be tempting to democratize the process of committee assignments in an effort to foster inclusivity or distribute the decision-making. However, I have found it best to avoid this impulse. Crowdsourcing committee assignments adds a lot of noise to the process. It can lead to additional complexity and confusion. It can make space for outsized influence from the loudest (and often most senior) faculty members. Be open to input and provide opportunities for feedback before final decisions are made, but you should make the decisions. A centralized approach from a conscientious chair ensures the process is efficient, fair, and optimal. Additionally, as chair you have a bird's-eye view of the department. While this may seem antidemocratic, I have found that the overwhelming majority of faculty are happy to have the process streamlined.

While committee assignment decisions rest with you, be transparent in your decision-making process. Not every choice will satisfy all parties, but clarity on how you determined assignments can mitigate dissatisfaction. Whether assignments are based on a rotation system, availability, specific skill sets, or other criteria, articulating the process to faculty is a good idea. Transparency here not only fosters a sense of fairness, but it also helps manage expectations and reduces the potential for discontent. People are generally more open and sympathetic to your decisions if they know you have a clear sense of why you are making them.

Faculty often see committee assignments as ancillary to their "real" academic duties of researching and teaching. It is something you do because you must. Faculty often express frustration that they are overburdened and inadequately recognized for committee work. You can address these concerns proactively. Acknowledge and celebrate exceptional service in tangible ways such as noting it in annual reviews or other departmental recognitions. Send out all-departmental emails thanking exceptional service and mention it at departmental meetings.

Successfully navigating the task of committee assignments requires you to consider both the practical needs of "right now" and the long-term vision of the department. It is an opportunity to build a culture of recognition, strategic engagement, and equality that can define the character of your department. As you approach this task, do so with the recognition that each committee assignment represents a chance to create a dynamic and efficient department.

REFLECTIONS

1. How have committee assignments generally been approached in your department in the past? What is working and what needs to be changed?
2. How is committee work perceived in your department? Are there any faculty members who you think might be difficult to work with during the committee assignment process? How will you approach those folks?

REFERENCES

Dettmar, K. (2024, February 12). *Ask the chair: How to cope with the service slackers*. Chronicle of Higher Education. https://www.chronicle.com/article/ask-the-chair-how-to-cope-with-the-service-slackers?sra=true

Fogg, P. (2003, December 19). *So many committees, so little time*. Chronicle of Higher Education. https://www.chronicle.com/article/so-many-committees-so-little-time

Chapter 50

Classroom Teaching Observations

While your role as chair is multifaceted, you can make an argument that the most critical component of the job is the oversight of teaching quality. As a new chair, observing and evaluating classroom instruction is not just about ensuring accountability; it is a symbolic move to your department that teaching matters to you, that you are invested in it, and that you intend to actively support your faculty in this area. Performing regular teaching observations is not merely a procedural task. It is a strategic move to establish your leadership. Teaching is ultimately your department's product. Effective teaching is the very essence of what academic institutions should deliver. It is a product that requires the same scrutiny and quality assurance as any valuable commodity in the marketplace. As a new chair, observing and assessing teaching firsthand is essential managerial practice. It demonstrates a clear commitment to the pedagogical experience of students and provides support and guidance (especially for junior faculty members).

Student evaluations often carry great weight in the evaluation of teaching. But they have their limitations. They often fail to capture the nuances of the teaching processes, and some research even suggests that there is very little correlation between student evaluations and what students learn in a class (Uttl et al., 2017). Student evaluations can also reflect bias toward minority groups (Kreitzer & Sweet-Cushman, 2021). Reviewing student evaluations should not be the sole way you engage your department's pedagogical product.

Classroom observations should be ingrained in the department's culture, not just as sporadic events, but as part of a systematic evaluation that faculty anticipate and prepare for. Unlike static student evaluations, teaching observations are dynamic. They can serve multiple functions beyond mere oversight. They offer opportunities to dialogue, mentor, exchange pedagogical strategies, celebrate, and foster a collaborative approach to classroom instruction. The significance of these observations lies in the fact that they are regularly scheduled and predictable. Having a structured schedule (perhaps biannually) establishes a rhythm and a norm, signaling that a classroom observation from the chair is a regular and expected part of the academic cycle. This predictability can remove the stigma of being observed, and it frames the experience as a normal aspect of pedagogical growth.

How you approach these observations is as important as the observations themselves. Communicate to your faculty that observations are not an audit. They are instead an important piece of an ongoing conversation that allows faculty members to reflect on and discuss their teaching both philosophically and pragmatically. Another benefit is that your visibility in the classroom communicates to faculty that their work is valued and that you are there not to judge, but to support and participate in their development. Many instructors will relish in the opportunity to showcase their instructional skills and welcome some meaningful engagement in their pedagogical process. Instructors who are doing good pedagogical work often love an audience.

To make the most of these observations, look beyond the content delivered and focus on the teaching process itself (Katal et al., 2022). Do not simply assess what is happening in the classroom but engage why an instructor chose certain teaching methods. How does a faculty member engage this particular group of students? How did the technologies used to enhance the classroom experience relate to the course content for the day? How does this instructor's instruction lend itself to certain pedagogical practices? When you offer constructive feedback, engage it at a deep level. For example, rather than advising a faculty member to "keep the PowerPoint slides simple," focus on how the visual complexity of slides might affect student comprehension and engagement and offer concrete suggestions for visual and informational display. Use your observations as part of a larger dialogue. Cross-reference what you see with patterns in student evaluations to gain a holistic understanding of pedagogical effectiveness.

As chair, it can become easy to think of your course offerings in terms of scheduling and rotations. Classroom observations keep you tethered to the experiential element of what your department is offering. It can keep you connected to your job as chair. Regular and sustained observations across all classes will give you a sense of your department's pedagogical strengths and areas of improvement, which makes it possible for you to lead informed discussions with your faculty about the general student experience in your department. You will notice trends and patterns that should be shared with faculty. It will allow you to keep your finger on the pulse of what is going on in your department.

If you teach, you should also open your own classroom up to observation. Invite your faculty to sit in and offer you feedback. Not only will you benefit from the feedback, but it also mitigates some of the power dynamics involved in observation. It communicates to your department that this is not an exercise in managerial control, but a mutual effort to cooperate in delivering an effective pedagogical experience to all students.

REFLECTIONS

1. How might a chair's classroom observation differ from a peer classroom observation? Will your colleagues welcome you into their classrooms?
2. Are there conflicting demands between a chair's classroom observation as managerial oversight and collaborative conversation? Why or why not? How might you handle any tensions in these demands?

REFERENCES

Katal, A., Singh, V. K., Choudhury, T., & Imran, F. (2022). Enhancing teaching and learning through peer observation: An Indian case study. *Education Research International, 2022*, 1–13. https://doi.org/10.1155/2022/7825178

Kreitzer, R. J., & Sweet-Cushman, J. (2021). Evaluating student evaluations of teaching: A review of measurement and equity bias in sets and recommendations for ethical reform. *Journal of Academic Ethics, 20*(1), 73–84. https://doi.org/10.1007/s10805-021-09400-w

Uttl, B., White, C. A., & Wong Gonzalez, D. (2017). Meta-analysis of faculty's teaching effectiveness: Student evaluation of teaching ratings and student learning are not related. *Studies in Educational Evaluation, 54*, 22–42. https://doi.org/10.1016/j.stueduc.2016.08.007

Chapter 51

Your Department's Approach to Online Education

In the last chapter I discussed the importance of hands-on classroom observation. Some of those insights are relevant to online course offerings, but others may not directly translate. However, considering the current (and likely future) state of higher education, it is critical that as chair, you closely examine your department's approach to online classes. The potential for creativity and strategic excellence is certainly embedded in online classes, but I have observed that many departments simply roll out online courses with little strategic planning or consideration. If this is the case for your department (hopefully it is not), then your new role as chair offers an opportunity to steer your department toward more deliberate and thoughtful engagement with online education. Quality control in online offerings is not just beneficial, but essential to long-term success. Although I'm reluctant to anchor this point with specific statistics since they ebb and flow and are likely to date this book rather quickly, it is safe to say that a substantial portion of student enrollment across the country are in online classes.

I have found that some instructors, while exceptional in the classroom, struggle to replicate their success online. Sometimes this stems from a lack of technological literacy required to successfully navigate and make an online class engaging. Other times it is due to the perception of online classes as somehow less "real" than the in-person version of the course. It is a powerful motivator to know that at a specific time you will be standing in front of a group of students waiting for a lesson. This motivation does not always exist in online classes. When the semester gets hectic, it is often easy to default to posting publisher materials and a discussion board and then checking out for the week—I've been there myself.

For all its faults, online education offers you more straightforward options for quality control than in-person classes. As a department chair, it is imperative that you have full access to all your department classes through your university's learning management system. Make it nonnegotiable and across the board. If there is pushback, question it. It is entirely reasonable that as chair you would play a part in assessing the quality of your department's online course offerings. To start shaping a coherent online education strategy, you first need to know what you are working with.

I have conducted a formal review of my department's online courses before. It was a very rewarding experience. While it may sound a bit formal, it is a vital step in understanding where your courses stand, and it can help spark some informed discussions. If your university has an office or division dedicated to the quality of online education, work with them to develop criteria by which to evaluate courses. For example, I checked if quiz questions could be easily found online with their corresponding answers. You can also see how many courses lean heavily on publisher content, have a clear schedule, or feature original instructor-developed and -provided content. My focus was on identifying what unique value instructors brought to their classes.

Use the insights from this process to start a conversation with your faculty about what constitutes quality online education. I have found a half-day retreat can be a good setting for this kind of conversation. Share your findings, such as percentage of classes lacking original material, and open the floor for discussion about whether everyone is satisfied with the current state of things. From there, work to develop standards and guidelines as a group. These should reflect your department's commitment to providing a quality educational experience for all your online students. Finally, offer support and resources. Ensure your faculty is aware of professional development opportunities. Bring in an expert to discuss quality online education at a department meeting. Ask one of your best online teachers to share some strategies with the group. Go out of your way to encourage and praise people when they pursue continuing education focused on online education.

Your goal is to lead the conversation in a way where your department feels engaged and has a sense of ownership. While you may lead the conversation, this is a collective responsibility. Some faculty may not even realize that their online teaching is lacking in some areas. By opening these dialogues, you can lead your department to deeper and more meaningful engagement with online education, its role in your curriculum, and how best to implement your strategy.

REFLECTIONS

1. How would you generally characterize your department's approach to online education? What is the strategy and who is responsible for it? What would you change if you could?
2. Consider some of the specific suggestions provided above, such as gaining access to your department's online courses, conducting a review, and initiating a conversation with your faculty? Does this seem feasible?

Chapter 52

Imposter Syndrome

If you are following this book on the recommended schedule, you are now well into your term as department chair. It is probably time to stop and do some introspection to ask yourself, "How am I coping? How do I feel at this point?" Reflecting on my first fifty-two days as chair, I can vividly recall being plagued with imposter syndrome. It weighed heavy on me as I became convinced that my department had severely overrated my abilities to do this job. I was left waiting for the inevitable unmasking of my inadequacies, a common phenomenon given that 36 percent of managers report feeling like imposters (Cristea, 2019).

This unease was compounded by the fact that I taught Organizational Communication. I was supposed to be an expert in all things management related. Each moment of doubt was more evidence of my shortcomings. The feelings were likely intensified by the pressures of academia (Cristea & Babajide, 2022; Breeze, 2018): the publish-or-perish mantra, constant peer reviews, and the brilliance and accomplishments of my colleagues. These are fertile grounds for breeding imposter syndrome. These feelings are even more exacerbated in minority academics (Simon, 2020).

Elsewhere in this volume, we have discussed the unique vulnerabilities of being a department chair. The onslaught of new responsibilities can amplify feelings of unpreparedness. While I am not a psychologist, take comfort from knowing that with time you will become more comfortable in this role.

Academic life follows cycles, reminiscent of the wisdom in Ecclesiastes 3:1: "To every thing there is a season, and a time to every purpose under heaven." The academic cycle is similar, and we will spend more time unpacking it later in this volume. There is a season for scheduling classes, a season for conducting annual reviews, a season for building budgets, and a season for conducting assessments. This can create the feeling that new challenges are coming at you rapidly, which can feel overwhelming. And as soon as you are done with one cycle, you need to learn how to handle a new one. The cycle of academic responsibilities can contribute to feelings of fraudulence. Each cycle brings new challenges and the fear of being exposed. However, embracing the cyclical nature of the job can help you recognize opportunities to grow and learn. Repetition breeds familiarity. With each cycle you will gather more evidence of your capability, gradually feeling more and more comfortable.

I have realized that striving to conquer imposter syndrome is futile. Instead, I have found peace in acceptance. Why view this self-doubt as something to eliminate? Might it be a sign that you care? Could it not indicate that you are a conscientious leader who is striving for improvement? Why shouldn't you be feeling some degree of imposter syndrome? Consider that the novelty of the new challenges you are accepting justifies a degree of imposter syndrome. It is a natural outcome of you pushing yourself out of your comfort zone. Embrace it as part of the growth process. This is not a one-size-fits-all solution, so find your own strategy.

Repeated exposure to the academic cycles will ultimately refine your skills, and soon chairing your department will come as naturally to you as giving a lecture. Imposter syndrome has one more gift—it cultivates empathy. Imposter syndrome is prevalent in academia, so colleagues of yours certainly feel it. Use any feeling of imposter syndrome that you have as chair as an impetus to reassure others (especially junior faculty). As a chair, you can transform imposter syndrome from a personal struggle into an opportunity to build a more empathetic and supportive culture.

REFLECTIONS

1. Are there elements of your new chair role that have created feelings of imposter syndrome for you? What tasks seem to cultivate those feelings? Are there any patterns in the tasks that cause you to feel especially fraudulent?
2. What do you think of the suggestion to embrace, rather than fight, feelings of imposter syndrome? Is this feasible? What are the benefits and drawbacks of such an approach?

REFERENCES

Breeze, M. (2018). Imposter syndrome as a public feeling. In Y. Taylor & K. Lahad (Eds.), *Feeling academic in the neoliberal university*. Palgrave Studies in Gender and Education. Palgrave Macmillan. https://doi.org/10.1007/978-3-319-64224-6_9

Cristea, M. (2019, November 22). *Overcoming the impostor feeling: How senior executives manage their insecurities* [Webinar]. Heriot-Watt University. https://pure.hw.ac.uk/ws/portalfiles/portal/42111976/Impostor_Feeling_Webinar.pdf

Cristea, M., & Babajide, O. A. (2022). Impostor phenomenon: Its prevalence among academics and the need for a diverse and inclusive working environment in British higher education. In M. Addison, M. Breeze, & Y. Taylor (Eds.), *The Palgrave handbook of imposter syndrome in higher education*. Palgrave Macmillan. https://doi.org/10.1007/978-3-030-86570-2_4

Simon, M. (2020). Stemming within a double minority: How the impostor syndrome affects black women Ph.D. students. *International Journal of Multiple Research Approaches, 12*(2), 185–201. https://doi.org/10.29034/ijmra.v12n2a2

Chapter 53

Your Relationship with Your Dean

"I don't want to be surprised by something like this again, Ben." My dean was kind and understanding but very clear. She did not like having personnel issues sneak up on her. "I thought I could handle this on my own. I didn't think it would make its way to you," I responded sheepishly. She took a breath and responded, "That's great. I love that you try to handle these kinds of things at the department level. But you have to give me a heads-up, so I am not blindsided when I hear about it from someone else. I run the risk of contradicting you, and it makes it seem like I don't know what is happening in my own college." I understood her point. And this is a lesson I have taken to heart. Now, any time I get the sense that something might make its way to the dean, I always give advance warning. This conversation, and the lesson I learned from it, encapsulates what I think makes an effective chair–dean relationship. Having a relationship with your dean built on open communication and trust is paramount.

As a new department chair, your position requires the ability to foster strong relationships within your academic community. Among these relationships, perhaps none is more critical to your success than the one you share with your academic dean. Your dean is your lifeline. Your relationship is not just important; it is imperative. It is certainly more important than your relationship with the president, chancellor, or provost. The reason is simple: your dean constitutes your immediate link to the broader institutional structure. Earlier in this volume, we discussed your role as a boundary spanner. Your dean is the boundary spanner between you and upper administration. Your dean is the person who can advocate for your department's needs, the one who can approve (or at least request) resources, and your primary ally in navigating the complexities of your institution. It is going to be very hard to get any initiative completed if you do not have your dean's support.

Relationships take work, and the relationship with your dean is no exception. Healthy relationships are built on trust, openness, effective communication, and shared vision. There are many ways to cultivate this kind of relationship. One of the most effective is to demonstrate reliability by getting done the things you are supposed to. Turn in reports, projects, reviews, schedules, and the like on time. Deans are busy, and they have only so much time to dedicate to each chair. Your political capital with your dean is precious; do not squander it on easily avoidable lapses that can undermine your credibility and your dean's trust in you.

Be supportive of your dean, and even go out of your way to do favors. Align your department's needs with the broader goals of the college. By taking your dean's side when appropriate and working together on initiatives, you reinforce a collaborative dynamic that benefits your department in the long run.

Every dean, like every person, has their own unique set of strengths and weaknesses. I have served as chair for five different deans, and every single one was different. It is crucial to try to understand what motivates your dean and how they operate within the institutional framework. This understanding can help you tailor your interactions and requests in ways that resonate. I have been optimistic and rosy up to this point. However, it is worth acknowledging that not all deans will be easy to work with. Some may present significant challenges. In such cases, maintaining a professional relationship is still in your department's (and your own) best interests. Open conflict should be a last resort, reserved for situations where the well-being of your department is at stake or an unacceptable injustice is being perpetuated.

Conflict management is a key part of any dean–department chair partnership (Towns, 2023). When you find yourself disagreeing with your dean, focus on finding common ground. Establish clear protocols for decision-making and prioritizing open dialogue. When agreement cannot be reached, defer to the dean's authority (unless absolutely necessary for the health of your department). In general, try to keep your disagreements with the dean behind closed doors.

Do not take your relationship with your dean for granted. This advice is not intended to suggest that you should be kissing-up. Instead, it is an encouragement to cultivate a partnership. This relationship is too important for your professional success and the long-term health of your department not to put in the necessary work. By being proactive in cultivating your relationship with your dean, you can build a framework for collaboration, which is essential for navigating the complexities of your role as chair.

REFLECTIONS

1. What is your dean's leadership style and priorities? How might this knowledge inform your approach to requests, proposals, and discussions with your dean?
2. What role does your dean play in your department's success? How can you make it easier for your dean to collaborate with you to support your departmental goals?

REFERENCE

Towns, L. (2023). *The dean–chair relationship: An examination of conflict management styles and relationship quality.* (ETC Collection for Fordham University. AAI29996334). Fordham University. https://research.library.fordham.edu/dissertations/AAI29996334

Chapter 54

Your Relationship with Your Dean Continued

In the previous chapter we explored why it is important to approach your relationship with your dean as a true partnership. Here, we are going to dig into that dynamic a bit deeper to understand the nuances of advocacy, collaboration, and mutually beneficial relationships. This chapter is going to focus on strengthening your relationship with your dean by positioning your department, and you as chair, as an asset by engaging in solution-oriented advocacy.

As discussed, your relationship with your dean should ultimately be characterized as one of mutual collaboration. But that collaboration should ultimately be geared toward advocacy for your department. We focused on the art of advocacy in an earlier chapter, and how we often mistakenly associate advocacy with loudness. The best chance you have of truly advocating for your department to your dean rests in cultivating a partnership based on a shared vision, respect, mutual support, and trust. I have worked with colleagues who believe that a good department chair should generally disagree with the dean as a matter of principle. Departmental advocacy is sometimes characterized as being noisy—the proverbial squeaky wheel. This is not your best avenue for advocacy though. Partnerships go two ways. You are not the only one with needs; deans have needs as well. And they need support from chairs. You should strive to be the kind of chair that your dean knows they can rely on for support when they need it. You must be willing to give. This fosters reciprocity.

The single best thing you can do to advocate for your department is to position yourself so your dean sees you (and your department) as an asset rather than a liability. Deans have hard jobs, and if they understand your department as a solution rather than a problem, they are far more likely to go out of their way to support you. Be the kind of department chair who shows up and is at recruiting events ready to impress, who comes to all-chairs meetings with suggestions, who follows through on requests, and who asks questions rather than argues. Be an asset. Demonstrate that you (and your department) being at the table makes things better. Help your dean solve problems, rather than create them.

Being an asset involves not only being competent and willing to work with your dean but also in rhetorically positioning your department to the dean. This means more than simply sharing updates or problems as they arise, but also engaging with your dean in meaningful dialogue about the future of your department and how it fits in with the larger landscape of the college. Highlight your department's successes and demonstrate how it contributes to student success, community engagement, and the overall reputation of the college. Moreover, be proactive in identifying opportunities for interdisciplinary collaboration, new funding, and innovative pedagogical ideas that benefit the entire university. By being proactive in such efforts, you position your department as a dynamic force within the college and make it more indispensable.

When problems arise, work with your dean rather than dumping a problem on their lap and demanding they fix it. More people collaborating on fixing a problem is better. Remember that your dean has a more comprehensive and broader understanding of the whole picture. Your problems may have wrinkles to them that you are not even aware of. I have worked with chairs who seem to believe that their role is to refuse to help, or worse, to obstruct. This is often couched in some vague notion of social justice, a distrust of authority, or the mistaken belief that department chairs need to be in perpetual conflict with the dean to show that they can stand up to power. Put yourself in the position of dean. Would you want to work with that person? Would you go out of your way to help a faculty member who acted that way? When you did help, you would likely do so begrudgingly.

You are better off working to be the kind of chair your dean wants to call in and ask advice from. Good deans want help, but they do not want to turn to chairs who are going to be difficult to work with. You want to be in the room when decisions are made that effect your department. The only way to make that happen is to position yourself so your dean wants you to be in the room when decisions are made that effect your department. Deans need help, so be part of the team.

Any smart dean will funnel resources and attention to departments that are aligned with the larger goals of the college. Smart resource management involves investing in your assets and limiting liabilities. So be an asset.

REFLECTIONS

1. This chapter warns against chairs who refuse to help or obstruct, sometimes under the guise of standing up to authority. How would you handle situations where you fundamentally disagree with your dean's decisions while still aiming to be constructive and collaborative?
2. What are your department's particular strengths that position it as an asset? What are your strengths as chair that position you as an asset? How can you consciously leverage these assets toward advocacy?

Chapter 55

Your Relationship with Your Office Associate

Jill, our office associate, didn't even look up when I walked into the office from my meeting. Her head was buried in a stack of papers and she was marking them with a pen. "What are you working on?" I asked. She paused and looked up. "Jeff asked me if I could grade these exams." I was surprised. Jeff was a senior faculty member in our department. He was well-liked and generally conscientious. But this rubbed me the wrong way. "How do you feel about doing this?" I asked Jill. "I feel a little uncomfortable since I am not teaching the class, but I don't think I can really say no." I assured her that I would discuss the matter with Jeff and advised her to prioritize some other tasks in the meantime.

I headed to Jeff's office and asked him about this arrangement. He was respectful and polite and explained that it was only the quantitative portions of the exam that he asked her to grade. I explained that this made me feel uncomfortable because it fell outside of the scope of Jill's position. Grading is inherent to the pedagogical feedback loop and should be done by instructors. Finally, as all instructors know, it is the worst part of the job. Offloading it to someone who makes significantly less money than a full professor seems unfair.

The last two chapters have focused on your relationship with your dean as an essential factor in your success as chair. We have established that that relationship should be built on trust and aligned goals. Your relationship with your office staff, and in particular your office associate, should be characterized by the same principles.

Your office associate is vital to your success. As a new chair, your office associate likely has a sense of institutional and operational knowledge that you do not. So, relying on them to help remind you when things are due or how you can log on to certain software is important. The office associate is also key for ensuring the operational efficiency of the department. They will maintain records, assist with scheduling, help plan events, and so on. Knowing that these are done well goes a long way toward shoring up your reputation in the department. Your office associate is also often the communication hub of the department. They are the first point of contact for students and outside entities. Their role in disseminating accurate information is essential for the functioning of the department. Finally, office associates are usually very good at providing support and problem-solving. Some of the best ideas I have ever had to improve the department have come directly from the office associate. They have a very different perspective than faculty. They are "in the weeds" in a way that faculty are not, which means they are often privy to operational inefficiencies that you and the rest of the faculty are not.

Like your dean, your relationship with your office associate needs to be cultivated. A healthy relationship with your office associate requires work and intentionality. It is important to approach the relationship remembering that they are often more vulnerable than faculty. The earlier example provided addresses this point. You must be willing to protect them and do what you can to ensure they do not get dragged into faculty disagreements. Be willing to say "no" on their behalf to unreasonable requests, like the one above.

It is also imperative that you both set clear expectations. Clarify how you envision their role and responsibilities and ask for feedback. For example, I once worked with an office associate who I received complaints about from other campus offices because they felt she was rude in emails. I read the emails, and I realized that she was emailing other campus offices with the same kind of familiarity that she used while emailing me. There were no greetings or pleasantries, subject lines were punctuated, and there was no sign-off. I had to have a conversation with members of the other offices and explicitly explain that because my office associate and I have a close working relationship and email several times a day, emails between the two of us can be informal, more like text messages. But a degree of formality was required when emailing other people on campus. These kinds of expectations should be clarified. They go both ways though. You also need to ask your office associate what expectations they have for you. How do they prefer to have you assign projects to them? Are they okay with emails after work hours? Are there professional development opportunities they might like to take advantage of? Do they need a weekly update from you? Is there some technology that might make it easier to do their job?

Finally, and maybe most importantly, show acknowledgment and appreciation. Regularly and publicly acknowledge the contributions they make. Give your office associate credit when they complete something. Take them out for lunch. Make sure they are included in the decision-making processes. These kinds of acts go a long way and help build a positive and strong relationship that ultimately helps you be a better chair.

REFLECTIONS

1. What role has your office associate played in your onboarding? What have you learned about their strengths and weaknesses through that process?
2. Thinking about the story that started today's reflection, how would you have handled the situation? Do you think that Jeff's request was appropriate?

Chapter 56

Your Relationship with Your Provost

A few chapters back we focused on your relationship to your dean; this chapter is instead focused on the next person up the chain of command—your dean's boss. Your relationship to your provost is characterized by a very different set of dynamics. In the previous chapters I have described your dean as your bridge to many departmental constituents. Given this, your relationship with your dean should be built on closeness, immediacy, mutual understanding, and trust. Your engagement to your institution's chief academic officer should embody a distinctively different tone and approach.

Given that there is generally an intermediary between you and your provost, this connection involves a different kind of relational labor than with your dean. You should operate with the ethos that nothing from your department should come to your dean as a surprise. That is not the case with your provost. Making sure your provost is not surprised is your dean's responsibility, not yours. While you certainly want to be warm and friendly, a healthy relationship with your provost should consist of a degree of distance. Operating within a clear understanding of roles and the established chain of command is in your best interest.

Your relationship with the provost should be built on an understanding of how they generally understand department chairs. Your dean's job is to work closely with chairs to help them solve problems. These often involve day-to-day operational issues, personnel concerns, and unforeseen hiccups. Provosts are instead generally concerned with upper-level managerial issues such as institutional strategy, state accreditation, university budgets, and board of trustee relations. If you are doing your job well as chair, your provost should generally not even really be aware. Showing up on the provost's radar repeatedly is generally a bad sign. Provosts need to trust chairs to autonomously carry out the strategic vision of the university and solve problems before they reach them.

The foundation of a strong relationship with your provost lies in the recognition and respect for the university's hierarchy. This is not to say that you need to adopt a subservient attitude. It instead means to operate with the understanding that if you bring issues directly to your provost, you are going to annoy them while also undermining your relationship with your dean. Only once in my eleven-year career as chair have I bypassed this chain of command, and it was warranted due to the situation. This should be a very rare occurrence.

You should also be aware that your relationship with the provost is more likely to be a relationship with the provost's office rather than an actual person. Provosts hold the academic leadership positions with the highest turnover rate (Callow, 2021). A provost appointment often serves as stepping-stone to higher ambitions or as a temporary commitment in service to the institution. Deans do not generally turn over as frequently as provosts (Prichard et al., 2020), so it is worth making the dean your primary conduit to upper administration.

The best way to stay in your provost's good graces is to keep your department running smoothly and to focus on revenue generation, growing enrollment, bringing in grants, and aligning with the university's financial and academic priorities. When you do interact with your provost, whether at meetings, walking across campus, or at sporting events, take those opportunities to build rapport. Ask about their current initiatives, find sincere avenues for expressing support, and look for connections between their strategic vision and happenings in your department. Linking your work to institutional priorities is a savvy way to positively garner your provost's attention.

Ultimately, if you're leading your department with integrity, following proper procedures, and working harmoniously with your dean, your provost should barely need to think about you. The provost–chair relationship should be largely indirect, with your dean stewarding that intermediary role. Respecting that hierarchy is key to upholding your dean's authority and ensuring your own lasting success. A good chair recognizes that keeping a healthy distance from the provost's office is the wisest path.

While maintaining that boundary is advisable, it is also important not to become completely disconnected. An effective chair will find ways to stay positively on the provost's radar through productive collaborations across departments, positive media attention, outstanding achievements, and praise from your dean behind closed doors. Recognize that while provosts are often transient, they still play a very influential role in shaping the academic direction and resource allocation for the university. While this is true, do not go out of your way to directly interact with or lobby the provost. Allow your dean to serve as your conduit for elevating high-level issues, concerns, or proposals.

Ultimately, the ideal chair–provost relationship should strike a balance. Work to remain respectfully independent as chair while staying aligned with the overarching institutional vision set by your chief academic officer. Striking this balance effectively will cultivate positive associations at both levels while reinforcing the proper chain of command.

REFLECTIONS

1. What does a healthy balance of departmental autonomy and alignment to the university's broader goals look like to you?
2. How do you plan to maintain a professional yet warm rapport with your provost while respecting the chain of command?

REFERENCES

Callow, B. (2021, March 31). *College administrator data/turnover rates: 2018–present*. Higher Education Publication. https://hepinc.com/newsroom/college-administrator-data-turnover-rates-2018-present

Prichard, A., Nadel-Hawthorne, S., Schmidt, A., Fuesting, M., & Bichsel, J. (2020). *Administrators in higher education annual report*. College and University Professional Association for Human Resources. https://www.cupahr.org/surveys/administrators-in-higher-education

Chapter 57

Supporting International Faculty

"I'll certainly be supportive and help, but these kinds of situations can sometimes be tricky," I explained. Lei sat across from me at the table in my office, her posture closed off, and her teeth gently catching her lower lip in an unmistakable sign of apprehension. It was clear the response she had just received from me was not the one she was hoping for. Trying to preemptively address her concerns, I elaborated, "I just sometimes think it is safer to wait rather than go up for tenure and promotion early. It can be a pretty stressful process for faculty. I have just seen plenty of early tenure cases go sideways, and I don't want that to happen to you." Lei waited a beat before answering and explained, "One thing you maybe are not aware of, is that my visa is expiring at the end of the year. US and China relations are very tense right now, and I am worried. I have to file for a visa renewal, and I believe my application would be stronger if I was no longer in my probationary period." Not only did her decision to go up for tenure now make sense, but I was also reminded that international faculty are often negotiating challenges that are not on the radar of those of who enjoy the comforts of living and working in their home country.

I want to start this reflection with an acknowledgment that your own positionality matters a lot in this area. As a US native and monolingual educator within an American university, my international professional experiences are fairly limited. While I lived overseas for a bit growing up, that experience did not wholly acquaint me with the multifaceted realities international scholars often face. Given this, I chair international faculty from a position that requires deliberate effort to bridge my gap in understanding the challenges that they face. You may be an international faculty member yourself, and if so, you are more intimately familiar with these challenges than I.

The value of having international faculty in your department is self-evident. They bring a global perspective and expertise to academic units. Their diverse pedagogical contributions are valuable to students preparing to enter a globalized professional workforce. There is also inherent benefit to having a diversity of cultural viewpoints represented in curricular decisions and research areas (Kim et al., 2011).

Fully realizing these benefits to your department requires support from you as chair. First and foremost, you must operate with an awareness that international faculty often face very different challenges than your domestic faculty. This may include feeling isolated and alone on campus (Munene, 2014). International faculty may be physically separated from their support systems and feel homesick. Additionally, they may be dealing with cultural translational issues. American education is different from higher education in other countries. It is often more informal. For example, in some cultures students may stand when a teacher enters the classroom (Jawaharlal, 2022). Additionally, international faculty may not have command of the same sociological or historical context that their students are operating with. Understanding your students is hard enough when you share cultural context with them. Finally, there are often pragmatic issues international faculty are dealing with. This includes visas, housing, securing a local support network, navigating the health-care system and benefits, understanding local banking practices, and so on.

Many international faculty do not receive the institutional support they need (Véliz et al., 2020). For this reason, it is important that as chair you do what you can to support international faculty. While you will not be able to solve every problem, as many are out of your control, you can do your best to communicate your support and to make your department feel like home for international faculty. Every international faculty member has different needs based on their home country and specific situation, but there are still some general principles to guide your support. The most important thing to remember is to provide clear and direct information. New international scholars may not be aware of processes that native faculty take for granted. How does tenure work? How are classes assigned? How are workloads negotiated? How does evaluation happen? I think it is generally a good idea to find an established international faculty member on your campus to serve as a mentor to help with these questions.

Communicate with international faculty before they arrive on campus. Ask what help they need in finding housing and setting up in town. Give them space to share if they have family who needs support when they start. Communication should go both ways. Ask about things like visa and work status. Show interest and ask if you can help with anything.

Finally, show emotional support. Encourage international faculty to participate by introducing them to people. Build a departmental culture of support and belonging. Acknowledge their vulnerability. Be aboveboard with everything (including the financial support your department may or may not be able to provide to support their work status). This can go a long way to building trust with your international faculty. Also be honest and transparent. Do not provide assurances that you may not be able to deliver on.

By providing both practical and emotional support, you can make your international faculty feel as if they are at home in your department. Reducing uncertainty and anxiety can go a long way to freeing up bandwidth so they can focus on the important work you hired them for. It is your responsibility as chair to foster an environment where all faculty, regardless of origin, can thrive in your department. By being mindful of the unique challenges that international faculty face, and proactively addressing them, you can affirm your commitment to diversity and inclusion while also strengthening your department as a whole.

REFLECTIONS

1. How familiar are you with the pragmatic issues that international faculty face? Do you understand the different kinds of visas, the application timelines, the renewal process, the financial requirements, and so on? What resources on your campus exist for you to familiarize yourself with this process?
2. Given the diversity in teaching styles and cultural backgrounds, how can you support international faculty in adapting to the American education environment while also valuing the unique pedagogical contributions they bring?

REFERENCES

Kim, D., Wolf-Wendel, L., & Twombly, S. (2011). International faculty: Experiences of academic life and productivity in U.S. universities. *Journal of Higher Education*, *82*(6), 720–747. https://doi.org/10.1080/00221546.2011.11777225

Jawaharlal, M. (2022, April 22). *Immigrant faculty need training in pedagogy, DEI*. Inside Higher Ed. https://www.insidehighered.com/views/2022/04/22/immigrant-faculty-need-training-pedagogy-dei-opinion

Munene, I. I. (2014). Outsiders within: Isolation of international faculty in an American university. *Research in Post-Compulsory Education*, *19*(4), 450–467. https://doi.org/10.1080/13596748.2014.955730

Véliz, D., Guzman-Valenzuela, C., & Pickenpack, A. (2020). Becoming a successful international faculty member in a striving university. *Current Issues in Education*, *21*(3). https://cie.asu.edu/ojs/index.php/cieatasu/article/view/1797

Chapter 58

Assembling a Search Committee

Garrett stood in my office doorway, his voice raised and his finger pointed at my face. "I deserve to be on this search committee," he insisted. "I am a senior member of this department and I have earned the right to participate in choosing our next colleague." While I was taken aback by how aggressive he was, I did not want to let him see that I was rattled, as I knew he would leverage any weakness. "I understand your desire to participate," I replied as calmly as I could, "but the search committee has already been formed. It is crucial that we get some fresh perspectives in the hiring process." I turned my back to Garrett and walked to my desk, sitting down. Garrett, voice raised even louder, retorted, "I am going to report this discrimination to HR!" With that, he stormed out of my office. After he left, our office associate, who had heard the yelling, came into my office to check on me. She rolled her eyes as I briefly explained the situation. "He has been on the last two search committees. Why does he think he is entitled to be on this one?" Garrett had an expectation that given his status as senior faculty member in the department, he should have the right of first refusal on all search committees. But I had reached a breaking point with his unhelpful behavior on search committees. During the last search, our outside committee member from a different department had resigned because he refused to work with Garrett anymore. On the one before that, Garrett had disparaged the dean to one of the candidates during a campus visit. In yet another search committee, he had tried to persuade a new hire not to accept our offer. He was also on the search committee that had hired me and spent much of my campus visit criticizing his departmental colleagues. His behavior was so egregious that one of my references reached out to me telling me how she was put off by his behavior and manners in the reference call. There was a litany of reasons why Garrett should not be on search committees anymore.

This incident, though more overt than usual, underscores how organizational dynamics can complicate the formation of search committees. Search committee formation is far too serious to be driven by these kinds of departmental politics. The process of hiring faculty is critical as it directly affects student instruction and departmental general well-being. Getting the hiring process right is also important because once a candidate becomes a departmental member, it can be extremely difficult to move on from that person if things are not going well. Think about every problematic faculty member at your university. Each one was selected by a search committee. While hiring is a serious responsibility, it is also a privilege. In most industries, employees do not get to choose their colleagues. We are very fortunate in this regard.

As chair, you likely do not get the final word on hiring decisions, but you do have a great deal of impact by choosing those who do the choosing. Forming a search committee is a vital but delicate task. There are a great deal of factors to consider, including disciplinary expertise, reliability, ability to work in a group, power dynamics, distribution of labor, commitment to diversity, and the interpersonal relationships of the group members (some people don't work well with others).

One of the most important elements to consider is the ways that the makeup of your search committee reflects your departmental needs and commitments. When groups make decisions about hiring candidates, they often engage in "culture matching" (Rivera, 2012). Groups tend to replicate themselves. There are steps you can take to mitigate this "culture matching," but even the best practices to do so are far from guaranteed to be effective. You should address this issue in the formation of the search committee by choosing a committee that has the capacity to be reflexive, ethical, judicious, and committed to ethical and transparent decision-making.

Do not pay attention only to who is on the search committee, but also to the power dynamics. Search committee formations will privilege some voices over others. Do your best to ensure that any single member will not dominate or have an outsized voice. This is especially important when you are working to ensure that a search committee consists of appropriate diversity. A committee skewed toward senior full professors from overrepresented demographics with one lecturer from an underrepresented group may satisfy your Human Resources checklist but it does not adequately demonstrate a commitment to diversity. Each member should have a real impact on decision-making to ensure fair and inclusive decision-making (O'Meara et al., 2020).

When assembling a search committee, you should also consider who is well-connected. Who might have graduate directors in their external network? Who can rely on their network to recruit? Additionally, who is likely to make a good first impression on candidates? The best candidates likely have multiple offers, so you need search committee members who will give candidates a positive impression of your department during the interview process.

As a new department chair, you are positioned uniquely to influence the future of your department through these critical decisions. The process of selecting a search committee goes beyond administrative duty; it is about fostering an environment where diverse perspectives are valued and where the culture of the department evolves constructively. Recognize that each member of the committee brings a particular set of values, biases, and experiences that will influence their decisions. Thus, balancing these elements becomes essential to achieving a fair and unbiased search process. Embrace this opportunity to mold the future of your department thoughtfully and inclusively. By doing so, you ensure that the hiring process not only brings in new talents but also contributes positively to the academic and communal life of your department.

REFLECTIONS

1. How have search committees been formed in the past in your department? What criteria have been used to decide who will serve? What role has departmental politics played?
2. What practices has your department or university committed to in efforts to address "culture matching"? What can you do as chair to address this issue?

REFERENCES

O'Meara, K., Culpepper, D., & Templeton, L. L. (2020). Nudging toward diversity: Applying behavioral design to faculty hiring. *Review of Educational Research*, *90*(3), 311–348. https://doi.org/10.3102/0034654320914742

Rivera, L. A. (2012). Hiring as cultural matching: The case of elite professional service firms. *American Sociological Review*, *77*(6), 999–1022. https://doi.org/10.1177/0003122412463213

Chapter 59

Candidate Selection and Search Committee Processes

I had just finished having breakfast with our prospective hire. He was great, exuding confidence, necessary expertise, and a commitment to collaboration. I left breakfast feeling like he was a strong contender for the position. I sent him on his way for a campus tour and headed down the hall to ask the search committee chair what she thought of our candidate. "He's sexist," she abruptly offered when I asked her opinion. I was taken back as I had not gotten this energy from him during my interaction. "He talked down to me during the entire car ride from the airport" she continued. Now concerned, I approached another search committee member to ask her opinion. "You are going to have a sexual harassment situation if you hire this candidate," she frankly explained. The first conversation was jarring enough, but hearing it from a second independent source really got my attention. A third female departmental member later echoed similar apprehension. Obviously, we did not hire this candidate, but this experience has been formative in how I approach the search process. I was primarily concerned that I had no reservations about the candidate. How was this possible? This experience reminded me of why we build checks and balances into the process. Even when being our most critical and looking for red flags, any one individual only has part of the picture. While having people with different perspectives serving on search committees is an essential component of ensuring the integrity of the hiring process, it is not enough. There must be intentionality built into the search process. Your job as chair is to oversee and ensure the search proceeds in a judicious, conscientious, and ethical manner.

The initial element that requires your attention is your search protocol. Your college or university may already have a step-by-step procedure for how searches should run. You should also have one for your department that specifies responsibilities, sequences of events, and involvement in various stages of the process. If your university or college already has one, your departmental checklist should be compliant but more detailed. If your department already has a search protocol, you should evaluate it to make sure it is up-to-date and reflects your departmental values. A checklist ensures that a committee is abiding by practices that ensure fairness. This checklist should include all elements of the search, including advertising and recruiting for the position. Special attention should be paid to ensuring you are recruiting in places that reach diverse populations (Bilimoria & Buch, 2010).

A critical item on the checklist is an official charge from the chair to the search committee. You need to be present at the first search committee meeting and explicitly communicate expectations. As chair, you can set the search committee priorities. Highlight the importance of process, go over your checklist, discuss fair and equitable hiring practices, and make sure the committee is clear about human resources and legal requirements about what can and cannot be said and considered. Use this opportunity to model the open and frank conversations you want the committee to engage in when approaching their tasks. An official charge from you also levels some of the power dynamics of a search committee. It provides a shared set of expectations that anyone on the committee (regardless of rank) can reference if they feel uncomfortable.

Your search committee should also openly engage in conversations about selection criteria. Criteria should be decided on prior to reviewing your candidate pool. What do you all want in a candidate, and how will you choose someone? Be wary of nebulous criteria such as "departmental fit." Unquantifiable criteria like this are how bias often gets smuggled into the selection process (White-Lewis, 2020). Also, your committee should use rubrics of some kind to ensure that all candidates are being evaluated on the same criteria. But also be wary of assuming that simply having a rubric eliminates bias. The rubric criteria itself can reflect bias (Culpepper et al., 2023). This is often more dangerous because committees often assume that there is no bias present in the decision-making process simply because a rubric exists. Given this, ensure that your rubrics are created with an awareness of potential bias that may be embedded. Make sure a rubric is created with a broad perspective and lots of options of input from multiple stakeholders.

Additionally, during your charge of the search committee stress that you expect open communication. There must be clear channels of communication whereby members feel safe to express concerns about process if this arises. Encourage a culture of transparency and honesty where difficult conversations about potential biases are welcomed rather than avoided.

Establishing a rigorous and fair search process is demanding, but it is crucial for the integrity of academic hiring. Hiring a new faculty member is far too important of a task to allow a committee to sort out during the process.

By being intentional and proactive in addressing the process up front you increase your chances of making a smart decision and conducting the search in a way that is just, equitable, and in compliance with the necessary legal requirements. It is far better to address these issues up front rather than to course-correct in the middle of a search. Attention to these processes not only sets you up for success in the search, but it also serves as an opportunity for you as chair to reaffirm your commitment to the principles of fairness, equity, professionalism, and justice.

REFLECTIONS

1. Does your department have a search checklist or protocol? When was it last evaluated? What are its strengths and weaknesses? What could be done to address weaknesses?
2. What does a strong charge from the chair to a search committee look like to you? Do you feel confident performing this duty? What should you include when charging a search committee?

REFERENCES

Bilimoria, D., & Buch, K. K. (2010). The search is on: Engendering faculty diversity through more effective search and recruitment. *Change: The Magazine of Higher Learning*, *42*(4), 27–32. https://doi.org/10.1080/00091383.2010.489022

Culpepper, D., White-Lewis, D., O'Meara, K., Templeton, L., & Anderson, J. (2023). Do rubrics live up to their promise? Examining how rubrics mitigate bias in faculty hiring. *Journal of Higher Education*, *94*(7), 823–850. https://doi.org/10.1080/00221546.2023.2168411

White-Lewis, D. K. (2020). The facade of fit in faculty search processes. *Journal of Higher Education*, *91*(6), 833–857. https://doi.org/10.1080/00221546.2020.1775058

Chapter 60

Your Increased Legal Liability

I like to start these reflections with a story when I have a relevant experience. I have one in mind that fits well here, but given this topic I am not keen to share it as it is far too sensitive and only opens me up to legal liability. So, I am going to dive right in without a framing story. The lessons here are very relevant, especially for new department chairs. When I first started my role of chair, I did not really understand just how precarious the increased legal liability was. I had a vague sense that there were now some new legal issues to consider, but it all felt very abstract. In the past eleven years I have become much more familiar with just how much exposure to liability is involved in being chair. I now realize that I should have been much more concerned at the outset. This is especially true given that your first year or two as chair is when you are most likely to make mistakes that could lead to legal intervention. The danger is greater as well as higher education has become increasingly litigious over the past several decades (Jesse, 2024). The trend is characterized not just by increased legal intervention in the usual areas, but an increase in legal intervention in all facets of academic and campus life (Guard & Jacobsen, 2024). Areas that used to primarily be academic may now be legal land mines. Understanding and navigating these changes is vital to your success. While many of the other reflections in this volume are about you engaging in best practices, this one is about potentially saving your career. One mistake can dramatically change your life.

I want to offer a caveat at this point. The increased legal liability is not necessarily a bad thing. Many people who were not afforded adequate legal protection in the past are now protected. That is good. And legal intervention is warranted when department chairs act inappropriately. In decades past, many chairs (who share a lot of demographic similarities with me) got away with egregious behavior that never would be tolerated today. A trade-off of this progress is that it increases legal liability for everyone, and honest missteps can often turn into legal issues. Additionally, there will always be people who seek to exploit this progress for their own benefit, even if unwarranted. For the purposes of this reflection, I am going to assume that you are a conscientious, ethical, and fair department chair doing your best to avoid legal entanglement.

I have had brushes with legal issues, and fortunately things have thus far gone my way. These include some run-ins with faculty who have threatened to sue, report me to various legal offices, or file grievances. Once I had to testify at a staff member's divorce proceedings (to testify that I had never noticed an alcohol problem), and I once had to consult with a personal lawyer about something that eventually blew over. I have witnessed colleagues have it much worse. I have seen fellow chairs sued, fired for discrimination practices, and have newspaper articles written about their legal issues. Some of these consequences were warranted due to bad behavior, but others have been the result of overly litigious faculty looking to leverage the legal system to their own ends.

You must operate with an awareness of limiting your legal risk. Issues that you may see as academic can quickly turn legal (Hustoles, 2012). You must include legal liability as part of your decision-making calculus. Areas to be especially careful of include: tenure and promotion, workloads, FMLA and ADA issues, the hiring process, and student privacy. These are all pretty clear, but the most minor of issues can turn legal as well. I have been threatened with legal action over office and classroom assignments. As chair, you represent the institution in a way you did not as a faculty member. This means that disgruntled faculty are more likely to see you as a part of the problem (Gomez, 2015). This means you will often have a target on you. Additionally, you now are required to make choices that you didn't have to before. As a fellow faculty member, it is fairly easy to commiserate with colleagues about the way things are. But as a chair, sometimes you have to make decisions that make people unhappy. You do not have the luxury of simply being annoyed about something.

There is another factor that significantly contributes to your increased legal liability—you are now liable for the behavior of those you supervise. You can be held responsible if you fail to take appropriate action to stop the problematic behavior of your direct reports. You may be unaware of the problematic behavior. But if you should have been aware, then you may be liable. You can also be liable for creating a general climate where inappropriate behavior exists. Several years ago, a departmental member interrupted another faculty member's class, and the instructor blamed me (and threatened legal action) for creating an environment where faculty felt they could interrupt classes. Thankfully, this went nowhere (this was an overly litigious faculty member who even Human Resources had taken to ignoring at this point), but it brought into focus the ways that the actions of others could fall on me.

In the next chapter we will cover some specific strategies for navigating your increased legal liability. Here I am just encouraging you to include legal liability in your decision-making. Failing to do so can carry a lot of risk, so it is worth you taking this very seriously.

REFLECTIONS

1. Do you feel nervous about increased legal liability? Have you felt it at any point thus far in your tenure as chair? How so?
2. Considering the potential for disputes to arise from even minor issues like office assignments, what strategies can you employ to manage and reduce conflict effectively? How might you balance being a decisive leader while limiting your legal risk?

REFERENCES

Gomez, Fernando C. (2015). *Legal issues department chairs often face.* Academic Chairpersons Conference Proceedings. https://newprairiepress.org/accp/2015/Plenary/3

Guard, L. H., & Jacobsen, J. P. (2024). *All the campus lawyers: Litigation, regulation, and the new era of higher education.* Harvard University Press.

Hustoles, Carol L. J. (2012). Through the eyes of higher education attorneys: How department chairs are navigating the waters of legal issues and risk management. *Dissertations,* 37. https://scholarworks.wmich.edu/dissertations/37

Jesse, D. (2024, February 26). *Your college's top lawyer has never been more powerful.* Chronicle of Higher Education. https://www.chronicle.com/article/your-colleges-top-lawyer-has-never-been-more-powerful

Chapter 61

Strategies for Navigating the Legal Aspects of Being Chair

I hit send on the email and got back to work. Not two minutes later the office phone rang, and caller ID alerted me that it was my dean, who was the recipient of the email I had just sent. When I answered there was none of the usual pleasantries of asking how my day was. She instead started in as if we were midconversation, stating, "Ben, please do not email about this topic. I do not want anything related to this in writing. Dr. _____ has accessed emails through the Freedom of Information Act before. Next time you have a question about this, please just pick up the phone and call me rather than email."

In the previous chapter we discussed approaching being chair with a general awareness of your increased legal liability. Here we are going to focus on some specific actions that you should take to mitigate risk. I do want to stress that this is not legal advice. Consult with a lawyer about any specific questions you have. Laws vary from state to state, and every institution has its own peculiarities (Euben, 2000). A lawyer can far better speak to your specific questions. These are instead general practices that may help limit your legal liability:

- *Know your university's email discovery process.* I have had my emails accessed twice. Once was for a divorce and the other for an internal investigation. Both were not the result of anything related to specific emails I had sent but were instead phishing attempts to find anything that could be used against me. Both instances yielded nothing of value to the requesting party, as I have been careful with university email. I was not even informed of the discovery request until after the fact. Know your university policies and state laws in regard to your emails. Never write an email that you would not be comfortable showing up on the front page of your local newspaper.
- *Complete your institutional legal training.* Stay up-to-date on all your mandatory (and optional) legal training in areas such as FMLA, Title IX, ADA,

hiring, and the like (Dusen, 2011). Laws and regulations frequently change, and these trainings ensure you are up-to-date. Take them seriously. Don't click through just to get them done. Not only do these trainings help you make smarter decisions, but if you mess up and do not complete mandatory training, you will likely increase your legal jeopardy.

- *Be proactive in compliance.* Be vigilant about complying with process and procedure in all areas of tenure, hiring, separation, leaves, workloads, and so on. When situations turn legal, process is the first place lawyers scrutinize. Did you overlook the faculty handbook section that requires you to notify a tenure candidate about outside reviewer requirements before they submit their dossier? Did you turn in an annual evaluation two days late? Does your collective bargaining agreement require you to consult with faculty before assigning classes? You must follow processes, or you will lose these battles, even if you made the correct decision.
- *Know your mandatory reporter role.* In many circumstances, you may be a mandatory reporter for problems you encounter. Take that seriously. When you hear anything at all related to issues of discrimination or sexual harassment, turn to the relevant offices immediately (Mezey et al., 2006).
- *Lay paper trails for later reference.* Establish documentation practices. It's critical to formally record the details of sensitive discussions or agreements. For instance, there was a faculty member known for being combative in legal matters who was approaching a precarious tenure evaluation. I had been diligent about providing guidance, advice, and assistance in her research submissions. When consulting with our legal department, they inquired about tangible evidence of such support. Informal conversations were deemed insufficient. They strongly recommended that I document offers of assistance with her via email every two to three months. This practice of documenting support would serve as concrete evidence, functioning as "Exhibit A, B, and C" in any legal challenge regarding her tenure support claims. Creating such a paper trail was a strategy endorsed by our legal counsel to ensure that, should a dispute arise, there would be a clear, defensible record of my efforts to assist.
- *Always consider the worst possible interpretation of what you say.* When having conversations, always imagine how they might sound to an outside observer without context. Remarks that might seem funny or lighthearted with friendly colleagues with whom you have inside jokes might take on a completely different connotation if isolated and spotlighted in legal proceedings or media coverage. Remember that it only takes one offended person to report such remarks.
- *Loop in legal sooner rather than later.* If you detect any sign of a potential issue, promptly involve legal, Human Resources, and your dean. Err on the side of caution; it's much more prudent to seek counsel and discover

your concerns are unfounded than to wish you had sought advice sooner (Gomez, 2015). Even if it turns out their input is not necessary for a particular issue, their expertise is often invaluable in preventing matters from escalating into legal disputes. They are employed by the university to handle such risks and are keen to be informed of any developments.

- *Know who to trust.* If you do find yourself in any kind of litigation, assess whether your interests are in harmony with those of Human Resources and legal departments. While it's common for a convergence of interests, it's not guaranteed. My training in human resources management has made me acutely aware that HR professionals are educated first and foremost to safeguard the institution. As a member of management, this often translates to your protection as well, although it is not a guarantee. If you are worried your interests do not align, get a personal lawyer immediately. If you think it is too expensive, rest assured that it is generally far more expensive in the long run not to hire a lawyer.

Navigating the complexities of these legal responsibilities can seem daunting, but approaching this challenge with proactive and informed strategies significantly reduces potential risks. While specifics will vary across different institutions and states, the principles of diligent compliance, proactive documentation, and strategic communication are universally applicable. Always prioritize transparency, maintain thorough records, and seek legal advice when necessary. By doing so, you fortify your professional integrity and safeguard your career against unforeseen legal complications. Remember, the goal is not simply to avoid legal pitfalls but to create a supportive and compliant academic environment.

REFLECTIONS

1. Where do you see the most potential for legal trouble in your role as chair? Which of the strategies mentioned above seem best suited to help you navigate it?
2. Do you know and trust another chair who has navigated legal issues related to higher education administration? If so, do you feel comfortable reaching out to them to ask for advice on how to avoid common legal pitfalls?

REFERENCES

Euben, D. R. (2000, February). *Hiring and promotion legal issues for department chairs.* American Association of University Professors. https://www.aaup.org/

issues/appointments-promotions-discipline%C2%A0/hiring-and-promotion-legal-issues-department-chairs.

Gomez, Fernando C. (2015). *Legal issues department chairs often face*. Academic Chairpersons Conference Proceedings. https://newprairiepress.org/accp/2015/Plenary/3

Mezey, S. G., Khalid, H., Marshall, D. R., & Goldenberg, E. (2006). 2005 Workshop for department chairs: Chairs and the law: Legal issues facing department chairs. *PS: Political Science and Politics, 39*(2), 303–309. http://www.jstor.org/stable/20451739

Van Dusen, V. (2011, April 11). Liability and litigation risks for colleges and schools of pharmacy. *American Journal of Pharmacology Education, 75*(3), 52.

Chapter 62

Hallway Diplomacy

I was engaged in general Monday morning chitchat with Laura, our departmental academic adviser, about the weekend. My wife, who works at the same university as I, was present for the conversation. Later that morning, she called me and asked, "Is everything okay with Laura?" I thought for a moment and answered, "I think so. Why?" My wife continued, "She seemed really bothered. I think you need to follow up and ask her if everything is alright." I had not noticed anything out of the ordinary about the way Laura was acting during our conversation, but I trusted my wife's intuition as she is generally more emotionally intelligent about these things than I. Later in the afternoon I circled back with Laura and asked if everything was okay. She confessed that it was not, and that she had received some concerning results on a health screening. The next morning, a faculty member who is close with Laura came to my office and told me that Laura had told her that I checked in on her. She mentioned that Laura had expressed that she was incredibly thankful for me asking her and that it meant a lot to her.

    I am struck by this story because it clearly mattered to Laura that I inquired and paid attention to her—so much so that she discussed it with other people. It also made me realize the impact that this kind of interpersonal care has. I teach in a communications department, so I certainly understand the value of interpersonal communication academically, but this experience served as a reminder that these principles hold true not just in the classroom. The fact that I was oblivious to Laura's emotional state made me realize that I need to be better in this regard. Thankfully, further medical tests for Laura revealed a false alarm, but the lessons here were not lost on me.

    Interpersonal communication skills are positively linked to managerial success (Rahim et al., 2020). It really does matter. Successful chair work is often framed as being good at paperwork, annual reviews, budgeting, scheduling, and advocacy. But fostering healthy interpersonal relationships with those in your department is part of your chair work as well. Like all your chair responsibilities, it takes effort, intentionality, and care. You need to find the time to engage interpersonally with the people in your department. Wander the halls and pop in when you see open office doors. Say "hi" and ask how the weekend was or how the family is doing.

Hallway diplomacy skills play a decisive role in your success (Holmes, 2005). I have a brilliant friend who served as chair. He was excellent at organizational efficiency, at advocacy, and at seeing big-picture problems. But he was far too abrasive and did not engage in this kind of relationship building. He was eventually voted out by his department because people did not enjoy working with him.

It can be difficult to find the energy and motivation to do this kind of work when you come into the office in the morning and have a long to-do list, but the benefits of putting in the effort are worth it. Much of your departmental culture is built in these moments. You can develop inside jokes, find out about people's personal lives, and foster a sense of camaraderie that can make the busiest days more enjoyable. This kind of relationship building can lead to increased collaboration, where ideas flow more freely and solutions are found more creatively.

Additionally, hallway diplomacy builds trust between you and your team. When you focus on interpersonal communication, your relationship to your colleagues is less transactional and is instead more personal and supportive. This makes you more approachable. Your colleagues will be more comfortable coming to you with concerns, problems, and issues if they feel that you care about them as people. Building these interpersonal relationships also helps when you need to ask for favors. You should not engage in hallway diplomacy selfishly or as a way to build relational capital to later spend on favors, but it is certainly a nice by-product of you fostering genuine connections with other people. Do not solely engage in office small talk with your friends. Actively seek out those who you are less close with. I think you will be surprised at just how far a few office visits to those outside of your inner circle will go.

The power of hallway diplomacy cannot be overstated. It goes beyond politeness and small talk. It is instead about crafting an environment where people feel valued. And it is worth engaging in not just so you are well-liked, but as a part of your approach to leadership that reduces uncertainty, fosters trust, and builds the infrastructure for collaboration and support. These moments of connection may seem small, but they are powerful. Just as we feel the need to learn and grow in our professional skills, we should strive to improve our ability to create genuine and caring interactions.

REFLECTIONS

1. Consider the balance between professional responsibilities and interpersonal interactions. How do you manage to integrate hallway diplomacy into a busy schedule without compromising task completion?
2. Think about a leader you admire for their interpersonal skills. What specific actions or behaviors make them stand out, and how can you incorporate these into your own leadership style?

REFERENCES

Holmes, J. (2005). When small talk is a big deal: Sociolinguistic challenges in the workplace. In M. H. Long (Ed.), *Second language needs analysis* (pp. 344–373). Cambridge University Press.

Rahim, A. R., Rasulong, I., & Wahjono, S. I. (2020). Interpersonal skills and the impact of managerial performance through organizational commitments. *Global Academic Journal of Economics and Business*, 2(4), 59–67. https://doi.org/10.36348/gajeb.2020.v02i04.001

Chapter 63

Keys to Relationship Building in Your Department

In the previous chapter we covered the role of interpersonal communication as a key to success of a department chair. Here we will focus on practical steps you can take to enhance those critical skills. In several chapters of this volume we have reflected on the limited managerial metaphorical toolbox you operate with as chair. We established that referent power (or power based on charisma) is the most readily available form of influence that you have at your disposal. Facilitating buy-in is the way to get things done as chair, and the most effective way to establish buy-in is to facilitate warm, friendly, and genuine connections with the people you work with. Interpersonal communication is central to this effort. Effective relationship building through interpersonal communication requires significant attention and effort, but there are plenty of practices you can implement that will make an immediate impact. I teach a class on interpersonal communication where we spend a whole semester discussing interpersonal communication theory and strategy. We do not have time for that level of engagement here, and there are plenty of resources you can seek out if you want to do a deep dive on the topic. Here we will boil down some of those lessons into a one-thousand-word reflection.

While interpersonal communication involves the sharing of information, its primary goal is not information transfer. Its principal function is to foster connection and meaning between people. Interpersonal conversationalists are engaged in a cooperative effort to build a bond. Interpersonal communication is much more about creating feelings and mood than it is about exchanging knowledge. As such, do not approach the hallway diplomacy we discussed yesterday as simply part of a strategic plan to further your career. Your best way to make people think you care about them is to actually care about them and be interested in them. Dale Carnegie (1936), in his timeless work *How to Win Friends and Influence People*, presented a series of principles, and one of them is "make people feel important, and do it sincerely." The desire to feel important to people is a human impulse. And you can cultivate that feeling in other people in interpersonal conversations. People generally leave conversations affected by how their conversational partner made them feel. Giving someone your full attention goes a long way.

One key element of making your colleagues feel important is active listening, which involves more than waiting for other people to be done speaking so you can take your turn. We often think of listening as a passive activity, but active listening challenges us to reframe it as something that takes effort. It involves a mindset whereby you are present, paying attention, and focused (Cabane, 2012). It involves physical cues such as eye contact, head nods, and mirroring body language to signal engagement. Active listening also entails responding with thoughtful feedback, cooperative overlap, and follow-up questions. Research shows that active listening is correlated to managerial success (Jonsdottir & Fridriksdottir, 2020; Kubota et al., 2004).

Uncertainty reduction theory (URT) offers some insight here on how to leverage your active listening efforts to interpersonal success. Much of the reason we communicate interpersonally is to reduce uncertainty, which generally causes anxiety and makes us feel isolated. URT posits that similarities between conversational partners tend to reduce uncertainty in interpersonal settings (Brashers, 2001). You should use what you learn in your active listening to find points of connections and similarities. Careers in higher education are often fraught with uncertainty. As a chair, reducing uncertainty and creating safety should be a goal. Identifying and highlighting points of connection can assist you in these efforts.

Social penetration theory (SPT) reminds us that while listening is important, self-disclosure plays an important role in interpersonal communication effectiveness (Mangus et al., 2020). Self-disclosure is a form of currency in relationships, and the mutual sharing of personal information is a structured process whereby interpersonal relationships are negotiated between parties. Ultimately, mutual self-disclosure is how relationships are built. When established social norms of self-disclosure are followed, trust is built slowly through the sharing of personal information. Sharing personal information about yourself creates intimacy and vulnerability. SPT reminds us that interpersonal relationships are generally not built on information dumps. Instead, similar pieces of information are disclosed at a rate that both parties find appropriate. Then gradually the information becomes more and more personal. So, do not always talk about work in the hallways. Ask personal questions about movies, hobbies, local sports teams, family life, what people are doing for the upcoming break, and so on. Be willing to share this kind of information back as well.

In exploring the role of interpersonal communication in managerial effectiveness, successful leadership goes way beyond just talking or playing the role. Good chairs have the ability to forge genuine connections, build trust, and ease the uncertainties that are often present within higher education. These communication strategies are not merely tools, but are instead the essence of a chair who is authentic and impactful. The real challenge isn't just to master a set of techniques, but to be a leader who instinctively nurtures these kinds of relationships through empathy, attentiveness, and mutual respect. This kind of leadership does not just enhance individual interactions but also builds a stronger department.

Effective department chairing is primarily about being human—about connecting, understanding, and growing alongside those in your department. This mindset can shift you from being an efficient manager to becoming an insightful leader who recognizes that the keys to true academic administrative effectiveness are found in the quality of the connections you make. This broader view of leadership emphasizes relational depth over procedural efficiency.

REFLECTIONS

1. Does relationship building as part of a managerial practice come easily to you or is it something you need to put a surplus of effort into? How can you evaluate the effectiveness of your interpersonal communication skills in managerial situations?
2. What does active listening feel like to you? When do you feel important to those in positions of power over you? What things does your dean, provost, president do to make you feel like they are listening to you, and can you do those same things for those in your department?

REFERENCES

Brashers, D. E. (2001). Communication and uncertainty management. *Journal of Communication, 51*, 477–497. https://doi.org/10.1111/j.1460-2466.2001.tb02892.x

Cabane, O. F. (2012). *The charisma myth: How anyone can master the art and science of personal magnetism.* Portfolio/Penguin.

Carnegie, D. (1936). *How to win friends and influence people.* Simon and Schuster.

Jonsdottir, I. J., & Fridriksdottir, K. (2020). Active listening: Is it the forgotten dimension in managerial communication? *International Journal of Listening, 34*(3), 178–188. https://doi.org/10.1080/10904018.2019.1613156

Kubota, S., Mishima, N., & Nagata, S. (2004). A study of the effects of active listening on listening attitudes of middle managers. *Journal of Occupational Health, 46*(1), 60–67. https://doi.org/10.1539/joh.46.60

Mangus, S. M., Bock, D. E., Jones, E., & Garretson Folse, J. A. (2020). Examining the effects of mutual information sharing and relationship empathy: A social penetration theory perspective. *Journal of Business Research, 109*, 375–384.

Chapter 64

Approaching Virtual Meetings

"Hey, Ben. Can you stay logged on to chat after this meeting is over?" The message from my associate dean popped up on the chat window of the college leadership virtual meeting we were both in. After everyone else had logged off, it was just the two of us in the virtual meeting room. "Are you upset during these leadership meetings?" she asked me. I was taken aback by the question. "No. Of course not. Why do you ask?" I responded. "You just seem like you might be troubled. You are often scowling during these meetings. A few of us in the dean's office were talking about it the other day."

This feedback was completely unexpected. I wasn't even remotely upset during the meeting. I had been making a concerted effort to actively participate and pay attention. This interaction really made me question what I was missing, especially since I had never gotten this feedback before. This exchange happened after COVID-19 broke out, when higher education was pivoting toward virtual meetings. I had been putting in effort to make sure I was getting the most out of all this new digital landscape we were all being shoehorned into. After the conversation, I asked several colleagues if they perceived me as upset during these meetings, and to my surprise they agreed, describing my facial expression as "intense." I decided to monitor and evaluate myself in the camera window in the next few meetings. As I tried to view my meeting performance through an objective evaluative lens, I could see their point. I realized that my efforts to show engagement in virtual meetings were sending the wrong message. I was leaning in, maintaining constant eye contact with the camera, and engaged in frequent nodding. All of these behaviors were likely being read as excessive.

While we covered meetings extensively earlier in this volume, virtual meetings merit their own chapter as they are becoming an increasingly important part of life in the university. This deserves attention here because you are likely attending many more meetings now that you are a department chair. Also, you do not simply represent yourself at these meetings anymore. You now represent your department. You must be attentive to the fact that your performance in these spaces will be read differently.

The conversation above with my associate dean prompted me to do some digging into virtual meetings. Given the prevalence of virtual meetings and the seemingly lack of understanding about how to approach them, I now cover this topic rather extensively in my business communication courses.

A common error is to treat virtual meetings as if they were essentially in-person meetings merely held in a virtual format. As famed media theorist Marshall McLuhan (1964) articulated, "The medium is the message." Virtual platforms fundamentally change the implications and ideologies of meetings, requiring us to adjust our approach. Do not try to replicate in-person meetings. Virtual platforms hold lower channel capacity, or informational/collaborative bandwidth (Smith, 2014). Virtual meeting participants do not have access to all the body language, subtle cues, and immediate feedback that are available in face-to face interactions. Participants in virtual meetings have more difficulty understanding the social dynamics of groups due to the lack of communicative signals, such as who is looking at whom, whose turn it is to speak, and nonverbal affirmations. This leads to a higher risk of miscommunication and reduced engagement for participants (Kuzminykh & Rintel, 2020b). The lack of communicative bandwidth has led to a phenomenon known as "Zoom fatigue" (Bailenson, 2021), which is the result of participants feeling the need to overcompensate the lack of communication channels. I think this is what was happening to me in the opening story. I was working hard to perform attentiveness through exaggerated facial expressions. "Zoom Fatigue" also drives virtual participants to engage in rampant multitasking such as checking email (Cao et al., 2021).

The challenges posed by the virtual format are offset by some advantages. Virtual meetings are more convenient, do not require travel time, provide chat functions for ongoing dialogue, allow for simultaneous meetings across geographical boundaries, and are more accessible. As with all mediums, there are trade-offs. In the next chapter, we will dive a bit deeper into specifics about how to approach virtual meetings as a department chair.

REFLECTIONS

1. How do you perceive your demeanor during virtual meetings? How do you imagine others perceive you? How do you want to be perceived during virtual meetings?

2. Have you experienced "Zoom fatigue"? Do you sense your department has "Zoom fatigue"? What strategies can you employ to address the lethargy that often accompanies virtual meetings?

REFERENCES

Bailenson, J. N. (2021). Nonverbal overload: A theoretical argument for the causes of zoom fatigue. *Technology, Mind, and Behavior, 2*(1). https://doi.org/10.1037/tmb0000030

Cao, H., Lee, C. J., Iqbal, S., Czerwinski, M., Wong, P., Rintel, S., Hecht, B., Teevan, J., & Yang, L. (2021). *Large scale analysis of multitasking behavior during remote meetings* [Paper presentation]. ACM CHI 2021, Yokohama, Japan. https://hci.stanford.edu/publications/2021/cao_remote/CHI2021-RemoteMeetingMultitask.pdf

Kuzminykh, A., & Rintel, S. (2020a). *Classification of functional attention in video meetings* [Conference session]. 2020 CHI Conference on Human Factors in Computing Systems, Honolulu, HI, United States. https://doi.org/10.1145/3313831.3376546

Kuzminykh, A., & Rintel, S. (2020b). *Low engagement as a deliberate practice of remote participants in video meetings* [Conference session]. Extended Abstracts of the 2020 CHI Conference on Human Factors in Computing Systems, Honolulu, HI, United States. https://doi.org/10.1145/3334480.3383080

McLuhan, M. (1964). *Understanding media: The extensions of man*. McGraw-Hill.

Ngien, A., & Hogan, B. (2023). The relationship between Zoom use with the camera on and Zoom fatigue: Considering self-monitoring and social interaction anxiety. *Information, Communication & Society, 26*(10), 2052–2070. https://doi.org/10.1080/1369118X.2022.2065214

Smith, R. (2014). Collaborative bandwidth: Creating better virtual meetings. *Organization Development Journal, 32*(4), 15–35. https://www.proquest.com/openview/729275e4afd30182386d144642aca183/1?cbl=36482&pq-origsite=gscholar

Chapter 65

Effective Strategies for Virtual Meetings

In the previous chapter we covered how to best think about virtual meetings. Here we will translate that overarching view into actionable strategies. You are likely not only attending more virtual meetings than before, but you are now more frequently responsible for leading them. This responsibility requires you to understand the nuances of virtual meeting formats. Navigating virtual meetings requires a conscientious adaptation of your normal meeting practices. As reliance on digital platforms for meetings is increasing, effectively managing this digital space is integral to your success as chair. We will start this reflection with specifics for how to effectively participate in meetings that you are not necessarily leading, although many of the things we cover there are also applicable to meetings you are running.

As I discussed in the previous chapter, I have firsthand experience with ineffectively managing facial expressions in digital meeting space. In virtual meetings, facial expressions are often amplified due to the way they are framed in a webcam. In a face-to-face meeting your facial expressions are part of a larger bodily context. In a virtual meeting, your face is not only front and center but also all that people see. Do your best to maintain a natural and relaxed expression. Use small nods and smiles to show engagement without coming across as too exaggerated.

Pay attention to your camera setup, your background, and your lighting. It is surprising how many smart and accomplished colleagues overlook these aspects of virtual meetings. Unlike a face-to-face meeting where the meeting space is generally out of your control, virtual meetings allow you the opportunity to carefully craft your backdrop. Your background is part of a semiotic system that communicates to others information about your professional identity, personal tastes, and organizational role. Every element of your frame is a sign that communicates meaning. Books, diplomas, minimalist decor, a picture, a preset digital background, and even a plain backdrop—all of these are symbols for others to interpret. Being strategic and intentional can project credibility, professionalism, and attention to detail. Conversely, a messy, homey, or cluttered background may signal disorganization or unprofessionalism. These background signals matter in how you are read (Tammaru, 2024). Position your camera at eye level to simulate face-to-face communication. Use a background that aligns with how you want to present yourself to others at the meeting.

Pay attention to your own "Zoom fatigue." Try to find times to take a break if you have multiple virtual meetings in a day. If you need a few minutes to recharge, turn your camera off to reduce the pressure to maintain eye contact and perform attentiveness. Finally, do your best to not multitask. Pay attention to what is happening. Important things are discussed at these meetings. Track what is being discussed and keep notes on actionable items.

The challenges of virtual meetings are exacerbated when you are tasked with leading them. The decision about the appropriate meeting format is itself a challenge. This decision should be informed by the goals of the meeting. I have found that virtual meetings suffice for quick updates or discussions. Face-to-face meetings are far superior when deliberating, decision-making, brainstorming, problem-solving, or any emotional complexity is on the agenda. I hold department meetings in person because I believe they are more conducive to team building. Not everyone in my department is thrilled by this, but as chair I understand that it is my responsibility to choose the modality that I believe is best for the department.

When you do lead a virtual meeting, do not simply replicate how you lead in-person meetings. Be aware of the lack of informational and emotional bandwidth in the medium and adjust accordingly. Communicate clearly, realizing that miscommunication is more likely in a virtual setting. I have found that clearly structured agendas are generally more important in virtual meetings. This helps maintain focus and engagement since participants have more temptations for distractions in a virtual meeting.

Managing participation is much more difficult in virtual settings. It requires more effort on your part due to the lack of nonverbal cues. It can be hard to know whose turn it is to speak and help with the flow. When leading a virtual meeting, you need to explicitly mark when people need to participate. This can help cue participants in and manage their effective participation. Also realize that it is much easier for people to fade into the meeting background and not participate. So be active and encourage those who have been silent to participate. Also ensure that everyone has a chance to speak since it is generally easier for larger personalities to speak over others during a virtual meeting.

Finally, have clear guidelines for virtual meetings. Do you want cameras on? Do you want people to formally raise their hands? How do you want the chat function to be used—for asking you questions or to have side conversations relevant to the topic being discussed? Establishing these protocols not only clarifies expectations but helps you maintain order and ensure everyone is engaged. This proactive approach can help you foster a more inclusive and orderly meeting.

The shift to increased virtual meetings necessitates a nuanced understanding of digital communication platforms. Addressing the limitations of virtual platforms for meetings will allow you to mitigate the downsides and leverage the benefits. Effective virtual meeting management can help you be a successful chair by getting the best out of the virtual meetings you run and by presenting yourself as an organized, engaged, and conscientious department chair.

REFLECTIONS

1. What do you understand as the benefits and drawbacks of virtual meetings? Which are best suited for your department meetings and why?
2. What is your most common backdrop for your virtual meetings? What does it convey about you? Is it communicating what you want it to?

REFERENCE

Tammaru, K. (2024). Analysis of communication in virtual meetings. In E. M. Tragel (Ed.), *Explorations in dynamic semiosis.* Theory and History in the Human and Social Sciences. Springer. https://doi.org/10.1007/978-3-031-47001-1_10

Chapter 66

Status-Based Inequality in Your Department

"I have never seen an institution where lecturers think they have so much influence in how a department is run." I took a sip of my coffee to conceal how annoyed I was at the implication of this suggestion. I had requested this one-on-one with a tenure-track faculty member to help her strategize about how to approach her upcoming tenure and promotion case, which was pretty shaky. The irony of this comment was reflected in the fact that this tenure-track faculty member was one of the most stagnant and least productive members of our department, and many of the lecturers she was disparaging were far more productive and engaged than she. But this flippant remark underscored an ideology that many tenure/tenure-track faculty subscribe to.

The entrenched divide between tenured/tenure-track faculty and non-tenured/tenure-track faculty deeply influences many of the dynamics of departmental life. I become particularly frustrated when folks on the tenured/tenure-track side of the divide not only enthusiastically accept it as a part of the natural order, but actively perpetuate this division as if it were a fundamental principle that justifies their place in the existing hierarchy. The way that some tenured/tenure-track faculty position themselves in relationship to instructors/lecturers is indefensible. Over the past several years we have seen more efforts to increase awareness of issues of inequity and injustice in university life. The divide between those with and those without the privileges of the tenure system is one place those concerned with these principles should be directing their efforts. The good news is that as chair, you can do something about this.

To be clear, I am not advocating that all faculty should necessarily have the same roles. There are some important differences between those in tenure/tenure-track positions and those who are not. This may include research expectations and taking on particularly politically challenging responsibilities where the security of tenure provides latitude to make unpopular (but necessary) decisions. I am instead taking objection to the ethos that those not tenured (or on their way to being so) are second-class departmental citizens. Instructors/lecturers are often treated as "separate but not quite equal" (Haviland et al., 2017) in university departments. I have often seen lecturers who have labored under this hierarchy for long enough that they seem to have internalized it.

While people in different positions have different responsibilities, as chair you need to do your best to ensure that everyone in your department is treated equally regardless of tenure status. This needs to start with you as chair. The best way to communicate the message that everyone is equal in a department is for you to embody this principle in your actions. This should be rooted in empathy for those in different situations. Most likely you are in a tenured position since you are chair (although there are exceptions), so this might require some work. Instructors/lecturers frequently encounter challenges related to their status within the department. Nontenure-track faculty often feel as if they are unconnected to the larger university structures (Bond, 2015). They may labor under a lack of professional respect as they are often excluded from significant governance and decision-making processes and lack access to professional development opportunities that are available to tenure-track faculty (Culver & Kezar, 2020).

Additionally, they often have their career opportunities limited in the university (Culver & Kezar, 2020). They cannot be promoted to certain positions. Even if one never wants to become dean, knowing you never could due to your status can significantly impact your sense of organizational value, personal belonging, and professional fulfillment. Nontenure/tenure-track faculty also do not enjoy the security that their tenure/tenure-track colleagues do, which may leave them feeling as if their employment is precarious. I have certainly found irony in this discourse since often instructors/lecturers are actually better teachers than the tenure/tenure-track faculty complaining. This is not always the case, but it often is. Research confirms this as well (Figlio et al., 2015; Tian et al., 2019).

Over the years, as I have become more experienced in my role as chair, I have become more confident in openly questioning the legitimacy of status-based hierarchy in my department. I have gotten into a few disagreements with some tenure/tenure-track faculty for questioning the legitimacy of this hierarchy. You may need to push back on your departmental culture if you want to be a conscientious and ethical chair in this regard. As to moving this beyond rhetoric, there are ways to operationalize a more egalitarian approach. Do not allow tenure/tenure-track faculty departmental privileges simply due to status. Tenure/tenure-track faculty should not have access to the best resources, the most desirable teaching schedules, the first crack at summer classes, or the ability to silence the voices of their colleagues. Put lecturers on important committees when you can and encourage them to participate in departmental deliberations. Finally, push back on the ideology of meritocracy in the university when you encounter it. Point out that nontenure/tenure-track faculty are generally treated with lower status due to systematic bias rather than as a true reflection of their professional worth (Purcell, 2007).

As I have said, the lessons here are not simply a matter of equity and justice. They are also a crucial step in increasing the sustainability of high-quality pedagogy in your department. The percentage of nontenure/tenure-track faculty are growing at universities, so finding ways to increase belonging and investment is not just the right thing to do. It is also essential to you building a supportive environment for an increasingly growing number of stakeholders in your department.

REFLECTIONS

1. Reflect on your own position here. Assuming you are a tenured chair, how might that position influence your perceptions and interactions with nontenure/tenure-track faculty. How can you cultivate empathy and understanding?
2. What are existing policies, practices, or norms within your department that might perpetuate status-based inequality? How can these be addressed to foster equitable treatment? How can you operate within your department culture to address these inequities?

REFERENCES

Bond, N. (2015). Developing a faculty learning community for non-tenure track professors. *International Journal of Higher Education*, 4(4). http://dx.doi.org/10.5430/ijhe.v4n4p1

Culver, K. C., & Kezar, A. (2020). *The impacts of 2020 on advancement of non-tenure-track and adjunct faculty.* Pullias Center for Higher Education, University of Southern California. National Academies Press. https://nap.nationalacademies.org/resource/26405/6_The_Impacts_of_2020_on_Advancement_of_Contingent_Faculty-Culver_Kezar.pdf

Figlio, D. N., Schapiro, M. O., & Soter, K. B. (2015). Are tenure track professors better teachers? *Review of Economics and Statistics*, 97(4), 715–724. https://doi.org/10.1162/REST_a_00529

Haviland, D., Alleman, N. F., & Cliburn Allen, C. (2017). "Separate but not quite equal": Collegiality experiences of full-time non-tenure-track faculty members.

Journal of Higher Education, 88(4), 505–528. https://doi.org/10.1080/00221546.2016.1272321

Purcell, M. (2007). Skilled, cheap, and desperate: Non-tenure-track faculty and the delusion of meritocracy. *Antipode, 39*(1), 121–143. https://doi.org/10.1111/j.1467-8330.2007.00509.x

Tian, Z., Wei, Y., & Li, F. (2019). Who are better teachers? The effects of tenure-track and part-time faculty on student achievement. *China Economic Review, 53*, 140–151. https://doi.org/10.1016/j.chieco.2018.08.014

Chapter 67

Fundraising and Interfacing with Donors

Fundraising is an area that most new department chairs are not thrilled to be involved in. The practice of asking for money often makes new department chairs feel a sense of anxiety (Perlmutter, 2014). While it may not be the responsibility you are most excited about, it is worth accepting as a part of your job. Department chairs have been increasingly expected to participate in fundraising activities due to the declining public investment in higher education and the rising costs of maintaining a competitive advantage in a saturated marketplace (Morse, 2013). For most chairs, fundraising is not a significant part of being chair, but you do get recruited to these efforts semiregularly. These opportunities offer significant benefits to your department and your reputation as chair.

You can take comfort in the fact that as chair you most likely do not have to ask directly for money from donors (Gearhart et al., 2018). Your university's development team will most likely handle the specific request. This is important not only because it may alleviate your anxiety, but also because the folks in those positions are trained in that task. They know how to do it diplomatically and effectively. Your job is much more about ensuring that the groundwork is laid for when the university's fundraising team makes the ask.

The way that you will primarily interface with the fundraising process is twofold. First, you may periodically be asked to identify departmental needs that can be presented to donors if they express interest. Most of the lists of needs you develop will go nowhere and they can feel like busywork, but they are still worth the effort. If nothing else, they are a good exercise for you to have thought through so you have talking points when you discuss your department. These lists should consist of funding projects that make sense for your department. Choose high-impact projects that directly affect students. Splashier and more headline-grabbing projects have a better chance of being funded. Also, be aware of perpetual support for any proposals you send forward. Many projects are amazing in theory but will require support that may eventually strain your department. Will you have to pay additional staff salaries, subscribe to expensive software, or divert faculty energy? Either avoid these kinds of projects or include the perpetual support as part of the costs.

Your other connection to fundraising will be building relationships with donors. Your fundraising team may be planning on asking for a gift, and they will ask you to be a primary point of connection between the potential donor and the university. This makes sense as the potential donor is often one of your alumni. You also have an "in the weeds" knowledge of the disciplinary impact as well as the students who might benefit from a potential gift.

In general, follow the lead of your development team for these kinds of projects. They have a sense of the big picture and will often know things you do not know about a potential donor's relationship to other university stakeholders. Also, they will usually have a file on potential donors and can tell you what their passions are, who their connections are, their business history, and what topics they are interested in. This is good info for you to build affinity. Donors like to support organizations that have connections to their own life experience and that promote their own preferences (Breeze, 2013). Knowing your potential donor can help you make sure you are able to find those points of connection that are instrumental to building affinity.

Your job with these donors is generally to keep them connected to your department. Engage them with some regularity. Send out updates on important departmental accomplishments and send them individual invitations to departmental events. Also, ask them to share their expertise with students. Donors like to know they are valued for more than just their money. Having them speak to students at an alumni event or as a special guest in a class goes a long way to making them feel connected. If they have given in the past, try to find opportunities to get them to meet with the students who have been impacted by their gift. You can thank them over and over, but seeing the impact of their gift goes much further.

While chairs have been called on to be more involved over the past years, fundraising is likely not going to be the most important part of your position. But when you are called on you really want to be able to do this well. Donations can make a serious impact on your department. They also can solidify your reputation as a special kind of chair. Donations get the attention of people across the university. Being significantly involved in securing a gift is good optics. Throwing yourself into fundraising opportunities when they arise can enhance the resources of your department and your effectiveness and visibility as chair.

REFLECTIONS

1. What are the fundraising priorities in your department? How comfortable do you feel being involved in developing initiatives around them?
2. What opportunities can you seek out to improve your understanding and skills in relationship to fundraising? Are there mentors or colleagues who can provide guidance?

REFERENCES

Breeze, B. (2013). How donors choose charities: The role of personal taste and experiences in giving decisions. *Voluntary Sector Review, 4*, 165–183. https://doi.org/10.1332/204080513X667792

Gearhart, G. D., Mamiseishvili, K., & Murry, J. W. (2018). Involvement of academic department heads and chairs in fundraising at U.S. public research universities. *Journal of Higher Education Theory and Practice, 18*(5). https://doi.org/10.33423/jhetp.v18i5.584

Morse, A. (2013). The plate that runneth over: An inquiry into department head fundraising role. *Research in the Schools, 20*(1), 15–22.

Perlmutter, D. D. (2014). *Don't fear fund raising, part 1*. Chronicle of Higher Education. https://www.chronicle.com/article/dont-fear-fund-raising-part-1

Chapter 68

Departmental Culture

As a department chair, your role goes beyond administrative duties, curricular oversight, and annual reviews. It also consists of building a departmental culture that is productive and positive. To use the language of organizational communication, academic departments in a university are "open systems." They are highly susceptible to environmental factors beyond the control of the individual actors in the system. These environmental factors include upper administrative decisions, enrollment fluctuations, the political climate in the community, disciplinary trends and new technologies, as well as many others. Although these factors are beyond your direct control, your leadership is crucial in how your department responds to both external and internal challenges (Gaubatz & Ensminger, 2017). As chair, you are responsible for facilitating an organizational culture that is healthy, safe, productive, just, and equitable. You cannot set your department's culture single-handedly, but you play a pivotal role in laying the groundwork for a strong and positive environment.

While policies and procedures are integral to shaping organizational culture, building a healthy environment requires much more than merely enacting rules. Successful cultures are built by how you engage people, how you acknowledge the efforts of your team, and the competence and knowledge you demonstrate to your department (Gordon & Patterson, 2006). Organizational culture is primarily about shared values and how they are performed. As a chair you can address your departmental culture by specifically attending to shared values. What are the principles that your department organizes itself around? What ideals drive the behaviors of people in your department? What behaviors are celebrated? What is punished? Who are the most influential people in your department and how do they wield that influence?

There are many shared values that your department can organize around, some healthier than others. You may have a departmental culture with values such as integrity, accountability, safety, creativity, collaboration, inclusivity, or excellence. Conversely, you could have a department that operates under the values of territorialism, hierarchy, secrecy, or conformity. Either set of values play a pivotal role in shaping the behaviors and outcomes within the department driving how people interact, make decisions, and achieve their goals. One set of values may encourage organizational performances geared toward innovation, support, and care while another rewards competition, individualism, and adherence to ridged structures.

If your departmental culture is built around values that you believe are suboptimal, recognize that one of your highest priorities is being an agent of cultural change. I once found myself taking on a new chair position with an organizational culture that I found to be very problematic. The primary values seemed to be seniority, assigning blame, preserving status, and mistrust of management. Those with less status routinely faced public harassment and belittlement for their attempts to improve the department, as these efforts threatened the exclusive claims to power through seniority and expertise asserted by some senior members.

I realized rather quickly that changing the culture was going to be a top priority. A top-down authoritative approach is generally not an effective approach to organizational change (Busher, 2006). Cultural change is a gradual process, and rushing it is likely to cause shock and resistance (Ford et al., 2008). You should seek to change culture slowly, methodically, conscientiously, and collaboratively. Begin the process by clarifying departmental values. Engage your department in conversations about what core values are important to them. Reflect on whether the current culture is aligned with those values and identify obstacles to achieving the desired core values. Often the obstacles to change are a vocal minority who are benefitting from the status quo.

In my own experience, I have found that significant culture shifts have been achieved by publicly addressing behaviors that contradict the desired departmental culture. For example, when a full professor publicly chastised a lecturer for "not staying in her lane," I responded in a department-wide email that I was proud of this lecturer for showing initiative. Reframing the behavior from territorialism to resourcefulness set the tone that as chair I was not interested in rewarding this kind of public beratement. This is but one example, and by itself it is surely not enough to change a departmental culture. But these kinds of performances, when repeated, empower those in your department to participate in creating the kind of culture people want. Every decision, interaction, email, and meeting is an opportunity to actively shape culture. Make sure in these moments you are embodying the values that define the very best of what your department can be.

REFLECTIONS

1. What are the current values that are at the heart of your departmental culture? How do you see those values in day-to-day operations?
2. What kind of department culture do you seek to create as chair? Where can you start? Are there departmental members who are likely to resist efforts to change the departmental culture?

REFERENCES

Busher, H. (2006). *Understanding educational leadership: People, power and culture*. McGraw-Hill Education.

Ford, J. D., Ford, L. W., & D'Amelio, A. (2008). Resistance to change: The rest of the story. *Academy of Management Review, 33*(2), 362–377. https://doi.org/10.5465/amr.2008.31193235

Gaubatz, J. A., & Ensminger, D. C. (2017). Department chairs as change agents: Leading change in resistant environments. *Educational Management Administration & Leadership, 45*(1), 141–163. https://doi.org/10.1177/1741143215587307

Gordon, J., & Patterson, J. A. (2006). School leadership in context: Narratives of practice and possibility. *International Journal of Leadership in Education, 9*(3), 205–228. https://doi.org/10.1080/13603120600797831

Chapter 69

Your Blind Spots

"Have you put together the search committee yet?" my dean asked me. "I have," I answered enthusiastically, proud that I had been on top of this task. I provided the names of four white faculty members and one Black faculty member, referring to the latter as our "diversity member." My dean paused and asked with genuine confusion, "What did you say?" As soon as the question left her lips, I realized how problematic the term "diversity member" was. I felt a deep sense of embarrassment, which was compounded by the fact that my dean was Black (for context, I am a middle-aged white guy). "We really need to address how we think about diversity in your department," she responded.

This conversation is frequently in the playlist of embarrassing moments to anxiously rerun when I cannot sleep at night and want to ruminate about mortifying things I have said in the past. My department had regularly used the term "diversity member" when discussing the makeup or assembly of search committees. It was part of the lexicon when I arrived at the department, and regretfully I never questioned it. This conversation with my dean turned into a learning moment for me as it pushed me to examine the assumptions that I (and my department) was laboring under when we used this kind of language. Since that conversation, I have retired it from my own vocabulary (it never should have been there in the first place), and I made a conscientious effort to mark it in the department as a problematic term we will no longer use.

Thankfully over the past several years more attention has been paid to inclusivity and diversity within the university system. Efforts toward building more diverse and equitable campuses have manifested in new administrative offices, initiatives, and training. While these are worthwhile endeavors, there is no substitute for a department chair focused on these ends. As I have mentioned in earlier chapters, 80 percent of institutional decisions at universities are made by chairs (Gonaim, 2016). The role of conscientious, knowledgeable, and empowered department chairs who are dedicated to enhancing equality and inclusion is crucial. While universities can establish and implement numerous diversity initiatives, their effectiveness largely depends on department chairs who actively execute and apply these strategies at the departmental level.

Much of the progress toward equality is nurtured in your department's organizational culture, which is comprised of the shared values, norms, rituals, and practices that constitute the psychological environment that your department operates within. Organizational culture guides and frames how stakeholders engage in sense-making. Symbols, jargon, dress codes, procedures, ceremonies, and language all play a role in both reflecting and shaping how a department engages its shared values. Culture is ephemeral while also influencing almost every facet of organizational life.

As a department chair, you should strive to do your part to help build a departmental culture that prioritizes inclusivity and diversity as shared values. Organizational culture is notoriously difficult to change, but as a leader in your department you play an outsized role in influencing the norms and values that promote inclusivity within your department (Bystydzienski et al., 2017). As such, paying attention to your own subjectivity and performance is essential if you want to build a just and equitable departmental culture.

The most obvious place to start is with an examination of your own blind spots. What are the aspects of your culture that are so engrained that you do not even notice them? The story above, with the term "diversity member," was clearly a blind spot to me. The department's use of that term, and my unreflexive acceptance of it, illustrated a host of ideologies about how we approached diversity. The term "diversity member" communicates that the value of one committee member is essentially their minority status rather than as a contributor to the core functions of the group. It also assumes that diversity can be achieved by a person's mere presence, rather than through a comprehensive and reflexive approach to considering the politics of representation. Diversity should be understood as an integral part of a committee's composition, rather than as an "add on." It also places an unfair burden on one individual to represent diversity on a committee while simultaneously simplifying the concept of diversity to people who look different while ignoring the myriad of ways that diversity manifests (socioeconomic status, political beliefs, sexual orientation, age, physical abilities, etc.). I would have consciously agreed to all of this, but I still threw around the term "diversity member" without thinking about its implications. Hence the blind spot.

There is a critical lesson here for department chairs in the essential role of language and awareness in promoting a departmental culture that fosters inclusivity. It is imperative to recognize and dismantle practices that may inadvertently marginalize members of our teams. Lead by example by interrogating where your own blind spots may be. Doing so publicly, humbly, and openly can move your department toward a commitment to diversity that is seamlessly integrated into departmental operations rather than treated as an afterthought or a checkbox. In the next chapter we will focus on some specifics for how you might address your departmental culture with this goal in mind. Your commitment to examining your own blind spots in relationship to departmental culture not only builds a more supportive academic environment but also sets the standard for everyone in your department.

REFLECTIONS

1. How would you grade your own departmental culture in terms of its commitment to issues of diversity and inclusion? Are there any long-standing practices within your own department that might contribute to exclusivity rather than inclusivity?
2. What can you do to identify your own blind spots? Are there practices you can engage in to increase your reflectiveness?

REFERENCES

Bystydzienski, J., Thomas, N., Howe, S., & Desai, A. (2017). The leadership role of college deans and department chairs in academic culture change. *Studies in Higher Education, 42*(12), 2301–2315. https://doi.org/10.1080/03075079.2016.1152464

Gonaim, F. (2016). A department chair: A life guard without a life jacket. *Higher Education Policy, 29*(2), 272–286. https://doi.org/10.1057/hep.2015.26

Chapter 70

Inclusivity, Diversity, and Departmental Culture

As we have reflected on over the past few chapters, organizational culture is the shared values of your department and how they are enacted in departmental daily life. As chair, you have an obligation to use your role to push your department to commit to a set of values that bring out the best in your team. Two of the values that you should certainly prioritize in this process are inclusivity and diversity.

The rationale for building your culture around these values is both pragmatic and ideal. It is not only the right thing to do, but creating a culture where everyone feels safe, included, and comfortable will make your department much more harmonious, help your department avoid groupthink, foster creativity, and help folks work better in teams. We have reflected on organizational culture from a bird's-eye view in the last few chapters. Here we will dig into some specifics on how to cultivate these values in your department.

- *Building an organizational culture needs to start with a recognition of your university and department's specific history* (Bystydzienski et al., 2017). As much as we would love to be able to flip a switch and change organizational culture, it does not work that way. Cultures are deeply rooted in history, and change is a gradual process of moving from where your department is toward where you want it to be through incremental change. An honest and fair assessment/reckoning with where your department is and how you got there is an essential part of the process. It helps you set benchmarks, understand what is feasible, and develop strategies for improvement. An honest assessment with your history not only allows for changes that are thoughtful and well-informed, but also sustainable.
- *Pay attention to the "cultural tax" that members of your department may be laboring under* (Guillaume & Apodaca, 2022). Efforts to increase diversity

and inclusion can have unintended side effects, like extra responsibilities disproportionately placed on minority faculty. The labor associated with diversity initiatives often falls more on minority faculty. Part of the problem is that the additional service activities assigned to minority faculty in the name of promoting diversity often do not align with professional advancement or significantly contribute to career success. Committee work does not move the needle on a tenure/promotion case the way a few more publications do. As chair, do your best to recognize and reward those service activities. Provide whatever resources you can to offset the "cultural tax." Also, be conscientious about how you distribute service work.

- *Your department's organizational design contributes significantly to culture.* Are there leadership opportunities that everyone has access to (Chun & Evans, 2015)? Are there pipelines to career advancement for faculty? Providing those opportunities makes space for those who may not have traditionally been chosen for leadership to pursue such roles and succeed. As chair, build transparent pathways for advancement that are accessible to all faculty members regardless of their background.

- *When evaluating faculty, do not fall into the "meritocracy myth," forgetting that circumstances play a big part in success* (Bystydzienski et al., 2017). This is not a call to lower expectations, but instead to remember that equity involves understanding and accommodating the varied backgrounds and challenges that your faculty members face. This awareness should guide both the evaluation and resource-allocation processes. Accomplishments are important and worth rewarding and recognizing, but remember that the playing field isn't always level. As chair, consideration of the full context of each faculty member's contributions and circumstances can foster a more inclusive and supportive department culture. This approach helps to recognize the diverse experiences within your department while promoting a sense of belonging and respect.

- *True commitment to diversity and inclusion is not achieved by patting yourself on the back after making sure there is someone who looks different on each committee.* You need to go a step further, ensuring that people who look and think the same are not in all the positions where the decisions are made. You need to have diversity represented in decision-making roles. Make sure people of different genders, sexualities, ages, ideological perspectives, races, backgrounds, socioeconomic backgrounds, and so forth are in important positions where they can genuinely influence outcomes and policy. You need to create a culture where diverse perspectives are not just present, but integral to the decision-making processes.

- *As chair, you can set the tone for this discourse.* Be open and visible about your priorities. Progress is rarely accomplished if people stay in their comfort zones. You should model a willingness to engage in uncomfortable conversations about these issues in thoughtful ways. Discuss inclusivity openly. Invite all viewpoints into the conversation, even those skeptical of the efforts.

Entire careers are built on studying how to best foster diversity and inclusion in organizations, so we are clearly just scratching the surface in these last few chapters. The one thing that I want to emphasize is that departmental culture change requires consistent and thoughtful effort from you as chair. Your role is pivotal in moving your department toward the values of diversity and inclusion. This is a dynamic process that will require you to engage in ongoing reflections, adaptation, open dialogue, and commitment. These reflections should come from a humble curiosity to identify your blind spots and work on them. The work will be continuous and your progress incremental, but the impacts of these efforts are well worth the investment.

REFLECTIONS

1. How would you describe the current organizational culture of your department in relationship to diversity and inclusion? What specific historical or contextual factors have shaped the culture?
2. How comfortable do you feel engaging in discussions of diversity and inclusion with your department? What can you do to foster an environment where these topics are discussed openly and freely?

REFERENCES

Bystydzienski, J., Thomas, N., Howe, S., & Desai, A. (2017). The leadership role of college deans and department chairs in academic culture change. *Studies in Higher Education*, *42*(12), 2301–2315. https://doi.org/10.1080/03075079.2016.1152464

Chun, E., & Evans, A. (2015). *The department chair as transformative diversity leader: Building inclusive learning environments in higher education*. Routledge.

Guillaume, R. O., & Apodaca, E. C. (2022). Early career faculty of color and promotion and tenure: The intersection of advancement in the academy and cultural taxation. *Race Ethnicity and Education*, *25*(4), 546–563. https://doi.org/10.1080/13613324.2020.1718084

Chapter 71

Enrollment Management

We have spent a considerable amount of time thus far reflecting on the ways that the department chair position has evolved over time. A department chair's role used to be primarily academic. A chair was an academic shopkeeper, ensuring the department's academic integrity. While you are still responsible for that, the role of the department chair has become increasingly managerial (Winter, 2009). Department chair success is now measured less by fidelity to the academic mission and more by budget and personnel management. Given this, it is no surprise that department chairs have become increasingly recruited into enrollment management efforts. In decades past, the responsibility for enrollment management primarily fell to the office of admissions or student success. As higher education has been experiencing seemingly perpetual enrollment challenges, the ethos has been "all hands on deck." This includes chairs.

Enrollment management is more than simply recruiting students—although that is a big part. It is about ensuring that students are attended to from the moment they express interest in your department until they graduate. This involves strategic planning, data analysis, and the development of initiatives that address student retention and success. You are now a strategic planner, a customer service representative, a public relations specialist, and a quality control expert. This multifaceted role requires attentiveness to the student (and potential student) experience.

Enrollment management is often conflated with outreach to potential students. While this is an important part of the enrollment management pipeline, it is not the whole picture. In the next few chapters we will reflect on various aspects of enrollment management. Before we discuss specific elements of how your job interfaces with enrollment management, we should build a foundation for those reflections. It is helpful to approach your enrollment management responsibilities with the sensibilities of a marketing manager. Marketing management is "the art and science of choosing target markets and getting, keeping, and growing customers through creating, delivering, and communicating superior customer value" (Kotler & Keller, 2015, p. 5).

Delivering "customer value" in an academic department needs to start with an understanding of both what customers want and what you can deliver. You need to understand your value proposition as a department. What does your department offer that would make students choose you over similar departments at other universities and within your university? Do you excel at internships, faculty expertise, facilities, connections with area organizations, curricular innovations, or other unique strengths? Before you can communicate your value proposition outwardly, you need to be able to accurately identify it. You need to approach the task of identifying your value proposition humbly, realizing that it may not be what you think it is. Often, the things we are proudest of are of little value to students. Also, things that we may not take that much pride in may be very important to students.

Listening to your students is the best way to identify and improve on your value proposition. There are several ways to do this, but I have found that your best tool is a formal focus group. Gather groups of students who can provide diverse perspectives, perhaps first-year students, transfer students, and outgoing seniors. Entice them with pizza and a promise that they are an essential part of helping guide departmental efforts to improve. Find someone with experience leading focus groups. It may be tempting to assume you can lead a focus group since it is just talking to people, but trust me that it is much better to find someone with some training or professional experience. Leading a focus group productively is harder than it looks. Someone at your university no doubt has the expertise.

Use the focus groups to find what drew these students to your department, what is important to them, what they have found most useful, and what they wish the department provided but does not. These findings can be generated into a report and presented to your department as the beginning of an extended conversation about what your value proposition is. Are you happy with this? What areas are worth diverting resources toward to improve your value proposition? How can you sustain your areas of strength? Finally, how can you include these findings as part of a comprehensive and strategic outwardly facing communication plan?

When you make sense of the data gleaned from the focus group, do so without expectations. It might make sense for you to have someone without an investment in your department do some of the sense-making work. This can be hard to give up as you likely want to have your efforts validated, your public predictions corroborated, your initiatives praised, and the efforts of those you cannot stand criticized. However, the goal of the focus group is not to further validate you as chair, but to listen. You can gain unbiased insights that might reveal surprising or uncomfortable truths, which are essential for genuine improvement.

I have seen many departments adopt an approach where they are the disciplinary experts and therefore the authority. Students will bend to departmental will and the authority of the faculty. However, a more effective approach is to view students as partners in the educational experience (Zeithaml et al., 2017). This means actively seeking their input, addressing their concerns, and continually reevaluating your department's value proposition in relation to their needs and desires. By fostering a collaborative relationship, you not only improve buy-in with current students, but you also have a more objective understanding of how to create and sell your value.

REFLECTIONS

1. What do you believe is your department's value proposition? What is unique about your department that other departments cannot boast?
2. Have focus groups been utilized to gather diverse student perspectives? If not, do you believe this is valuable? Is this feasible?

REFERENCES

Kotler, P., & Keller, K. L. (2015). *Marketing management* (15th ed.). Pearson.

Winter, R. (2009). Academic manager or managed academic? Academic identity schisms in higher education. *Journal of Higher Education Policy and Management, 31*(2), 121–131. https://doi.org/10.1080/13600800902825835

Zeithaml, V. A., Bitner, M. J., & Gremler, D. D. (2017). *Services marketing: Integrating customer focus across the firm* (6th ed.). McGraw-Hill Education.

Chapter 72

Recruiting New Students

While marketing encompasses more than just recruiting, promoting your program to potential students remains a key responsibility. Few things will define your success more than getting new students into your major. There are plenty of outside influences that you cannot control, such as economic conditions, demographic trends, and industry demand. Successful recruiting involves responding effectively to these influences in ways that clearly communicate your departmental value proposition.

An additional component to consider is that your university has a marketing and communications team. Strangely, departmental relationships with these offices are not as collaborative as one might hope. I have found that they can be rather territorial and cold when asked to help with department-specific outreach initiatives. I hope your experience is different than mine, but it has been this way at all three universities where I have served as chair, so I assume it is a norm rather than an exception. Regardless, they are still a resource and should still be consulted. Stay friendly with them. Also, consult the branding guides they provide. While you may do your own thing in terms of departmental outreach, you do not want to be out of alignment with the university's branding and messaging.

There are a variety of outreach channels that you must pay attention to as chair. You will need to manage a multifaceted approach across recruiting events, social media outlets, job fairs, high school visits, mailers, and your website. You need to ensure that there is coherent messaging across all these points of contact with potential students. Your value proposition should be articulated consistently from one channel to the next.

For face-to-face points of contact like on-campus recruiting events, individual campus visits, high school visits, and job fairs you need to find ways to tell your story. Do not just *tell* potential students what your department does, *show* them. Put effort and energy into promotional materials. Have a nice table to set up, showcase equipment, display student work, bring current students to talk, and engage potential students in disciplinary-related activities. You need to project energy and enthusiasm. Success in these events is driven by the emotions you create. You need students to feel connected to what you are doing and to want to be a part of it. Ask questions of potential students: What are they looking for in a program? What are their passions? What projects have they worked on in high school classes? Showing that you are interested in them will go far.

Also, pay attention to the dual audiences at these events. You are not only speaking to potential students, but also to parents. So, while energy and enthusiasm are important, parents are often the ones more interested in long-term career prospects, curricular rigor, and educational value. Address their concerns by highlighting your program's strengths in these areas. Discuss alumni success stories, job placement rates, and the support services your institution offers to ensure student success. Offer concrete examples of how your curriculum prepares students for the workforce and higher academic pursuits. By balancing the emotional appeal for students with the practical assurances for parents, you can create a compelling narrative that resonates with both audiences. This dual approach will help build a strong connection and leave a lasting impression on everyone involved. Finally, recruit other faculty to attend these events. Align these kinds of recruiting events with their expertise (Furback, 2021). Get them at these events to talk about things they find interesting and valuable.

For your non-face-to-face points of contact, the key goal is to move potential students to face-to-face interactions. Try to entice students to come see you. One method I have used in the past is to have our mailers double as a coupon for a free departmental T-shirt. This encourages students to hold on to the mailer so they can exchange it when they come visit us. We have covered social media elsewhere, so we won't focus on it here except to say keep your branding consistent. Parents are more likely to scrutinize mailers, so focus on career prospects that ensure students are not living with their parents after graduation. If they look good for you, include employment facts from the Bureau of Labor statistics about industry outlook and average starting industry salary. Include recent alumni testimonials and photos of students doing things other than sitting in a classroom. Make sure your department website has a clear "schedule a visit" button that is easily accessible. Get students in the door.

When you get students in front of you, do not focus heavily on curriculum. Focus instead on opportunities and outcomes. Promote student clubs, internships, facilities, and faculty expertise. The absolute best thing you can do is to get potential students talking to current students. Find those students of yours who are excited about your program and get them in front of potential students. Similarity breeds trust, and current students are much more like potential students than you are.

As chair, you are now responsible for the overall strategy in recruiting. Do not feel like you need to do it all yourself, but you are the one who drives the overall approach. Over the past few years I have taken to implementing a recruiting and retention committee (that I serve on) where we can have open conversations and workshop ideas. Collaboration and a collective approach not only lighten the workload but also enhance the effectiveness and cohesiveness of recruitment efforts. Successful recruitment involves creating a unified strategy that leverages the strengths and insights of the entire team.

REFLECTIONS

1. How would you describe your department's overall current recruiting strategy? What is most and least effective about your strategy? What changes might you make as chair?
2. Do your faculty feel buy-in to the recruiting process? Do they participate? What strategies can you use to encourage them to participate?

REFERENCE

Furback, S. (2021). *Faculty involvement in student recruitment and its impact on enrollment* [Doctoral dissertation, University of Nebraska]. ProQuest Dissertations Publishing. https://www.proquest.com/openview/2bbbd05b6bec3e3b281266dc19ad5458/1?cbl=5324452&pqorigsite=gscholar&parentSessionId=8XAX0LZWPXnBqk3zmzc13e0Y4D3mBLT6rVwQoeeekyM%3D

Chapter 73

Retention

Retention is an essential part of your enrollment strategy. While bringing in new students is critical, it is arguably more important to focus on the ones you already have. The well-worn maxim in marketing is that retaining an existing customer is five times more profitable than recruiting a new one (Pfeifer, 2005). The primary reason for this is the acquisition cost of acquiring new customers. It takes five times more resources to attract a new customer than it does to keep one you already have. Additionally, existing customers already have cultivated loyalty, and they are more likely to make future purchases over the course of their lifetime than newly recruited customers. Due to the design of higher education, I am skeptical that the "five times more valuable" model holds up exactly since students are not lifetime customers (they matriculate out) and they do not purchase additional products due to existing loyalty. While five times more valuable is a bit aggressive of a formula to apply to higher education, the underlying principle still holds. Retaining students is generally more cost beneficial than recruiting new ones. The costs associated with attracting new students is substantial: marketing materials, faculty effort that could be spent improving classroom experiences, advertising, recruiting events, swag, and the like. Retaining students can generally be achieved with fewer resources than needed for bringing new ones in.

Additionally, investing in retention strategies generally improves student outcomes, which improves the reputation of your department and makes it more attractive to future students. Satisfied students are more likely to become engaged alumni, which can lead to donations, positive word-of-mouth, and community partnerships. While the exact ratio may differ, the core idea that retaining students provides superior value is highly relevant to you as a chair. Also, many of the factors that drive student retention are well within your abilities as chair to address.

Retention is complicated and unpredictable. Given this, it is worth initiating some efforts to gain whatever information you can about why students leave your department. Identify those students who have fallen through the "leaky pipeline" (Metcalf, 2010) to determine the key factors driving their departure. You are likely to have difficulty tracking them down to talk to them, but look for trends. Are there characteristics that many of the students leaving your department share? Do higher- or lower-achieving students leave? What about athletes? Do "at-risk" students leave your program at a higher rate? Do they have financial difficulties?

While retention is difficult to get a handle on, there are two things we know with relative certainty. The first is that student engagement and social integration leads to higher retention (Burke, 2019; Aljohani, 2016). For this reason, find ways to use your position as chair to build community. Hold a networking event with alumni and students. Have a pizza party with a career panel of area industry experts. Hold a student club gathering with faculty advisers from student clubs and recruit new members. Have a welcome party at the beginning of the year. Host a departmental event for homecoming. Provide whatever resources you can for student clubs. I have held an open office-hours event before where all faculty have been in their offices at a set time. Students needed to meet with every professor they were in class with that semester and have them sign a sheet. We then held a drawing for a gift card out of those who made it to all their professors. You can find your own event like that. Whatever it is, try to make your students feel like they are part of a family.

The other thing we know with relative certainty is that quality academic advising is related to retention (Tudor, 2018; Drake, 2011). Superior advising helps students feel as if they have a comprehensive sense of where they fit in to the program. It helps ensure that students' engagement with the department is connected to their career goals and passions. Advising is a chance for students to feel connected to their adviser as a representative of the department. It is an opportunity for them to feel listened to and to receive practical advice. You may either have a departmental adviser or have faculty do advising. Either way, you absolutely must do whatever you can as chair to ensure quality advising is happening in your department. This is the lowest of hanging fruit to effect retention. If you have a full-time adviser in the department, then have lots of conversations with that person about what constitutes effective advising. If faculty do the advising, have trainings and specific instructions on how people should approach advising. Make it exceedingly clear that faculty should not act as if advising is an ancillary part of their job that they have to get out of the way so they can research and teach. Advising is essential. Have conversations about how you all can deliver superior advising in a way that makes students feel as if they are integrated into the department.

Many factors are out of your control in terms of retention. You cannot help it if a student wants to move to a new city, receives an athletic scholarship elsewhere, or has a change in their financial situation. But pay attention and address what you can. Doing so will, over time, minimize the number of students who leave your department.

REFLECTIONS

1. Has your department done any analysis into trends of why students leave your department? If not, should you engage in those efforts?
2. How would you assess the state of advising and community in your department? Where do you see the need for improvement?

REFERENCES

Aljohani, O. (2016). A comprehensive review of the major studies and theoretical models of student retention in higher education. *Higher Education Studies, 6*(2), 1–18. https://doi.org/10.5539/hes.v6n2p1

Burke, A. (2019). Student retention models in higher education: A literature review. *College and University, 94*(2), 12–21. https://eric.ed.gov/?id=EJ1216871

Drake, J. K. (2011). The role of academic advising in student retention and persistence. *About Campus, 16*(3), 8–12. https://doi.org/10.1002/abc.20062

Metcalf, H. (2010). Stuck in the pipeline: A critical review of STEM workforce literature. *InterActions: UCLA Journal of Education and Information Studies, 6*(2). https://escholarship.org/uc/item/6zf09176

Pfeifer, P. E. (2005). The optimal ratio of acquisition and retention costs. *Journal of Targeting, Measurement and Analysis for Marketing, 13*(2), 179–188. https://doi.org/10.1057/palgrave.jt.5740142

Tudor, T. R. (2018). Fully integrating academic advising with career coaching to increase student retention, graduation rates, and future job satisfaction: An industry approach. *Industry and Higher Education, 32*(2), 73–79. https://doi.org/10.1177/0950422218759928

Chapter 74

Transfer Students

I met Emma when she visited our department the previous semester. She was thrilled about the idea of moving from the community college she was currently enrolled at to our four-year major. As she toured our facilities, she excitedly asked questions about what a typical day would look like in our department. What were the students like? What kind of classes would she take? Would she get to use our media equipment regularly? Her enthusiasm was contagious. She enrolled that very day. When I ran into her the during the first weeks of the following semester, I asked her how she was doing. Much of her enthusiasm had waned. She was overwhelmed. Not as many of her credits had transferred as she hoped. Additionally, she said she was struggling to keep up with all the new responsibilities and expectations. She felt lonely as she didn't know many people and she was disappointed that she had to take some prerequisites before she could get into her lab classes. This was all very different from both her community college experiences and from what she was expecting in our department.

Feeling guilty that maybe I had oversold my department, I wanted to make this okay for her. I set up a meeting with her academic adviser and myself to review her credits and see if there was anything we could do to get some more credits transferred. I also reached out to a senior who was very active in the department and asked if he could get her plugged in. Emma went on to become an active, well-liked staple of our department. I am not crediting her success with my intervention, but I like to imagine that it played a role in smoothing her transition.

Emma's experience is not all that uncommon and should serve as a reminder that attentiveness to transfer students is an important and often overlooked part of the enrollment management responsibilities that you have as chair. Simply getting transfer students enrolled in your program is only half of the equation. You must also concern yourself with providing a seamless transition. First impressions matter. Facilitating a smooth transfer experience is key to building a healthy relationship with your transfer students. This starts with attempts to understand their motivations and experiences. There are vertical (two-year to four-year institutions), horizontal (four-year to four-year institution), and reverse (four-year to two-year institution) transfer students (Hossler et al., 2012). All these likely come in with different experiences, expectations, and needs. For example, Emma came to our department as a vertical transfer student interested in a bachelor's degree after completing her general education courses at a cheaper institution. A horizontal transfer student likely has different motivations. Did they transfer to your department because of some area of specialization you offer? Your facilities? Financial reasons?

If you are at a four-year institution, I strongly recommend that you reach out and make connections with your counterparts at the community colleges in the area. Find out what their students are looking for. Make them partners. What kind of curricular alignment can you enact so students will have a clear pathway with minimal credit loss? Additionally, what kinds of areas are attractive to students in these programs? Building goodwill through collaboration can manifest some very positive results in both recruiting and transfer student success.

Be attentive to the "transfer shock" that transfer students experience as they move from one academic environment to another (Ivins et al., 2017). It can be disorienting and confusing to come to a new place where everyone seems to know each other, and you are the outsider. Transfer students also may not have a cohort they went through orientation with. Try to make them feel at home immediately. Meet them and encourage them to come see you with issues. Introduce them to faculty and students in their areas of interest. Have a transfer student welcome event where you get to know them. Personally engaging and showing interest is one of the most impactful actions you can take as chair to mitigate the "transfer shock." Let transfers students know they have an ally in the chair's office.

On the systematic level, actively be involved in your institution's transfer programs. Know the statewide articulation agreements as they relate to your major (Education Commission of the States, 2022). Help shape a transfer-friendly curriculum. Credit loss is one of the key drivers of transfer student dissatisfaction (Taylor & Jain, 2017). Remove curricular obstacles at the institutional level so transfer students do not have to stress about them.

Supporting transfer students requires a proactive and empathetic approach. Understanding and caring about their experience and unique needs can significantly impact their well-being, satisfaction, and educational experience. As chair, these are all things you can directly affect. Use your influence and power as chair to build a department that is not just transfer student friendly, but transfer student centered. Paying attention to the interests of transfer students will benefit all your students.

REFLECTIONS

1. How can you best address the issue of "transfer shock" in your department? What initiatives can you engage in to create a seamless transition?
2. What is the transfer student onboarding process at your department? What does the experience likely look and feel like? Are there any transfer students you can discuss the transfer student experience with?

REFERENCES

Hossler, D., Shapiro, D., Dundar, A., Ziskin, M., Chen, J., Zerquera, D., & Torres, V. (2012). *Transfer and mobility: A national view of pre-degree student movement in postsecondary institutions.* National Student Clearinghouse Research Center. https://nscresearchcenter.org/wp-content/uploads/SignatureReport2.pdf

Ivins, T., Copenhaver, K., & Koclanes, A. (2017). Adult transitional theory and transfer shock in higher education: Practices from the literature. *Reference Services Review, 45*(2), 244–257. https://doi.org/10.1108/RSR-08-2016-0048

Taylor, J. L., & Jain, D. (2017). The multiple dimensions of transfer: Examining the transfer function in American higher education. *Community College Review, 45*(4), 273–293. https://doi.org/10.1177/0091552117725177

Whinnery, E., & Peisach, L. (2022). *50-state comparison: Transfer and articulation policies.* Education Commission of the States. https://reports.ecs.org/comparisons/transfer-and-articulation-2022

Chapter 75

Students Switching Majors

A substantial portion of communications majors do not begin their academic journey in this field. Communications is sometimes referred to as a "found major" given the number of students who start in a different department. This often happens because students take a class and fall in love with the discipline, or they start in another major (often business, sociology, or psychology) and find that it is not what they were expecting. We are fortunate that we have a discipline that is connected with interesting technologies and is tied to a robust job market. I only bring this up to bolster my credibility on this issue. I talk to a lot of students about switching from another major to communications. As chair, this is another area of enrollment management to pay attention to. It is also the last one we will cover in this volume.

Compared to the other areas of enrollment management (recruiting, retention, and transfer students), navigating the process of students coming into your department has some political complications. The first is that students from other in-house departments finding their way to you is not always as valued as other forms of enrollment management. I have been told by an upper administrator that my department's major count did not justify equal resource allocation because although we had many majors, many were already enrolled at the university. Given this, our major was not given credit for attracting students to the university.

The second way that this issue is politically complicated is that you cannot be seen as reaching out to poach students. I made this mistake early in my tenure as a chair. I had a list of students who had initially expressed interest in majoring in communications but ultimately chose another discipline. I invited those students to a departmental beginning-of-the-year party. Several chairs complained to the dean, and I learned my lesson rather quickly. It is not worth fracturing a relationship with other units in hopes of encouraging students to switch to your major.

Do not go out of your way to recruit students to change from another major to yours, but be prepared to make the switch seamless when the opportunity presents itself. When students come to you interested in switching majors, approach the conversations with emotional intelligence. While these kinds of conversations may be routine for you, they are anything but for the student. For them, these decisions are often associated with anxiety, confusion, and uncertainty. Maybe they just discovered that the thing they have wanted to do since childhood does not actually match their skill set. Perhaps they have just realized that the reality of their future is different from what they imagined. They may be dreading a conversation with a parent about their potential major change. Be soft, open, friendly, and warm. I find it helpful to approach these conversations with normalizing the idea of major switching. Approximately one-third of college students switch majors at least once during their academic career (Denice, 2021). I always try to explain that this is the benefit of going to college. You get to try things out to see what fits. There is nothing embarrassing with shopping around a bit.

Always start these conversations with questions. Rather than giving a stump speech about your department, ask what they are looking for. What is it about your department that led them to your office? How do they envision their future career? What are they looking for in an education? What isn't working in their current major? Avoid the temptation to use this as an excuse to badmouth another department, regardless of how you actually feel about it.

After finding out what the student wants, talk pragmatics. The biggest barrier is often students' concern that a switch will delay their expected graduation date (Liu et al., 2021). When possible, be flexible substituting prerequisites. Minimizing the cost of switching increases the value of not just your department, but the entire university as it accommodates increased diversity of academic experience (Astorne-Figari & Speer, 2019).

Do not engage in a hard sell. Your job is to help them figure out if your major is the right fit for them, not strong-arm them. As much as we all want more majors, keep in mind that they are already at your university. They are already contributing to the overall well-being of your institution. Engaging in hard-sell tactics, especially when they may already be feeling vulnerable, is not responsible academic leadership. The goodwill you burn by appearing to "poach" students is not worth whatever local benefits your department might gain from an additional (student already enrolled at the university) major. The irony is that avoiding the hard sell is in fact sound strategy as it engenders trust in the students who do make the switch.

Ultimately, the goal is not simply to increase numbers at the expense of overall institutional health. It is instead to genuinely support students in finding their best academic fit. As chair, you will likely be the first point of contact for students interested in your major. Engage in these conversations with an ethos of care, integrity, and understanding. By balancing strategic thinking and empathy, you can effectively manage major switching with positive results for both students and the institution.

REFLECTIONS

1. How can you ensure that you approach conversations about switching majors with empathy and understanding? What strategies can you use to normalize the idea of major switching?
2. What are the most common reasons students switch to your major? What are the most common concerns they express about the switch? How can you incorporate this knowledge into how you approach these conversations?

REFERENCES

Astorne-Figari, C., & Speer, J. D. (2019). Are changes of major major changes? The roles of grades, gender, and preferences in college major switching. *Economics of Education Review*, *70*, 75–93. https://doi.org/10.1016/j.econedurev.2019.03.005

Denice, P. A. (2021). Choosing and changing course: Postsecondary students and the process of selecting a major field of study. *Sociological Perspectives*, *64*(1), 82–108. https://doi.org/10.1177/0731121420921903

Liu, V., Mishra, S., & Kopko, E. M. (2021). Major decision: The impact of major switching on academic outcomes in community colleges. *Research in Higher Education*, *62*(4), 498–527. https://doi.org/10.1007/s11162-020-09608-6

Chapter 76

Crisis Communication

The situation was quickly spiraling out of control. The curriculum committee had made some suggestions for curricular revisions. Two faculty members were opposed to the changes but were clearly outnumbered. Given the fact that they did not have the votes, they decided to mobilize students toward their goals. These faculty members circulated committee documents to current students and told them that these changes would limit their educational opportunities. One morning I woke up to an email from several students addressed to the entire faculty expressing concern. The two faculty members had directed the students to come to the next department meeting to voice their objections. The school newspaper picked this up and published a story on the situation, which quickly spiraled and grew increasingly public. The rumor mill did what it does and soon we were getting feedback that students believed the curricular change meant that their major was going away and they had to transfer to other programs. Students threatened to leave, and we were in a full-blown crisis.

Thankfully, these kinds of public crises do not happen all that frequently. When they do, you need to be ready to respond quickly. The relative infrequency of this kind of crisis is no excuse for not being prepared, because when a crisis does materialize the consequences are dire. Risk management not only considers the frequency of an event, but also the potential severity of the impact. When you find yourself in a crisis, there are some guidelines to follow to help you sort through how to manage it.

- *The first thing I did in the crisis above was to reach out to an expert.* Being that we are a communications department, we are fortunate to have a faculty member whose expertise includes crisis communication. If you do not have a crisis communication expert in your department, reach out to the

communications or business department and ask if they have someone who can help you develop a plan.
- *Crises are stressful.* You will likely feel emotional. You need to regulate your emotions and act wisely (Guy et al., 2013). Acknowledge and accept your emotions, but do not make decisions based on them. In the crisis above, I was seething with anger at the faculty members who involved students. I wanted to tell the students that they were being manipulated by these faculty members, but I bit my tongue because I knew that was unproductive.
- *Develop a plan immediately* (Marsen, 2020). Time is of the essence. Crises rarely get easier to deal when left unattended. Crisis communication plans should be flexible, as situations can change quickly, but even the exercise of developing a plan forces you to think through key aspects of the crisis.
- *Identify key stakeholders and engage in two-way communication with them* (Ozanne et al., 2020). Address their concerns directly. Stakeholders are generally emotional as well in a crisis, so be cognizant of that and address their emotions. If they are anxious, then reassure. If they are angry, then apologize/explain. Showing genuine care for the concerns of stakeholders can go a long way in deescalating the issue. In the crisis above, the dean, the curriculum committee, and I had an all-student meeting with our majors. We provided pizza and soda, and we went in with a three-minute opener and then took questions. The end result not only helped alleviate concerns, but also it was a good opportunity to connect with our students, and some of the most worked-up students turned into some of the biggest advocates for the curricular changes.
- *Engage in multichannel communication.* Find lots of ways to get your message to diverse audiences. Use as many channels as feasibly possible to communicate. This can include social media, direct conversations, email, and press releases. In our crisis, we used a variety of channels. We sent out department-wide emails where I encouraged students to come see me with any questions. I contacted a local news channel that had a former student of ours as a reporter and secured a story framing the curricular changes as exciting. We put out positive messages on all our social media feeds assuring everyone that our curricular changes were about staying relevant.
- *Crisis communication is not only about outward-facing communication.* You also need to pay attention to internal communication (David, 2011). This means ensuring that everyone on your team is on the same page. You must communicate with your team about the strategy. The best way to ensure consistent outward messaging is to make sure everyone in your department understands what the message is. Have specific talking points. In our crisis, I sent out an email to the department detailing the plan and

providing talking points. I also asked faculty members to send all students with questions to me so there would be fewer points of contact.

Hopefully you never need the info provided here. But when you do, you really do. Successfully leading your department through a crisis is likely going to be one of the more rewarding accomplishments you have as chair. Effectively engaging in crisis communication not only can help put out the fire at hand but can also ultimately strengthen your department by building cohesion and trust.

REFLECTIONS

1. What steps can you engage in now to ensure that you and your department are equipped to handle a public-facing crisis if one appears?
2. What are your takeaways from the crisis recounted in this chapter's reflection? How would you have responded to this situation?

REFERENCES

David, G. (2011). Internal communication—Essential component of crisis communication. *Journal of Media Research*, *4*(10), 72–81. https://www.mrjournal.ro/docs/R2/10MR7.pdf

Guy, M. E., Newman, M. A., & Emel Ganapati, N. (2013). Managing emotions while managing crises. *International Journal of Emergency Services*, *2*(1), 6–20. https://doi.org/10.1108/IJES-07-2012-0033

Marsen, S. (2020). Navigating crisis: The role of communication in organizational crisis. *International Journal of Business Communication*, *57*(2), 163–175. https://doi.org/10.1177/2329488419882981

Ozanne, L. K., Ballantine, P. W., & Mitchell, T. (2020). Investigating the methods and effectiveness of crisis communication. *Journal of Nonprofit & Public Sector Marketing*, *32*(4), 379–405. https://doi.org/10.1080/10495142.2020.1798856

Chapter 77

Public-Facing Events and Public Speaking Anxiety

In the introduction to this volume, I shared the story of my first department meeting as chair when I froze and had to leave the room. I teach public speaking classes, which made this failure even more traumatizing and embarrassing. For the next few years, I found myself dreading public-facing events. I was filled with anxiety any time I had to give a speech, even if it was a simple introduction. I know my experience is shared by many as public speaking is one of the most feared situations in the world (Ebrahimi et al., 2019).

While it may not be your favorite professional responsibility, you need to accept it as an important part of being chair. While much of being chair is tied to managing personnel, budgets, curriculum, scheduling, and so forth, being an outward-facing public presence representing your department is also essential. Occasionally being in the spotlight is part of your job. You will need to introduce faculty at events, present awards, speak at departmental happenings like roundtables, lead alumni events, address faculty senate about departmental initiatives, and represent the department at university-wide ceremonies.

Being nervous about these events is perfectly understandable. The added pressure of representing the department can compound anxiety. Anxiety about public speaking is driven primarily by a concern that other peoples' expectations are high combined with fear of high social costs associated with failing (Clark &Wells, 1995). "What will people think of me if I screw this up?" This generally leads to anxious public speakers avoiding both public speaking situations altogether and making safe choices when they are forced to do it (Hofman, 2007). Perhaps you just stick to the facts and don't use humor, or you avoid eye contact, or rush through your speech as quickly as possible. This avoidance creates a self-perpetuating cycle of self-perceived weakness in public speaking, which only reinforces the very behaviors that lead to avoidance in the first place.

Much of the anxiety I felt about my responsibilities at public-facing events was a result of my new position. Public speaking anxiety was not something I generally struggled with before I became chair. I enjoyed it. But that changed dramatically when I became chair. My best guess is that I felt less pressure when I was simply representing myself rather than my entire department. The department had chosen me to represent them at these events, so they expected me to be good at it.

While you may not enjoy the public-facing elements of being chair, there are significant benefits to doing them well. You can inspire your department, impress alumni, attract students, and project an air of confidence in relationship to your department. You can also more successfully advocate for resources and support from upper administration. There are also personal benefits as effective public speaking skills are linked to career success (Schraeder, 2019). Public-facing speaking events are opportunities to impress deans, provosts, and those outside of the university who might have interesting opportunities. Effective public communication rarely fails to get someone's attention.

I used to understand my public speaking anxiety as a barrier to effectively handling public-facing events. I spent a lot of time thinking about how to alleviate public speaking anxiety. I tried exercising vigorously before a presentation, using positive visualization, varying my delivery techniques, working with a licensed therapist, and a few approaches I don't want to put in writing here because I am scared you will judge me. None of it worked. My anxiety remained. I eventually changed my approach from trying to eliminate my public speaking anxiety to simply accepting it. Rather than doing whatever I could to get rid of anxiety, I prepared to give a speech while feeling it. Acceptance provided a lot of relief. I know now that I am not going to overcome anxiety; I am instead going to be incredibly anxious while giving a speech—and that is okay.

Anxiety is part of the package when it comes to speaking in public as chair. It is a result of caring and wanting to do well, so it has a silver lining. This realization allowed me to redirect my attention away from trying to manage my own emotions and to instead focus on the message itself. I could prepare and rehearse focusing not on how I would feel (I already knew that), but instead on what I wanted to communicate. This allowed for increased preparation of the message, which made me feel more prepared and less nervous.

If you feel anxious about your newfound public speaking responsibilities as chair, you are in good company. Most people do, and department chairs are people. My anxiety has abated some as I have been doing this for a while, but I still feel incredibly nervous before public speaking in my capacity as chair. Most chairs approach these public-facing events reluctantly. This is not a reason to avoid them though, as this will only increase your anxiety for the events you cannot get out of. Embracing the anxiety and preparing to give presentations while nervous can free you from feeling anxiety about your anxiety. You can instead focus on preparation, your message, and your audience. This can make it a more manageable, and even rewarding aspect of your role as chair.

REFLECTIONS

1. Have you noticed a change in how you feel about public speaking now that you are a chair? If so, what is driving those changes? If not, what does that tell you about your relationship to your chair position?
2. Reflect on the following statement: "Acceptance provided a lot of relief. I know now that I am not going to overcome anxiety; I am instead going to be incredibly anxious while giving a speech—and that is okay." How can accepting your anxiety change your approach to public speaking?

REFERENCES

Clark, D. M., & Wells, A. (1995). A cognitive model of social phobia. In R. G. Heimberg (Ed.), *Social phobia: Diagnosis, assessment, and treatment* (pp. 69–93). Guilford Press.

Ebrahimi, O. V., Pallesen, S., Kenter, R. M. F., & Nordgreen, T. (2019). Psychological interventions for the fear of public speaking: A meta-analysis. *Frontiers in Psychology, 10*, 488. https://doi.org/10.3389/fpsyg.2019.00488

Hofmann, S. G. (2007). Cognitive factors that maintain social anxiety disorder: A comprehensive model and its treatment implications. *Cognitive Behaviour Therapy, 36*(4), 193–209. https://doi.org/10.1080/16506070701421313

Schraeder, T. L. (2019). Public speaking and presentation skills. In *Physician communication: Connecting with patients, peers, and the public* (pp. 113–137). Oxford University Press. https://doi.org/10.1093/med/9780190882440.003.0003

Chapter 78

Your New Raise

The additional compensation for being chair fluctuates widely between institutions. The average chair receives a 10 to 20 percent bump in salary over their faculty salary (Bichsel et al., 2017). This salary bump can occur through converting from a nine-month employee to a twelve-month employee, from a stipend, or both. I know some chairs who do not receive any additional financial compensation and others who receive more than the amount cited above. If you do not receive additional financial compensation for serving as chair, apologies as this is not going to be applicable to you.

The thing to keep front and center is that your new chair pay bump is not permanent. Every year there is a 19 percent turnover of department chairs (Higher Education Publications, 2023). This means the average chair has a tenure of about five years. "Average" means that many will serve for a far shorter term. When I tell people I have been in the position for eleven years, I usually hear some version of *"Wow,* that is a long time!" These positions rotate frequently. Often the rotation out of the position is not in your control. You may experience a life situation that necessitates you stepping aside. Maybe a new dean comes in and wants to shake things up. Perhaps you mishandle a crisis, and your department thinks they would be better off with a different chair. I have a very good friend who was three years into his term when he was very unexpectedly removed. The following year another good friend had to resign from being chair to focus on a family member's health. It happens.

You need to manage your new raise with this in mind. Do not use your new salary to make long-term financial commitments based on the assumptions that your pay increase is indefinite. For example, do not buy a more expensive house that saddles you with a higher monthly mortgage payment that is hard to maintain if you lose your raise. Avoid purchasing a fancy car with a loan or enrolling your child in a more expensive daycare or a private school. These kinds of purchases generate future obligations, and their price tag is tied to a salary that can go away at any moment.

Also, resist the temptation to generally increase your lifestyle habits. Eating at fancier restaurants, going on extravagant vacations, or picking up expensive hobbies are certainly enjoyable, but these habits can be difficult to sustain if your new chair salary increase goes away. Your tenure as chair may be shorter than you plan, and managing the salary reduction can be painful if you have become accustomed to a certain lifestyle. It will feel like you are losing something.

It is wiser to use your salary bump to build your financial foundation. Make smart choices that allow you to reap the rewards of your increased salary while also safeguarding your financial security. Build an emergency fund or pay off existing debt. These moves increase your financial flexibility regardless of whether you keep the chair position long-term or not. Alternatively, use your raise to add to your retirement savings.

This is not only financially prudent, but it increases your peace of mind and gives you professional flexibility. If you need to keep your salary to make monthly payments, you are in a situation where you are forced to do whatever you can to keep the chair position. Your hands are tied in complicated situations. You cannot walk away from the position if you need or want to. If your position is threatened, you will be forced to react out of financial fear rather than what you think is right. By setting yourself up to benefit from, but not be beholden to, your new raise you can get the best of both worlds. You can enjoy the financial benefits of your raise while maintaining the freedom to make decisions that are best for you and your career without financial pressure. This balanced approach will ensure that you will be prepared, regardless of the length of your chair tenure.

REFLECTIONS

1. Where is your new raise best allocated? Where can it do the most good for your financial future?
2. How can you resist the temptation to increase your lifestyle based on your new salary?

REFERENCES

Bichsel, J., McChesney, J., & Calcagno, M. (2017). *Faculty in higher education salary report: Key findings, trends, and comprehensive tables for tenure track, non-tenure track teaching, and non-tenure track research faculty; academic department heads; and adjunct faculty at four-year institutions for the 2016–17 academic year.* College and University Professional Association for Human Resources (CUPA-HR). https://www.cupahr.org/wp-content/uploads/2017/07/Faculty2017_Overview.pdf

Higher Education Publications, Inc. (2023). *College administrator data/turnover rates through 2022.* https://hepinc.com/newsroom/college-administrator-data-turn-over-rates-through-2022

Chapter 79

Formal Discipline

With a flushed face and raised voice, the union representative looked directly at me and forcefully stated, "If you pursue this, we are going to take you to court. We will fight it all the way to the top." The faculty member, whose behavior had led to this meeting between him, Human Resources, the dean, me, and union representation, sat smugly to the side with a smile. He clearly enjoyed seeing this lawyer threaten me. After the meeting was over, I immediately asked the Human Resources personnel how to make sense of that threat. I received instructions not to worry about it. "She is just trying to scare you into backing off." I felt reassured. The HR representative continued, "We need to implement some formal discipline here—it is warranted." As much as I would have loved to back down and be done with the situation, I knew he was right. "Okay, let's talk next steps," I begrudgingly responded.

We have spent considerable time in these reflections focusing on how to maintain a collegial, open, and productive departmental environment. When successful, focusing on these values should help maintain harmony, increase buy-in, and aid in conflict resolution. But despite your best efforts, there will be times when formal discipline of faculty members will be a necessity. Sometimes, collegiality, gentle reminders, and polite requests simply do not have the desired effect. If this is the case, it might be time to initiate formal discipline.

This area of personnel management is one of the most hated responsibilities of being a department chair (Wolverton et al., 2005). I have had to initiate it several times, and I can verify that it takes an emotional toll. While Human Resources and the dean can be very helpful in the process, they do not usually have to have daily interactions with the person to whom the discipline is directed. You do. And these interactions can be uncomfortable. Additionally, as we have discussed in previous chapters, most new chairs already feel awkward about the power dynamic and changing relationships to their colleagues (Deal, 2014; Berdrow, 2010). Few circumstances crystalize this change more than the process of formal discipline.

While you may hate it, it is now part of your job. It is necessary not only to address the behavior of the individual violating the rules but also to maintain the overall health of your departmental culture. People notice bad behavior, and your faculty will generally not be happy if bad behavior is not addressed. This can lead to discontent, loss of trust in you as a leader, and a sense of apathy. Formal discipline should be pursued when all other avenues have failed. It is not a first resort. It should be a tool to address egregious examples of behavior that hinders the mission of the department, harasses colleagues or students, threatens the health of the institution, or aggressively undermines leadership or initiatives reached through democratic consensus.

When you get the sense that formal discipline might be a distinct possibility, begin the process of documenting everything. Keep records of meetings, incidents, emails. This documentation helps provide a clear record, supports your actions if questioned, and ensures transparency. Additionally, let your dean and Human Resources know that you think there might be a need for formal discipline as they can provide valuable (and more objective) insight about whether it is warranted. The earlier they are looped in the better. Be 100 percent honest. Acknowledge your own culpability and shortcomings with them. Did you send an email you shouldn't have? Did you yell at the faculty member in the hallway about this? It is better to identify your faults upfront rather than have them come out later in an investigation.

Know your institution's procedures for formal discipline thoroughly. Familiarize yourself with the faculty handbook and collective bargaining agreement if you have one. Be vigilant about compliance. Failure to follow procedure is often how these cases are lost.

Every university has different procedures, but it is common that there will be a letter addressed to the employee explaining the violations. It is often accompanied by a meeting and a statement of expectations for how the employee can improve. Keep the letter and meeting free of emotion. Focus on what happened rather than how it made you feel, provide the specific policies that were violated along with a clear explanation of what actions constitute the violation, and include a clear plan of action for improvement.

Try to frame these positively. Avoid accusations. Instead, simply point out how the behavior did not meet expectations. Offer support and resources to help and acknowledge if any effort or progress has been made. Finally, focus on the benefits of the proposed corrective plan of action by saying something like, "By improving in these areas you will be able to leverage your expertise to contribute to student success in the following ways . . ." I have found that using this kind of tone tends to make people less defensive and more willing to follow through.

While formal discipline is certainly not enjoyable, it is an important part of maintaining a healthy department. By approaching it methodically, transparently, and with the help of your support system, you can handle the process successfully. Doing so ensures it is an effective tool when you need it.

REFLECTIONS

1. Do you feel uncomfortable engaging formal discipline? What aspects are you most and least comfortable with?
2. How familiar are you with your university's policies about formal discipline?

REFERENCES

Berdrow, I. (2010). King among kings: Understanding the role and responsibilities of the department chair in higher education. *Educational Management Administration & Leadership*, *38*(4), 499–514. https://doi.org/10.1177/1741143210368146

Deal, J. (2014). From faculty member to department chair: Making the transition to administration. *College Music Symposium*, 54. https://www.jstor.org/stable/26574360

Wolverton, M., Ackerman, R., & Holt, S. (2005). Preparing for leadership: What academic department chairs need to know. *Journal of Higher Education Policy and Management*, *27*(2), 227–238. https://doi.org/10.1080/13600800500120126

Chapter 80

One-on-One Meetings

As a new chair, you likely understand the importance of putting effort and energy into leading department meetings, which are one of the places where the role of the chair is most visible. While regular meetings with your entire department are essential, an equally important aspect of your role is often overlooked: one-on-one meetings. Here I am not referring to walking the hall and dropping in on people's offices. I am instead referring to a set-aside dedicated time that you spend with your faculty members individually. You should have regular time set aside for one-on-one meetings. The frequency of these meetings will vary depending on the number of faculty in your department, but aim to have a one-on-one with each faculty member at least once a year. These meetings should be proactively scheduled to check in with faculty rather than to address specific concerns or issues as they arise.

One-on-ones are important in any management setting, but they are especially important in academic settings. Unlike many other organizational settings, faculty operate rather autonomously. They do not take daily direction from a manager. This can create some distance between faculty members and chairs. This volume has addressed the importance of chairs creating buy-in with faculty due to the structure of higher education. One-on-one meetings offer valuable opportunities to foster this buy-in. One-on-ones are much more effective than larger meetings at building relationships (Flinchum et al., 2023). Much of this is because employees are more likely to feel as if they can be emotionally vulnerable in a one-on-one meeting (Islam & Zyphur, 2005).

The work you do in one-on-one meetings goes far beyond simply transferring information. These meetings are an opportunity for diplomatic work, coalition-building, trust-garnering, and making faculty feel valued. You are also likely to obtain very valuable information, as one-on-ones are often perceived as less intimidating, allowing employees to express their opinions more freely (Morrison, 2011).

To get the most out of one-on-one meetings, you need to put some effort into them. Schedule them at specific times and give the faculty member your full attention. Avoid distractions and put your phone away. Come prepared with a flexible agenda that you have discussed in advance and asked for input on, but let the conversation be guided by the faculty member. Doing so can reveal a lot about what is important to the faculty member.

Ask lots of questions. Do not dominate the conversation. You should do much more listening than talking. As chair, you have plenty of time to have your voice heard. Let this space be primarily for someone else's voice. This is not a chance for you to push an agenda, but instead for you to connect and learn about your faculty. Giving your undivided attention and listening will make people feel heard and communicate that you care about and value your faculty. You may want to ask for advice about a situation. You may also want to solicit advice. Show your faculty that you want their input. Inviting suggestions for how you chair not only helps you crowdsource your problem-solving, but it also makes people feel valuable. Your faculty will have different vantage points than you, and that can lead to some valuable ideas you may not have considered.

The location of the meeting can also impact its effectiveness. If your relationship with the faculty member allows, consider getting out of the office. Meet over lunch, coffee, or even happy hour. Walking meetings are another excellent option as they are associated with several benefits such as increased creativity and egalitarianism (Clayton et al., 2015). Getting out of the office can foster a more productive and collegial atmosphere.

There are many benefits to intentional and well-structured one-on-one meetings. They will build relationships, create a sense of belonging, provide valuable information, and improve communication. Taking the time to meet individually with your faculty will demonstrate that you are committed to their success and that you appreciate their individual contributions. One-on-one meetings offer unique opportunities that you will not find anywhere else in your professional life to connect with your faculty on a deeper level.

REFLECTIONS

1. What role have scheduled and regular one-on-one meetings between chair and faculty had in your department? If none, do you feel comfortable initiating this practice as chair?

2. Given your department's size and makeup, what is the optimal frequency for which you should be holding one-on-one meetings with your faculty?

REFERENCES

Austin, J. B. (2016). *Master the one-on-one meeting.* Harvard Business School Working Knowledge. https://hbswk.hbs.edu/item/master-the-one-on-one-meeting

Clayton, R., Thomas, C., & Smothers. J. (2015). How to do walking meetings right. *Harvard Business Review.* https://hbr.org/2015/08/how-to-do-walking-meetings-right

Flinchum, J. R., Kreamer, L. M., Rogelberg, S. G., & Gooty, J. (2023). One-on-one meetings between managers and direct reports: A new opportunity for meeting science. *Organizational Psychology Review, 13*(4), 478–505. https://doi.org/10.1177/20413866221097570

Islam, G., & Zyphur, M. J. (2005). Power, voice, and hierarchy: Exploring the antecedents of speaking up in groups. *Group Dynamics: Theory, Research, and Practice, 9*(2), 93–103. https://doi.org/10.1037/1089-2699.9.2.93

Morrison, E. (2011). Employee voice behavior: Integration and directions for future research. *Academy of Management Annals, 5*(1), 373–412. https://doi.org/10.1080/19416520.2011.574506

Chapter 81

Maintaining Your Scholarly Agenda

I was sitting down to write an earlier chapter of this volume, excited that my calendar was wide-open for the day. I had plans to get a lot of writing done that day as the deadline for submission was approaching faster than seemed possible. About ten minutes into writing, our office associate came into my office asking, "Did you see that email?" I hadn't, so I opened my inbox to find an email from a faculty member informing me that she was visiting Germany over the summer and had to have an unexpected medical procedure. She could not fly for several weeks, which meant that she would be missing the first three weeks of the semester. I immediately knew that my day dedicated to writing had evaporated. The rest of the day was spent talking with the faculty member, the dean's office, faculty labor relations, and Human Resources and identifying possible replacements for the first few weeks of the class.

This is a common tale in the life of a chair. We have spent time in this volume reflecting on the ways in which your agenda can become easily co-opted by the needs of departmental stakeholders. The constant cycle of addressing timely departmental needs takes its toll most significantly on your scholarly or creative agenda. Attention to research and creative endeavors are usually the first thing department chairs cut when they lose hours that they thought they would have in a day. This makes sense as these deadlines are often more flexible, there are fewer people affected, and it is easy to promise that you will make it up tomorrow. The problem is that when tomorrow comes, the same distractions (with different details) exist. Before you know it, months have gone by, and that project is no closer to completion.

The loss of scholarly/creative productivity is one of the biggest concerns that potential department chairs have about accepting the position (Armstrong & Woloshyn, 2017). This fear is not unfounded. Most chairs I know bemoan their inability to maintain the level of research/creative productivity they used to have when they were a faculty member. I complain about it too. The irony is that some degree of scholarly/creative success probably got you into the position in the first place. Research shows that people who find themselves in chair positions have generally enjoyed more scholarly success than the average faculty member, but their productivity dramatically drops once they make the transition to chair (Zelle et al., 2017).

The shift in priorities is understandable given the varied responsibilities that you have in front of you. The day-to-day demands of managing a department will consume much of your time and attention. This change in focus and frequent interruptions often relegate research and creative work, which require sustained focus and deep thinking, to the background. When you do carve out time for research, switching gears can be difficult.

Accept that your research productivity may drop, but it should not vanish. You need to put some effort into keeping it alive. I have gotten much better about prioritizing my own scholarly agenda over the past few years. It takes effort, but it is well worth it for a few reasons. First, being department chair is likely not a forever position. You need to prepare for post-chair life. This means staying active to ensure you can be promoted and stay competitive. Secondly, you are likely more passionate about your creative/research projects than you are your chair duties. Carving out time to focus on them will keep you connected to your discipline and keep your mind engaged. It can infuse some life and meaning into the administrative tasks of being chair.

In my own efforts to stay research active, I have been inspired by the work of Cal Newport (2016), particularly his book *Deep Work: Rules for Focused Success in a Distracted World*. I highly recommend it. In it, he reminds us that engaged analytical and creative work requires an intense degree of focus. You cannot achieve the necessary level of focus when multiple demands are pulling your attention in different directions. Administrative tasks require a different kind of attention than research/creative tasks. When you move between these kinds of tasks, your brain needs to switch gears. This takes time and mental energy. The ping-pong method of bouncing between tasks is suboptimal since you cannot maintain the necessary level of focus to do the *deep work* well.

There is no way around it. You must intentionally set aside time for yourself without distractions to focus on your research—even if it is just a few hours a week. Turn off your notifications, put your phone away, close your door or go to a coffee shop if you are worried people will knock. Be open about it with your department. Tell them what you are doing. They should be sympathetic considering they are all in academia as well and likely value their own research productivity. No one should begrudge you focusing on your own intellectually satisfying projects. When you are in the space, work.

Do not check your email, text people, play games, and so on. Take advantage of the distraction-free space you have created because it is limited.

It took me a few years to realize how important this advice was. Not only has the practice of setting aside time helped me increase my scholarly productivity, but it has also provided some much-needed intellectual respite from my chair duties, which has made me less resentful of them.

REFLECTIONS

1. How have you found the balancing act between your administrative duties as chair and your scholarly agenda? Has your scholarly agenda been impacted by your new role? How much less scholarly/creative productivity are you willing to accept as chair?
2. Can you implement any of the suggested strategies to maintain your research/creative agenda? What can you do to ensure you have space for the kind of *deep work* necessary to maintain it?

REFERENCES

Armstrong, D. E., & Woloshyn, V. E. (2017). Exploring the tensions and ambiguities of university department chairs. *Canadian Journal of Higher Education, 47*(1), 97–113. https://doi.org/10.47678/cjhe.v47i1.186470

Newport, C. (2016). *Deep work: Rules for focused success in a distracted world.* Grand Central Publishing.

Zelle, B. A., Weathers, M. A., Fajardo, R. J., Haghshenas, V., & Bhandari, M. (2017). Publication productivity of orthopaedic surgery chairs. *Journal of Bone and Joint Surgery, 99*(12), e62. https://doi.org/10.2106/JBJS.16.00587

Chapter 82

Higher Ed in Flux
Chairing through Uncertain Times

The state of higher education is in flux, and universities are experiencing perpetually stronger headwinds. The particulars may change, but as of this writing higher education is sorting through how to operate in the face of decreasing enrollments, challenges to free speech on campus, lower state funding, college closings, and an artificial intelligence revolution. The health and stability of higher education has become increasingly more responsive to market pressures (Buller, 2015). As chair, you are responsible for setting the direction and priorities of your department. Doing so while failing to stay abreast of the latest macrodevelopments is akin to navigating a ship through turbulent water without a compass.

As a faculty member, you likely had the luxury of disengaging from the broader discourse about higher education challenges. You could likely put your head down and focus on your research, teaching, and immediate academic community. As chair, you now have a responsibility to deeply engage these issues, understand their implications for your department, and lead your faculty in conversations about those implications (Gano-Phillips, 2022; Kruse, 2020). Staying abreast of the broader discourse is essential to you being a proactive leader in guiding your department through the challenges, uncertainties, and opportunities in the ever-changing world of higher education.

Staying plugged in is imperative. You owe it to your faculty and students to be the most well-versed individual in your department. You should be subscribing to and reading outlets such as *The Chronicle of Higher Education* and *Inside Higher Ed*. There are also several excellent podcasts about higher education. The ones I subscribe to and enjoy are *Leading Improvements in Higher Education*, *Campus*, and *The EdUp Experience*. Higher education podcasts are great ways to feel like you are having a conversation with higher education leaders. You will get an inside track into what the folks in the upper administrative offices are talking about and how they are making decisions. Additionally, when you attend conferences, try to go to some panels or workshops about higher education. Most national conferences will have some version of these. As tempting as it may be to solely attend niche panels specifically focused on research that interests you, don't overlook roundtables about the state of higher education as they offer valuable opportunities to stay plugged in.

While you need to keep informed, you also need to ensure that your faculty are aware of what is happening at the macro level. You need to provide this context for your faculty when macro trends are influencing decision-making. When faculty only hear these messages from upper administration, they are much more likely to be skeptical. The headwinds are real, and as a leader you have an obligation to communicate them to faculty. You need to have an informed team who understands the challenges. Your faculty and staff are unlikely to feel motivated to engage in being part of the solution to these challenges if they do not see you actively participating in the conversation.

When you get bad news about budget cuts or organizational restructuring, it can be tempting to throw up your hands and blame upper administration. While this might take some heat off you, you are shirking your leadership responsibilities when you do this. Instead, explain the broader context and frame the decisions as part of the university's strategic plan to address an ongoing crisis. By framing the decisions around long-term goals, potential opportunities, and organizational health, your faculty are more likely to see the challenges as manageable and to be willing to contribute to the efforts. This approach does not mean you have agreed with all the decisions that upper administration makes. We have seen plenty of incompetence in high-level campus decision-makers over the past few decades. But it is instead an invitation to engage with these decisions in productive ways rather than unproductive ones.

While upper administrators certainly make mistakes, the challenges facing higher education that they often cite to justify their decisions are quite real. Your department needs to take them seriously. Failing to move the conversation beyond complaining is not productive. Lamenting the situation is fine, but as chair you must lead the conversation beyond that. You need to inspire your faculty to do something in response.

Use your department meetings to engage these issues. When you read relevant articles, send them to your department. When faculty return from conferences, ask them to update the department on what they learned about the state of the discipline. Have a beginning-of-the-year retreat focused on the state of higher education. The point of these conversations is not simply to talk about the state of things for the sake of having talked about them. It is instead to foster forward thinking about how your department should be operating given the reality of the situation. You do not need to have all the answers. But you should be the one pushing the conversation in productive ways.

REFLECTIONS

1. What are the trends and challenges you see posing the biggest challenges to your university? What can you do to stay abreast of the ever-changing landscape in higher education?
2. What does productive conversation with your department about the challenges facing higher education look like to you? How can you, as chair, move the conversation from complaining to responding?

REFERENCES

Buller, J. L. (2015). *Change leadership in higher education*. Jossey-Bass.

Gano-Phillips, S. (2022, October). *Expanding responsibilities of department chairs: Deans' roles in facilitating professional development*. ACAD Leader. Association of College and University Educators. https://acad.org/resource/expanding-responsibilities-of-department-chairs-deans-roles-in-facilitating-professional-development

Kruse, S. D. (2020). Department chair leadership: Exploring the role's demands and tensions. *Educational Management Administration & Leadership*, 1–19. DOI: 10.1177/1741143220953601

Chapter 83

Your Department Website

Few responsibilities crystalize the frustrations and challenges of being department chair more than managing your department's website. Your role is usually unclear. You receive instruction that you are responsible for enrollment management, which would presumably involve overseeing the department website. But you are rarely looped into any conversations about the institution's digital strategy. You likely do not receive the necessary training in design principles, digital storytelling, or navigating the necessary design software. Unless your discipline is graphic design, digital communications, or computer science, you probably have limited expertise. You must work with the marketing and communications team, who you have no managerial authority over and who are generally understaffed and pulled in many other directions. You have all the responsibility but none of the power. The website is a critical communication tool, but you have very limited control over it.

Chairs always seem to be frustrated about their relationship with their department website. They never seem happy with where it is. In most other managerial positions, you would communicate your ideas to a marketing or digital communications team, and they would execute your vision. Infusing any kind of innovation into your department website is instead usually a Herculean effort that tests your patience and resolve. You need to find the time to be a web designer, which is a full-time job, on top of your other administrative responsibilities. You must gain access to necessary university-wide resources and support systems while managing slow-moving bureaucratic structures. You must learn the branding guide to ensure you are not running afoul of the university's master digital strategy. Given these factors, it is no wonder that chairs often throw their hands up and passively manage the website whenever necessity dictates.

While I am sympathetic to departmental website apathy, I would encourage you to put some effort into your department website. It is a key factor in managing your departmental reputation, attracting potential students, and helping current students find valuable information. It is your front door to the outside world. No one is going to enroll because of your website, but it is your first impression to a lot of people. Given its importance, you probably want to invest some time in the website. Do not spend hours and hours on it if there is no payoff, but try to be proactive and explore what you can and cannot accomplish.

Academic website effectiveness is different from that of general commercial websites. A commercial website is primarily geared toward attracting new customers. While you certainly want your website to attract students, it's also likely accessed by alumni, parents, community members, news organizations, current students, and institutional members looking to find information (Abifarin et al., 2019). You need to provide comprehensive information about your programs, research activities, faculty, and opportunities. Given this, departmental websites must fit in a lot of information, and they can quickly become cluttered. Navigability is an absolute must. Aim for a clean home page with clear links to relevant information and easy pathways back to the home page. Do not dump all your information on your home page. You want to drive engagement, and making people feel confused and lost is a surefire way to drive them away.

Keep your audience in mind. The website exists for outside stakeholders, not internal politics. Website design can get surprisingly political. One instance that stands out is when a senior faculty member got loudly upset with me for reorganizing the order of the faculty listing based on alphabetical order rather than faculty rank. She loudly accused me of discriminating against her now that she was not at the top of the faculty ranking. But I held firm, explaining that the page exists primarily for students to find their professor's contact information. Students do not care at all about the rank of their instructors. They care about finding their instructor, which is easier when arranged alphabetically. I have also had faculty claim that their area of expertise should be more featured on the website and complain that someone else was asked to be in a photo and they were not. The overall point here is that a website designed primarily to avoid political disagreement will likely be suboptimal.

Overall, you need to consider how you want your website (and especially your home page) to align with the story you are trying to tell about your department. Are you selling yourself as a new and cutting-edge department that is on the front line of innovation? Are you a department with a rich history and tradition that prides itself on long-standing excellence? Is your department close-knit and one that emphasizes personalized education and strong faculty–student relationships? Does your department have strong ties to industry, providing students with exciting internship opportunities and a high job-placement rate? Is your department social-justice oriented, and does it advocate for equity and inclusion? Your website should reflect your story through its design, content, and user experience.

The single best thing you can do to enhance your website is to get some feedback. Find someone who constitutes your ideal audience and ask them to navigate your website in front of you. I have a seventeen-year-old son, so I am fortunate to have an in-house tester on stand-by. Watching him navigate my departmental website and then asking him questions is very valuable.

Overall, your ability to make significant changes to the website might be limited. But do not ignore the responsibility. Do what you can. Small changes are still worth it. Issues such as navigability are usually within your ability to affect. Even minor adjustments can significantly improve the user experience and make your website more effective and welcoming.

REFLECTIONS

1. How do you feel about your current department website? What are its strengths and weaknesses? What easy fixes can you make to improve it?
2. What is the process for making changes to your department website? Who approves changes? Who has access? What are the parameters you are operating under when making changes?

REFERENCE

Abifarin, F. P., Imavah, S. A., & Olobashola, A. S. (2019). Design effectiveness of academic library web sites: A comparison of university, polytechnic, and college sites in Nigeria. *The Electronic Library, 37*(3), 577–591. https://doi.org/10.1108/EL-08-2018-0159

Chapter 84

Beyond Reluctance

Chairing toward Unexpected Opportunities and Growth

A few years into my tenure as chair I realized that we did not have ample opportunities to showcase student research. I took it upon myself to organize an event to fix this. It was considerable work, and I coached several of the students who presented their research. I MCed the event (which was a big swing considering that I was still dealing with a lot of public speaking anxiety). A student of mine who I worked with was interning at a local business and invited the owner of the organization. After the event, the owner reached out and asked for a meeting with me. He told me that he was impressed with how organized the event had been and my remarks at the beginning. He explained that he had recently signed a consulting contract and he wondered if I would like to be involved. This turned into a fairly financially lucrative opportunity that spanned a few years. I never could have foreseen or mapped out this opportunity. It was only through pushing myself that it fell in my lap.

As we are starting to move toward the end of this volume, I want to shift the focus. Up to now, our reflections have primarily concentrated on how you can be an effective chair for others. Many of these reflections have started with self-examination, but with the end goal of becoming a better chair for the benefit of your team. In this chapter and the next, I want to focus on you for your own sake. Early on in this volume we discussed the common assumption that a good chair is often supposed to be a reluctant chair. It is often considered bad form if someone actually wants the position. The underlying principle in that assumption is that a chair should not be in the position for personal gain. It should be a sacrifice.

While there is certainly sacrifice involved, there are also personal benefits. While there are occasional material benefits (as illustrated in the story above), the most significant rewards are often found in the personal growth the position offers. Being in this position is an adventure (Hess,

2013) that will change you (Cranford, 2020). You should recognize the position as an opportunity to grow. Much like weightlifting will build your muscles, being a department chair will build your leadership skills, your emotional intelligence, your resilience, and your problem-solving abilities. Your time as chair is an invaluable opportunity to grow both personally and professionally.

The chair position is especially fertile ground for growing. The ambiguities, challenges, and paradoxes that you must navigate are especially good at pushing you. As I have mentioned many times in the volume, being a department chair is not like most management positions. You are forced to be both management and colleague, and this is a very difficult tightrope to walk effectively. But, like everything, the more you do it the better you get at it.

Personal growth does not just happen though. You must lean into it. One of the most important ways to do this is to continually stretch yourself. I spent my first few years as chair being far too safe. I would go out of my way to avoid rocking the boat. I avoided difficult conversations. I would, to the detriment of everyone, flee from conflict. I sought safety in established rituals and operating procedures—even when I knew there were better ways to do things. I was far too concerned with maintaining status quo in the name of self-preservation. As I got further into my tenure, I became more interested in taking risks. And this is when the position became more interesting and fulfilling. Stretching yourself involves saying yes to things that seem uncomfortable. Engage in the things that will test your abilities. This doesn't mean you should always say yes to things if your plate is full; instead, it means that you should not say no to things because they are a stretch.

The cyclist Greg LeMond famously said about racing, "It never gets easier, you just get faster" (LeMond & Hom, 2014, p. 122). This quote aptly applies to your role as department chair. Every difficult conversation, budget crunch, public speaking opportunity, and political challenge is an opportunity for you to become a more well-rounded person. These things do not necessarily get easier, but you get better at handling them in ways that lead to positive outcomes. Like a cyclist peddling uphill, they are all opportunities to push your limits and get better. You can then take on bigger challenges, which you then get better at as well.

Continually engaging in challenges not only sharpens your skills, but it also transforms your own perception of your abilities. You will get better at juggling the responsibilities, handling the emotional complexities, and managing your stress. The more you lean into the challenges, the better you will get at handling future challenges. The things you get better at by being chair translate to many areas of life. I have found that I have grown in my abilities to be direct with people, make difficult decisions, and not lose sleep over people being unhappy with me. The first year as chair is scary. Accept that it is often anxiety producing. It would be strange if it wasn't. And rather than look for safety, look for growth. Consider your discomfort a guide, teaching you to effectively face even more substantial challenges in the future.

REFLECTIONS

1. What are the aspects of the chair position that make you most stretched? How about the ones that make you most comfortable? How can you identify opportunities to lean into challenges that make you uncomfortable?
2. What specific leadership skills do you want to build over the next year? What are opportunities that you can identify that might help you build them?

REFERENCES

Cranford, J. S. (2020). Leadership: Reflection in action—Why chairs need to perform self-evaluations. *The Department Chair*, *30*(3), 1–3. DOI: 10.1002/dch

Hess, Jon A. (2013). The risks and rewards of serving as a department chair. *Communication Faculty Publications*, 13. https://ecommons.udayton.edu/cmm_fac_pub/13

LeMond, G., & Hom, M. (2014). *The science of fitness: Power, performance, and endurance*. Academic Press.

Chapter 85

Contemplating the Pursuit of Upper Administration

This chapter is a bit more abstract since I have never been a dean (or an associate dean for that matter). I am open to that career trajectory if the situation is right, but so far the opportunity has not presented itself. Thus, this advice will be more hypothetical rather than based on experience. As I wrote in the previous chapter, this reflection is about you and your career trajectory. It is not about what you can do for others as chair, but instead what being chair can do for you.

The position of department chair is often the stepping-stone to upward mobility in higher education. This makes sense considering the worst upper administrators I have ever had to work with did not have experience as chair, which left them out of touch with the realities of department management. Their lack of understanding about the constraints that department chairs operate within was very frustrating. In general, it makes sense for upper administrators to have their leadership informed by time spent in the weeds of departmental operations. Considerable space in this volume has been dedicated to reflecting on just how challenging the chair position is. It is often referred to as the most difficult job in higher education. I have had more than one dean tell me that it was harder to be chair than dean. This is because many of the more challenging day-to-day minutia as well as the direct personnel engagement are handled by chairs (Jenkins, 2018). You can oversee rather than directly manage the details of many issues. I think those deans were probably downplaying the difficulty of being dean, but I understand what they were getting at. Being dean can be quite rewarding as you have increased ability to use your talents to help more people across campus (Williams, 2020).

The potential for upward mobility is a significant draw for many when considering the chair position. When I was having trouble deciding if I wanted to take my first chair job, someone I respected advised me to go for it since it could open career opportunities. Even though you are likely new at being chair, it is not too early for you to begin considering whether you want to use your time as chair as a springboard. Use your time as chair to explore whether you want to be in the dean's office. As chair, you have an opportunity to test out your skill set, interest, and priorities and to see if they align with those of a dean.

Start by assessing what you excel at and what is most rewarding. Are you better at the direct interaction with students and faculty or with the strategic planning and problem-solving? Do you prefer working on the budget or scheduling classes? Deans will be much more involved in managing budgets and long-term strategic planning (Whitaker, 2022; Jenkins, 2018). Pay attention to which tasks make you feel more fulfilled and where your strengths lie. Consider what you want your workday to look like. While chairs have many responsibilities, they generally have more flexibility about when they need to accomplish tasks. Deans have more rigid schedules filled with many meetings (Jenkins, 2018). If you are the kind of person who hates meetings, maybe being dean is not for you.

You should not set your aim for a higher administrative role simply for the sake of advancement. Pursuing a deanship should stem from genuine interest, belief in your abilities, and a desire to serve your institution (Dettmar, 2024). Doing it because it is the next step has the possibility of making you miserable. At this point you may be feeling so overwhelmed by your chair responsibilities that the idea of being dean sounds unappealing. But I would encourage you to hold off on that assessment for a while. You will get better at being chair the longer you are in it, and you may find yourself enjoying some of your chair responsibilities more than you imagined. Forming an opinion about whether you enjoy being chair in the first year is like deciding how you feel about learning a new language after just the first few lessons. It is daunting at first, but as you become more fluent, you might find joy and satisfaction in gaining mastery and connecting in a new way.

There is no downside to keeping your options open. You can always decide later that remaining chair is what makes you happy. Build in optionality for your future self. Do not loudly declare that you would never want to be dean. Try to engage in some increased administrative burdens. Perhaps there is a university-wide committee or some project the dean's office might have for you to give you a sense. Keep an open mind. Approach your career trajectory with flexibility, recognizing that you may be surprised at what ends up being of interest to you.

REFLECTIONS

1. How have you been thinking about the possibility of upward advancement? What is driving that assessment? Could you see yourself as dean some day?
2. What does keeping your options open look like to you? Are there specific things you can do to maintain flexibility for your future self?

REFERENCES

Dettmar, K. (2024, May 9). *Ask the chair: "Should I apply for a deanship?"* Chronicle of Higher Education. https://www.chronicle.com/article/ask-the-chair-should-i-apply-for-a-deanship

Jenkins, R. (2018, July 5). *Do you "really" want to be a dean?* Chronicle of Higher Education. https://www.chronicle.com/article/do-you-really-want-to-be-a-dean

Whitaker, M. (2022, March 14). *Before you move into senior administration.* Chronicle of Higher Education. https://www.chronicle.com/article/before-you-move-into-senior-administration

Williams, D. (2020, Winter). *Take my dean, please: Advice from a happy chair-turned-dean.* Modern Language Association Profession. https://profession.mla.org/take-my-dean-please-advice-from-a-happy-chair-turned-dean

Chapter 86

Embracing Feedback

Learning to Listen and Adapt

"Ben, what were you thinking sending that email?" My dean asked me this question as soon as I picked up the phone. It was in the early days of COVID-19, and everyone was scrambling to accommodate the sudden shifts. I had received an email from a student who was complaining about his classes being moved online and demanding a refund. I forwarded the email to all the chairs in my college with a note that we all had to get on board with some consistent messaging about these moves to address the uncertainty that students were feeling. The response was predictably chaotic with chairs quickly offering various suggestions, finger-pointing, and panic.

My dean was not happy. "Why didn't you send this to me, and we could have had a conversation about it? This is only adding to the confusion, not helping to resolve it." I felt myself getting angry. "I can email whoever I want" I initially thought. But I responded, "It felt relevant. I'm sure the other chairs have students who feel the same way. I was just trying to get a conversation started." My dean paused, and retorted, "If you want to start a conversation, we need to think about how to frame it productively. There have been some behind-the-scenes complications you are unaware of, and your email has exacerbated these issues." I wanted to reply that that was her problem, not mine. I had been a chair for several years at this point, and I knew what I was doing. I instead bit my tongue and begrudgingly acquiesced. Reflecting on the incident later, I realized she was correct, especially as the pandemic progressed and the university's response became a political hotbed. In hindsight, sending that email was a mistake and likely created more problems for my dean.

If I was wrong, why my initial hostility? It was likely caused by both "identity triggers" and "social triggers" that are common responses to unwelcome feedback (Stone & Heen, 2014). The feedback conflicted with my self-perceived identity as a manager with expertise in organizational communication aware of optimal information flows in a network (identity trigger). The fact that this was coming from an authority figure meant the feedback implicated certain power relationships and that it challenged my perceived role and authority within the organization, which evoked a defensive reaction (social trigger). The dynamics of hierarchy often amplify the impact of feedback from superiors, potentially leading to an initial hostile response to protect one's status and self-concept.

When you became chair, you probably realized that offering feedback was a core component of the job. You may have spent less time considering how vital it is to accept and adapt to feedback before accepting the role. Adapting to feedback is an essential part of being good at being chair. Gmelch and Buller (2015) explain that academic leadership growth is "first and foremost an inner journey. Self-knowledge, personal awareness, and corrective feedback must be part of the strategy for each leader's development" (p. 11). Feedback is how you course-correct for what is not working and know to keep doing what is working.

Accepting and incorporating feedback is difficult. It may be relatively easy to do in theory, but when your actual actions are implicated, it becomes difficult. I have become much better about accepting feedback in the past few years. I used to feel very threatened when I would receive anything other than glowing feedback. I wish I could go back and tell my past chair self to relax. You will not be perfect, and it is okay to have people point out ways you are not.

The role of chair makes it particularly difficult to accept feedback. As academics, we have probably experienced significant negative feedback. We have all spent time working on projects or manuscripts only to have a reviewer or editor torch it. I found that kind of feedback less personal though. It is on paper behind the veil of blind review. Being chair already feels vulnerable, even when it is going well. You do not have a great deal of managerial power, you can be removed at any time, you may feel awkward about occupying a position of authority. Negative feedback hurts more when you do not feel safe and secure.

While it may be difficult, you need to learn to not just accept, but embrace feedback. Productively listening to and incorporating feedback is linked to managerial success (McCarthy & Garavan, 2007). You will make better decisions, have a better sense of what your team needs, and be more trusted and credible (Zenger & Folkman, 2019).

Hear what is actually being said rather than filling in your own narrative. Listen logically rather than emotionally (Stone & Heen, 2014). Let go of your ego and understand that honest feedback is a gift and an opportunity to do better. Even if you disagree with the feedback, do so because you have analyzed it carefully rather than because you feel threatened. Listen actively and ask follow-up questions. Model how you want your own department to respond to your feedback.

Do not just accept feedback. Seek it out. Doing so is a managerial superpower. You will grow and learn. You will also do your part to foster a feedback culture (Stone & Heen, 2014) where feedback is a regular part of making your department and university better.

REFLECTIONS

1. Have you received any negative feedback in your position as chair yet? How did it feel different from scholarly feedback? Did you experience any emotional triggers?
2. How do you expect your faculty and staff to respond to feedback? How can you model that ideal response in your own practice?

REFERENCES

Gmelch, W. H., & Buller, J. L. (2015). *Building academic leadership capacity: A guide to best practices*. Jossey-Bass.

McCarthy, A. M., & Garavan, T. N. (2007). Understanding acceptance of multisource feedback for management development. *Personnel Review, 36*(6), 903–917. https://doi.org/10.1108/00483480710822427

Stone, D., & Heen, S. (2014). *Thanks for the feedback: The science and art of receiving feedback well*. Viking.

Zenger, J. H., & Folkman, J. (2019). *The new extraordinary leader: Turning good managers into great leaders* (3rd ed.). McGraw-Hill Education.

Chapter 87

The Value of Classroom Engagement

I have had three chair positions at three institutions over the past eleven years, and each time the course load has reduced. In my first stint as chair, I taught three courses per semester, in my second I taught two, and now I teach one class every term. This makes sense as each institution was significantly different, and each position has become more administratively focused. Additionally, with more experience I was able to negotiate lower course loads with each institutional move.

While there are certainly additional changing variables at each institution, it also feels intuitive to me that some of the differences in the experience of being chair have been related to the amount of time I spend in the classroom per week. When I taught three courses per semester, I was burned out. It was incredibly hard to focus on big long-term projects with that course load. But there were silver linings. I felt incredibly close to my students. I had a good sense of what they were interested in and talking about. I knew their concerns. I was attentive to their stress when it was finals week and could feed off their energy at the beginning of the year. My favorite moments of most workdays are the few minutes I spend making chitchat with my students at the beginning of class. Now that I teach one course per semester, I have much more time to focus on both administrative and strategic tasks, but it would not be honest if I claimed that I was as close to my students.

Being in the classroom has its benefits. It keeps you tethered to the ultimate mission of your department. It also keeps you connected to the work of the other faculty in your department. You evaluate them on their teaching, so it makes sense that you would benefit from keeping your own pedagogical skills honed. Being in the classroom offers professional growth opportunities. It makes you better at many things such as time management, public speaking, and organizational skills (Gibbs & Coffee, 2004; Postareff &

Lindblom-Ylänne, 2008). I have also found that teaching keeps me sharper. Explaining theoretical concepts to students who are hearing them for the first time is an excellent opportunity to practice critical thinking and communication skills. Preparing lesson plans and finding new course materials also increases your subject mastery and keeps you current in your discipline (Prince et al., 2007).

There are also numerous emotional and psychological benefits from being in the classroom. These benefits are increased for you as chair. Teaching is a rewarding experience, as you have the ability to make an impact that you can see. You can have positive interactions with students and see them understand and apply new concepts. This is all very rewarding. Teaching can also increase motivation and your own sense of self (Postareff & Lindblom-Ylänne, 2008).

These are all excellent benefits even if you are not a chair, but now that you are, you can truly appreciate and enjoy them much the way a resident of Seattle is more thankful for a sunny day than someone who lives in Tampa. I have found the classroom a respite from the stresses and administrative tasks of being chair. Email is unavailable. There are no drop-ins with urgent issues to handle. You can be passionate without being too corny. Students (generally) listen respectfully as we talk about ideas and their future. I know there are frustrations and challenges to being an instructor, but I have found that they pale in comparison to those of being chair.

While I have spent less and less time teaching over the trajectory of my chair career, I have certainly appreciated my time in the classroom more and more. Every chair position is different, and your course load is often out of your control. I am certainly not recommending that you need to go take on a higher course load in the name of self-development or emotional satisfaction. Instead, value your time in the classroom. Consider avoiding teaching online classes so you can have face-to-face time with students. There may be a temptation to frame your chair duties as your primary professional focus and teaching as secondary. Do not fall into this framework. Put time, effort, and energy in your classes and savor the change of pace that comes from being in the classroom. Do not see teaching as a distraction from your chair responsibilities.

REFLECTIONS

1. How can you maintain a strong connection to your students despite the reduced classroom time now that you are chair? What strategies can you employ to ensure you remain engaged with the pedagogical mission of your department?

2. What do you see as the emotional, professional, and psychological benefits of teaching? How can they influence your approach and attitude toward your administrative responsibilities?

REFERENCES

Gibbs, G., & Coffey, M. (2004). The impact of training of university teachers on their teaching skills, their approach to teaching and the approach to learning of their students. *Active Learning in Higher Education*, 5(1), 87–100. https://doi.org/10.1177/1469787404040463

Postareff, L., & Lindblom-Ylänne, S. (2008). Variation in teachers' descriptions of teaching: Broadening the understanding of teaching in higher education. *Learning and Instruction*, 18(2), 109–120. https://doi.org/10.1016/j.learninstruc.2007.01.008

Prince, M. J., Felder, R. M., & Brent, R. (2007). Does faculty research improve undergraduate teaching? An analysis of existing and potential synergies. *Journal of Engineering Education*, 96(4), 283–294. https://doi.org/10.1002/j.2168-9830.2007.tb00939.x

Chapter 88

Leading Meaningful Assessment

As chair positions have become progressively managerial, the task of overseeing curricular assessment has fallen increasingly under their purview. Assessment has become an important part of university life (Kuh et al., 2014). Forty-four percent of department chairs report that they are responsible for overseeing assessment in their department (Weaver et al., 2019). It is a significant part of many chairs' jobs.

It is not surprising that this task would fall to the chair, as most faculty are not particularly thrilled with the labor of doing curricular assessment (Joyner, 2016). This is often the result of faculty feeling as if it is busywork that is unlikely to make much of an impact. Assessment is a lot of work, and its impact is usually limited. Additionally, it is not particularly valued, as much of the labor is hidden from your colleagues. Rarely do faculty get promoted because they are good at leading assessment. Much of the disdain for assessment is understandable. Alexander (2000) explains the rise of assessment culture on campus as being rooted in the changing relationship between government and higher education. Universities have been pushed to increase accountability at the same time they have had reductions in funding. Governmental demands for assessment have often had a judgmental connotation to them.

The performance assessments required often do not align with the goals of the institution. Complex pedagogical goals are reduced to simple outcomes. Feuerstein (2015) has argued that this has led to assessment being a kind of ritual that is more about verifying compliance than enriching students. Many faculty seem to have adopted this stance, as assessment is viewed as something we have to do rather than something that we should be doing. According to Feuerstein, department chairs are caught in this performative assessment ritual where the task must be done so we can all verify that it has been done. The disconnect between our educational goals and the mechanisms for assessing them is not likely to breed passion.

While all of this is true, your oversight of the assessment process is a reminder that your role has changed. You are no longer simply a faculty member who can complain about this and move on. Now that you are chair, you own it. If something is broken, you now have an obligation to address it. Assessment does not have to be your favorite part of the job, but you should not approach it with the same negativity that faculty often do. As an academic leader you have a responsibility. While the current state of assessment may not live up to its potential, we should all be able to agree that the general principle of figuring out what our students are learning in their time at a university is a good thing.

No one is expecting you to fix the state of assessment or be its biggest cheerleader. But try to make it better and don't participate in the general complaining that is often associated with assessment. As a new department chair, use your position to move toward an assessment process that is a more pleasant, rewarding, and valuable experience rather than a bureaucratic necessity. There is no doubt that when done well, assessment is a very valuable tool for a department. What department would not benefit from knowing whether students are mastering the learning objectives in your classes? Most successful companies implement product assessment because they know they need to be delivering value. Higher education, especially given the numerous headwinds it is facing, could benefit a lot from meaningful assessment as part of the feedback loop.

Engage your faculty by having conversations with them about what assessment should be. How could you use assessment as a strategic tool to align your department's educational activities with broader university goals and student needs? Ask your faculty how they could envision an assessment that enhances the pedagogical quality and improves student outcomes rather than simply fulfilling an administrative requirement.

As a department chair, embracing the managerial aspects of assessment allows you to lead significant changes. By spearheading a constructive approach to assessment, you can shift the perception from a mundane task to an integral part of academic enhancement. This leadership role enables you to integrate assessment meaningfully into the department's culture, ensuring it contributes effectively to both teaching quality and student learning outcomes. Furthermore, your forward-looking stance on assessment can set a powerful example, emphasizing the department's commitment to continuous improvement and academic excellence. In doing so, you highlight the critical role of academic leadership in fostering an environment where assessment is not just a requirement but a valuable tool for achieving educational goals and advancing the university's mission.

REFLECTIONS

1. What role does assessment currently hold in your department? Does the assessment process align with the department's educational goals? What needs to change?
2. What is your department's attitude toward assessment? Is it productive? If not, what can you do to make it better?

REFERENCES

Alexander, F. K. (2000). The changing face of accountability: Monitoring and assessing institutional performance in higher education. *The Journal of Higher Education, 71*(4), 411–431. https://doi.org/10.1080/00221546.2000.11778843

Feuerstein, A. (2015). Rituals of verification: Department chairs and the dominant discourse of assessment in higher education. *Journal of Higher Education Theory and Practice, 15*(6), 38–51. http://www.na-businesspress.com/JHETP/FeuersteinA_Web15_6_.pdf

Joyner, H. S. (Melito). (2016). Curriculum mapping: A before-and-after look at faculty perceptions of their courses and the mapping process. *Journal of Food Science Education, 15*(2), 63–69. https://doi.org/10.1111/1541-4329.12085

Kuh, G., Jankowski, N., Ikenberry, S., & Kinzie, J. (2014). *Knowing what students know and can do: The current state of student learning outcomes assessment in U.S. colleges and universities.* National Institute for Learning Outcomes Assessment. https://www.learningoutcomesassessment.org/wp-content/uploads/2019/02/2013AbridgedSurveyReport.pdf

Weaver, L. D., Ely, K., Dickson, L., & DellAntonio, J. (2019). The changing role of the department chair in the shifting landscape of higher education. *International Journal of Higher Education, 8*(4), 175–188. https://eric.ed.gov/?id=EJ1223225

Weiner, W. F. (2009). Establishing a culture of assessment. *Academe, 95*(4), 28–32. https://eric.ed.gov/?id=EJ861803

Chapter 89

Gossip, Trust, and Leadership

I was whispering in hush tones to our office associate about a faculty member's new tattoo. I try not to be judgmental about such things, but this was objectively terrible. The graffiti lettering, the cookie-cutter positivity message, the fact that it was one art piece spread across both forearms that made no sense unless the arms were held next to each other, the pastel colors, and the large size all combined for a disastrous tattoo. The piece was made all the worse by his peacocking around the office with his sleeves rolled up showing it off and talking loudly about what it meant to him. Everyone in the department was talking about it. "What was he thinking?" I asked our office associate, trying to hold in giggles. "I think he's going through a midlife crisis," she offered. Another faculty member walked in and upon seeing us gathered, asked, "Are you guys talking about Mark's tattoo? It's a cry for help. Should we all give him a hug and ask if he's okay?" We all laughed again and went our separate ways. I headed to the mail room adjacent to the front desk only to see Mark checking his mail. With raised pitch and too much enthusiasm, I offered "Hey Mark!" I tried to assess if he had heard us gossiping. He quietly responded, "Hey Ben" and left. I could tell from his response, which was very different from his usually loud affect, that he had heard at least some of our conversation.

While I will stand by my assessment of the tattoo, I learned a lesson that day. I had been caught gossiping before. Who hasn't? But it felt different this time now that I was his supervisor. It felt especially bad considering he heard me gossiping about him to his peers. The new power dynamics changed how I viewed my relational responsibilities in relationship to my colleagues. The guilt I felt was a reminder that with the chair position comes a responsibility to build a supportive and positive environment. My role had changed, and my words carried more weight.

Gossip is "informal and evaluative talk in an organization about another member of the organization who is not present" (Kurland & Pelled, 2000). It is a part of organizational life. There is no way around that. Fourteen percent of all workplace break chat consists of gossip and 66 percent of all workplace conversation is about other people (Cole & Dalton, 2009). Unsurprisingly, gossip is often framed negatively. It can also lead to toxicity, hostility, and negative career advancement for employees (Cheng, 2024; Kuo et al., 2015). Other scholars point out positive effects. It can strengthen relationships and help deter bad behavior in organizations (Ferrari, 2015). Gossiping about the boss can build community and cohesion (Ellward et al., 2012).

You cannot regulate the speech of others, but you may need to rethink your own participation in gossip. Gossip can make you feel good. You are sharing a worldview and a point of reference with someone. It can help you bond and feel like you are in the in-group. But now that you are in a managerial position, gossip should not be a foundation on which you build solidarity with direct reports. There are a few reasons for this.

Your reputation is vital for your effectiveness in the chair position. Having a reputation as a chair who is fair and impartial is essential. Speaking about those you supervise when they are not there to fill in perspective is a bad look. You control resources and review people. You must have the appearance of being judicious, which involves being transparent and hearing multiple sides of the story. Gossip also creates in-groups and out-groups that can lead to ostracization (Carrim, 2019). When you gossip with someone, the bond you create comes at the expense of another faculty member whom you are also responsible for supervising. This is a surefire way to build animosity. Gossip may be less destructive when peers are gossiping about peers, or you and someone you supervise are gossiping about someone higher up the organizational hierarchy. But no good will come from you and someone you supervise gossiping about another person you supervise. I worked with an associate dean once who would constantly gossip about people when I was in his office. I was always cautious with him because I assumed he would gossip about me when someone else was in his office. It was hard to trust him.

Finally, your team must know that they can come to you with delicate issues and you will maintain confidentiality. If they feel that their private concerns might become fodder for office gossip, it undermines their confidence in your leadership and can seriously impact morale and productivity. If you are careless with departmental gossip, your team will be hesitant to speak to you about things that are sensitive.

You do not need to be the gossip police. You are not going to stop gossip in your department. That is simply an unachievable goal and trying is a bad look. Instead, just remove yourself nonjudgmentally from conversations that veer into gossip. Find an excuse to leave. If it is a conversation with only two of you and you cannot find an excuse to leave, just offer a short quip like, "Well, you never know the whole story" or "I'm curious what _____ would have to say back to that." Avoiding being implicated in gossip is a great way to inoculate yourself from a whole host of problems and is bound to make your job easier.

REFLECTIONS

1. Since being chair, have you found that conversations centered around gossip feel different than when you were a faculty member? Why?
2. Do you agree that you should avoid gossiping with those you supervise about their peers? Why or why not? Under what conditions might gossip be appropriate or helpful?

REFERENCES

Carrim, N. M. H. (2019). Minorities' experiences of office gossip. *SA Journal of Industrial Psychology, 45*. https://doi.org/10.4102/sajip.v45i0.1562

Cole, J. M., & Dalton, J. (2009). *Idle women's chat? Gender and gossip*. Social Section, The Annual Conference of the British Psychological Society, University of Kent, Kent, UK. https://www.researchgate.net/publication/268686656_Idle_womens'_talk_Gender_and_gossip

Cheng, B. (2024). How negative workplace gossip undermines employees' career growth: From a reputational perspective. *International Journal of Contemporary Hospitality Management, 36*(7). https://doi.org/10.1108/IJCHM-2024-1234

Ellwardt, L., Wittek, R., & Wielers, R. (2012). Talking about the boss. *Group & Organization Management, 37*(4), 521–549. https://doi.org/10.1177/1059601112450607

Ferrari, F. (2015). In praise of gossip: The organizational functions and practical applications of rumours in the workplace. *Journal of Human Resources Management Research*, 1–8. https://doi.org/10.5171/2015.854452

Kuo, C.-C., Chang, K., Quinton, S., Lu, C.-Y., & Lee, I. (2015). Gossip in the workplace and the implications for HR management: A study of gossip and its relationship to employee cynicism. *International Journal of Human Resource Management, 26*(18), 2288–2307. https://doi.org/10.1080/09585192.2014.985329

Kurland, N. B., & Pelled, L. H. (2000). Passing the word: Toward a model of gossip and power in the workplace. *Academy of Management Review, 25*(2), 428–438. https://doi.org/10.5465/amr.2000.3312928

Chapter 90

Chairing through the Tenure Process

As chair, guiding candidates through the tenure/promotion process is a key responsibility that requires diplomatic skill, an understanding of policy and procedure, and meticulous attention to detail. The stakes are high as someone's career (and life circumstances) is directly affected. The process is fraught with liability for both you as chair and your institution. All of this can make for a confusing and stressful process.

The tenure process is comprised of three intertwined components running concurrently: a legal process, a peer-review process, and a political process (Harris, 2018). We will briefly address each and your obligations to them. The legal aspect is clear, as employment law is directly engaged. Tenure guidelines and processes are not simply academic, they are legal and exist to protect both candidates and the institution. As I have echoed elsewhere in this volume, you must familiarize yourself with every step of the tenure/promotion-review process in advance and follow it to the letter of the law. Check your faculty handbook, your university policies, your college and department elaborations, and your university's collective bargaining agreement (if it has one). When candidates challenge tenure decisions, process is often the first place their lawyer will look. You are now responsible for overseeing much of this process. There are several legal cases of tenure decision challenges where department chairs were implicated. I would encourage you to read about some of them so you can understand how these things can go wrong. There are plenty of examples where chairs thought they were helping when they were in fact opening themselves up to legal jeopardy.

The peer-review process relates to discipline-specific criteria. How strong is the candidate's work? Your relationship to this part of the process is crucial. You need to ensure that the review is conducted with impartiality and confidentiality and is comprehensive. If a candidate's tenure is on the horizon but not yet here, engage them in conversations about their work early so you can coach them. When it is time for review, ensure the process (but not the deliberation) is transparent. Frame the candidate's work in fair ways for external reviewers. Your goal should be to make certain that all evaluations are squarely based on merit and the established academic standards of your discipline.

The political aspect of the tenure process involves navigating complex interactions and negotiations between various stakeholders. As we all know, tenure and promotion are not always decided solely based on merit. Political dynamics can significantly influence outcomes. It is often the most hazy and difficult part of the process to control. As chair, you need to help the candidate navigate this space by coaching them to make wise decisions. Additionally, this is often the process that causes the most stress for candidates since it is more nebulous. Approaching the political process of tenure as chair requires a nuanced understanding of the interpersonal and institutional dynamics at play. Do not get involved in backdoor politicking but do try to keep your finger on the pulse. Facilitate open communication and encourage candidates to build healthy relationships with all departmental members, not just those they like. Finally, emphasize the values and goals of the department in conversations with those doing evaluating. This can help create an environment where political processes, which are unavoidable, do not detract from the integrity of the process.

The tenure process is usually messy enough, and the lines between these legal, peer-review, and political aspects can get very blurry. What happens in one aspect of the tenure process can complicate another. For example, candidates often want reassurances. It can be very tempting to offer support in the form of "I'm sure you'll be fine" or "I've got your back." Never say, and especially do not email, these kinds of statements. It may feel like you are giving emotional support, but these kinds of statements can complicate things as they blur the legal and peer-review process. You need to formally evaluate the candidate, and these kinds of statements are informal evaluations that can hold weight in the event of a legal challenge. "But the candidate's chair assured him he would be fine" is not the kind of statement you want to hear a lawyer say. Offer encouragement in the form of giving specific feedback and guidance without promises. That kind of support is constructive and legally defensible and keeps the different aspects of the process separate.

You walk a fine line as a chair between being responsible for coaching the candidate while also safeguarding institutional and disciplinary standards. When in doubt, seek guidance from other chairs. Your first tenure case as chair is likely going to cause some stress, as the stakes become very clear. Remember that the process is not only stressful for you as chair but also for the candidate. Be attentive to the three aspects of the process, but also help the candidate manage the emotional aspect by making sure they feel confident in the integrity of the process.

REFLECTIONS

1. Which of the three components of the tenure process do you feel most comfortable interfacing with as chair? Which do you see as the most complicated?
2. How familiar are you with the tenure and promotion processes at your university? What are the aspects you feel most and least familiar with?

REFERENCE

Harris, M. (2018). *How to get tenure: Strategies for successfully navigating the process*. Routledge.

Chapter 91

Justifying Your Decisions

"Just don't answer her." This advice from Mary, a human resources personnel staff member, landed with the force of hammer smashing a glass. The idea had never occurred to me before. I bit my lip, furrowed my brow, and vocalized my confusion. "What do you mean?" I asked. I was in her office because a difficult faculty member was unhappy with a decision I had made. In response, she had sent out an email to the entire department demanding that I explain why I had chosen this course of action. I was defensive and wanted to strategically think about how to respond in a way that showed that I was not going to be bullied and let my team know that my decision-making was sound. My dean had suggested I speak with Mary, who was "good at this kind of thing."

Mary's suggestion was so surprising because it questioned a premise I was operating under. My decision matrix was centered around *how to respond*, not *whether to respond*. In thinking about how to respond, I was operating under the framework that a response was warranted in this situation. "I'm not required to justify my decision?" I inquired. Mary continued, "There is nothing in the faculty handbook that requires managers to explain their decisions. Generally it is good practice, but there are times when it is not the smartest course of action."

That moment was a turning point in how I handled situations with difficult faculty members. The advice was valuable, but exposing the premise under which I was leading my department was even more so. I had always felt a need to justify decisions when pushed. I believed (and still do) in the virtues of open management. But the practice of always being willing to offer a justification is not always the wisest course of action. There are three reasons why I have come to understand this.

First, we have spent many chapters in this volume reflecting on the ways that chairing a department is vulnerable—and responding to demands that you justify your actions can make you feel even more exposed. Constantly feeling like you need to explain and validate your decision-making process can make you feel psychologically unsteady. Feeling as if you are under attack and need to defend yourself is not conducive to your emotional health, which is important if you are going to handle this position well.

Second, it can create some unhealthy power dynamics in your department by undermining your authority as chair. This can make it hard for you to lead effectively. The philosopher Louis Althusser (1970/1971) explained the idea of *interpellation*, which is the process by which individuals are transformed into subjects by being hailed through social interactions. For example, imagine a police officer yells, "Hey You. Stop!" and you stop and answer "Me?" Through that social interaction you have been interpellated into the matrix of the state under the authority of the police officer. Even if the officer was calling someone else, your response constitutes an acceptance of their authority. Similarly, by acquiescing to bad faith demands for justification, you tacitly acknowledge the legitimacy of the demand. This person is, presumably, not your boss. But they might as well be.

Finally, it never works. Those who make bad faith demands for justification are never satisfied. You will provide it, and it will fuel further demands. They will pick up on one element of something you said and run with it. Then you will need to provide new justifications. It turns into a justification loop and your time is better spent focusing on other things.

There are some caveats to this advice that I want to explicitly state. I am only discussing bad faith demands for justification. I am not referring to good faith genuine questions from faculty. Good faith queries are excellent opportunities to gather feedback, show accessibility, crowdsource problem-solving, and build relationships. Those should be welcome as they are a gift. But some faculty will demand justification to score political points or to undermine you. These are often public and are always mean-spirited. Be judicious in sorting through which examples fall into which categories. Simply disagreeing with someone does not mean their request for a rationale was made in bad faith. I trust that you can decipher when these demands for justification are in good or bad faith.

Also, do not use this advice as an excuse to dodge questions that make you uncomfortable. I am not suggesting that you avoid hard questions about your leadership. Do not stubbornly assume you are always right or avoid engaging in conversations about your decision-making to avoid being reflexive about your actions.

Most requests for explanations are made in good faith, and it is usually wise to give people the benefit of the doubt until they have given you a reason not to. Your ability to discern between when it is best to engage in constructive dialogue and when you need to draw your boundaries is critical for all leaders—but especially for you as a chair given the vulnerability of the position. When appropriately deployed, your silence will speak much louder than a justification. Selective and wise engagement helps preserve your authority, reduces unnecessary conflict, saves you time, preserves your emotional well-being, and maintains focus.

REFLECTIONS

1. Have you faced any demands/requests to justify decisions you have made as chair? Did you feel compelled to respond? What does your impulse tell you about your leadership style?
2. How do you manage the power dynamics in these circumstances to balance the competing demands of drawing boundaries and maintaining open lines of dialogue with your faculty?

REFERENCE

Althusser, L. (1971). Ideology and ideological state apparatuses (Notes towards an investigation). In B. Brewster (Trans.), *L. Althusser, Lenin and philosophy and other essays*. Monthly Review Press. (Original work published 1970)

Chapter 92

The Calculus of Change

"Last day before summer. Time to give final exams!" my colleague excitedly said as I passed her in the hall. The end-of-the-year energy was in the air, and everyone was in a good mood. But I was confused at her statement; exams were scheduled for next week. I was lecturing in my class today, not giving final exams. I was new to this institution, so I asked the office associate if she knew what was going on. "Oh, yeah," she replied, "most faculty give exams on the last day of class and don't make students come in for the scheduled final exam. You are one of the few who holds final exams during the scheduled final exam session."

I was incensed. "But aren't we required to report all missed class periods? No one has reported to me they are not holding exams." Our office associate, still sitting and not looking up from her computer screen, offered, "Yeah, technically. But this has been the way it is for several years. The students don't complain about starting their summer early." I left the conversation contemplating this injustice. Students were paying for class time. We should be meeting during every scheduled class time unless there is an emergency or unforeseen circumstance. We promise students a certain number of contact hours. Missing one class does not jeopardize that, but it set a precedent that I found concerning. I was new to this department, but this was the kind of quality control that I had promised in my interview. This was low-hanging fruit.

I reached out to another chair in my college that I had become friendly with. I told him about what I had discovered and asked for advice on how I should approach it. Given that it was the end of the semester, I figured I would address this issue in the first department meeting at the beginning of the next semester. My colleague informed me that his faculty generally didn't meet during exam week either. He agreed with me that faculty were being lazy in this regard, but he had given up the fight a long time ago. I spoke with a few other chairs to ask if this was standard practice in their departments, and I came to realize that this was common.

While I still held convictions that this practice was lazy and disadvantaged students who were paying for an education, I gave up the cause at this point. As chair, you now need to wisely choose what causes you dedicate energy to. University life is full of inefficiencies, suboptimal processes, and institutional norms that do not align with your own values. It may be tempting to assume that you will clean all of these up, but it is simply unfeasible to address every problem you identify. Change takes effort, energy, and political capital.

We have spent considerable space in this volume reflecting on just how limited and tenuous your influence and managerial power are as chair. You cannot mandate change. You need to change hearts, and as Buller (2019) wisely reminds us, "No unit of a college or department is ever ready for as much change as it claims to be" (p. 17). There are times when you may need to begrudgingly accept the status quo. Do not think of this as approval of the problematic organizational norm, but instead an acceptance of your limited managerial power.

This advice is not only about self-preservation, but also about the best interests of your department. Fighting every fight that you feel strongly about may cause more disruption and damage to your department than the problem you are trying to fix (Ness & Samet, 2010). Change is, by definition, disruptive. Given these factors, be judicious in choosing what battles you fight. Ask yourself, "Is the juice worth the squeeze?" Is the potential result of fixing the issue worth the effort? How long has the norm been in place? How widespread is it? What kind of political maneuvering will you have to do to address it? How strongly do you feel about the problem? What is the impact (financially, emotionally, operationally) of the norm you'd like to change? And finally (and usually most importantly), what are the odds that you can change it?

In the example above, I never ended up addressing the exam time issue. I knew that I would likely be unsuccessful and risked losing the support of my department. This decision, like all decisions about such matters, required careful consideration about the potential consequences, available resources, and long-term goals. No students or faculty were complaining. The practice spread across other units and no department had yet collapsed as a result. Not every issue warrants immediate intervention. Prioritizing what you try to fix allows you to conserve your energy and political capital for endeavors that you believe will have the greatest impact on your department. Being a good chair involves not only being able to successfully identify problems and solutions, but also in discerning when to let go of something and focus on what matters in the grand scheme.

REFLECTIONS

1. How would you have handled the situation? Are there organizational norms in your department you disagree with? What are the relevant factors in deciding whether to challenge them?
2. Reflect on the advice from Buller regarding the readiness of units to change. Do you agree? How does this insight inform your approach to addressing organizational norms?

REFERENCES

Buller, J. L. (2019). *The essential department chair: A comprehensive desk reference.* Jossey-Bass.

Ness, R. B., & Samet, J. M. (2010). How to be a department chair of epidemiology: A survival guide. *American Journal of Epidemiology, 172*(7), 747–751. https://doi.org/10.1093/aje/kwq268

Chapter 93

Parent Complaints

A police officer, in full uniform with her gun holstered, stood towering over my desk. She yelled, "My daughter is going to lose her scholarship because of this! Her instructor is targeting her." I was terrified. "She only needs another ten points on the assignment. The instructor has it out for her and is trying to make her lose her scholarship!" From my seat behind the desk, I managed to stammer "I'll look into it." After she left, our office associate came in to check on me. "What was that?" she asked. After discussing, she insisted, "You need to call the university chief of police. It is scary for her to be in your office yelling at you, especially when she is in uniform and has a weapon." I heeded her advice, and the police chief was taken aback at the story. "I'm so sorry, Dr. Myers. That is utterly inappropriate. I will discuss the situation with this employee."

The next day, the irate police officer, still in uniform, returned. Expecting an apology, I was instead met with another confrontation. She shut my office door uninvited and snapped, "Think you can get me in trouble by complaining to my boss?" Her sarcasm was biting as she continued, "And you mentioned feeling uncomfortable because I had my gun. What did you think I was going to do, shoot you over this?" Asserting her parental rights, she proclaimed, "I have every right to defend my daughter from being unfairly targeted." When she left, I immediately phoned the police chief again to update him on this interaction. He was flabbergasted and promised me that this was the last I would hear from this officer. It was. She was fired a few months later for a separate incident that involved harassing a student.

Parents will complain sometimes. As chair, these complaints will usually fall to you. The incident above is extreme, and thankfully I have had no other experiences with parent complaints that have approached this level of intimidation or inappropriate behavior. But this story should serve as a warning that as chair, you should be prepared for anything.

Like many aspects of being a department chair, handling parent complaints involves walking a fine line. Eye rolls often accompany stories about parent complaints. It is easy to label these parents as helicopter parents who cannot let their child be an adult. There is some truth in this sentiment, and it can be annoying when parents get involved in resolving conflicts that students should be managing. As chair, you do need to realize that parents of students are stakeholders in your department. However demanding they may be, they often have invested both financially and emotionally in the educational experience of students in your department. They have often saved money or taken on debt. Even if they are not financing their child's education, they likely care deeply about how their child is being prepared for their career. While the above story about the police officer is clearly egregious, as a parent myself I understand the impulse to use whatever resources you must to help your child.

Beyond sympathy, there is a pragmatic reason to approach parent complaints with grace. You also want to cultivate goodwill with all departmental stakeholders. Having angry parents does not put good energy out there. It is not great to have parents complaining about your department to their friends at dinner parties. That can have an impact on your department in ways you will never even know. You want parents bragging about their child's experience in your department.

Approach parent complaints with a customer service mindset. Showing that you are reasonable, friendly, and happy to talk goes a long way. Usually, you are not going to be able to fix their complaints, but showing that you care can diffuse a lot of situations. Parent concerns tend to be about three things: grades, course content, or instructor conduct. When complaints are about grades, you can easily fall back on the Family Educational Rights and Privacy Act that prohibits you from speaking about this. Be polite and friendly but explain that you are legally forbidden from conversations about grades. Complaints about course content are often political. Maybe parents do not approve of a topic being covered in class. You can applaud parents for taking an interest in what their child is learning. Explain that academic freedom allows professors to explore a wide range of topics and that exploring different perspectives is an important part of the educational process. Encourage parents to talk with their child about how to raise these questions in the classroom. I have found that in these cases, parents are usually more concerned than the student is. When complaints are about instructor conduct, take them seriously. Listen and investigate thoroughly. Withhold any judgment until you have all the facts. Remember that parents are secondhand witnesses and that students may conceal parts of a story to hide their own academic shortcomings.

Being sympathetic does not mean you need to accept unacceptable behavior though. Parents who complain to a department chair are usually the loudest kind. Do not allow yourself to be walked over or bullied. Be respectful but firm when behavior crosses the boundary of appropriateness. I have had parents threaten to go to the university president, call their congressional representative, or contact the local news. This is fine. These parties are less responsive to such complaints than parents anticipate.

Parent complaints are generally few and far between, but you will encounter them from time to time. In general, aim to balance compassion and assertiveness. Effectively handling parent complaints will help you manage your department's reputation and show that you take seriously the concerns of all your stakeholders. Strive to turn these interactions into opportunities to reinforce your commitment to both excellence and fairness.

REFLECTIONS

1. How would you handle a situation where a parent is visibly upset or confrontational? What strategies can you use to deescalate tension?
2. Do you agree that you should approach parent complaints with a customer service mindset? What are the benefits and drawbacks of such an approach?

Chapter 94

Balancing Academic Leadership and Academic Management

As chair you occupy dual roles as both an academic leader and an academic manager. These roles overlap in some areas, but each carries distinct responsibilities and requires a different skill set to effectively pull off. As an academic leader, you are responsible for setting a visionary direction for your department, inspiring faculty, and fostering a departmental culture that prioritizes excellence and innovation. Conversely, your role as an academic manager requires you to oversee administrative operations, attend to the budget, abide by proper policy, and complete necessary paperwork and reports on time. Managing your roles as both leader and manager can be a struggle.

Being an academic leader involves finding ways to strategically guide your department toward its academic mission. You need to display vision, enthusiasm, and strategic thinking. This involves pursuing excellence through setting goals and aligning them with your university's broader objectives. When you are acting as an academic leader you are concerned with questions such as how your department's curriculum can be aligned with industry trends, tactics for advocating for resources, and methods for inspiring students and faculty to reach their potential. You are directing the creative and intellectual energies of your department. This requires a proactive approach to building and nurturing partnerships and increasing your department's footprint and a deep commitment to educational excellence.

In contrast, being an academic manager primarily necessitates a focus on immediate operational tasks such as course scheduling, managing staff, annual reviews, and policy compliance. Rather than the long-term vision necessary for academic leadership, managerial duties require an eye for detail, organization skills, discipline, and an ability to handle logistical challenges. Being a good academic manager involves ensuring the department functions smoothly with minimal disruption.

Balancing these two roles is not always easy, as they both require different kinds of energy, attention, and focus (Kurniawan & Puspitaningtyas, 2013), which are often in conflict (Arntzen, 2016). A consistent theme in this volume has been on the ways in which unforeseen circumstances that require immediate attention often hijack your workday. These are usually managerial tasks. When you are putting out fires, scheduling classes, and trying to get annual reviews completed, it can be easy for leadership to fall by the wayside. However, to be a successful chair you need to succeed at both being a leader and a manager. Finding ways to successfully balance these competing demands is essential.

You need to prioritize and plan. Have running lists of both long-term visionary projects and day-to-day priorities. Set aside specific time to work on both. This involves intentionality. It can be very easy to focus on the things that need to be done tomorrow, but if you continually do that you will never accomplish the things that need to be done a year from now that position your department for long-term success. Whenever possible, delegate administrative tasks. Ask your office associate or another faculty member to help. Some things you need to do yourself, but when you can, try to offload routine managerial tasks so you can dedicate adequate focus to leadership activities.

When we compare academic leadership and academic management, we often inherently frame the management side of the equation negatively. We associate it with bureaucracy and busywork. We privilege and prioritize leadership. But doing managerial tasks well is also very important. When faculty and staff know that the day-to-day operations of the department are well under control, it frees everyone up from worrying. This is a very valuable service to provide to your team. While it is often the managerial tasks that "get in the way" of the more leadership-oriented projects, do not dismiss this as trivial work. A department chair who does not ensure that the day-to-day operations are completed is not leading effectively. Both aspects are critical to the successful functioning of an academic department.

The true challenge lies not in choosing between leadership and management, but in harmonizing them. There should be synergy between the two. Your strategic vision should inform how you approach operational tasks, making sure they are aligned with your department's goals. Conversely, a well-managed department provides a stable platform from which your department can safely engage in big-picture thinking.

The tensions and overlaps between managerial and leadership tasks are examples of how multifaceted the role of department chair is. By mastering balance and attending to both managerial and leadership tasks, you can create a department that can thrive.

REFLECTIONS

1. Have you felt competing pulls from your managerial and leadership responsibilities? How have those been resolved thus far?
2. What can you do to find ways to harmonize your managerial and leadership responsibilities? What support systems are available to help?

REFERENCES

Arntzen, E. (2016). The changing role of deans in higher education—From leader to manager. *Universal Journal of Educational Research, 4*(9), 2068–2075. https://doi.org/10.13189/ujer.2016.040918

Kurniawan, A. W., & Puspitaningtyas, Z. (2013). Leadership in higher education: Academic leader or manager? *Buletin Studi Ekonomi, 18*(1), 1–6. https://www.researchgate.net/publication/258277325_LEADERSHIP_IN_HIGHER_EDUCATION_ACADEMIC_LEADER_OR_MANAGER

Chapter 95

The Academic Cycle

Being in higher education is a unique experience. The highly regimented cyclical nature of our profession is a blessing and a curse. Some people find comfort in the annual cycle while others find the monotony boring. As chair, you will find yourself even more tethered to the academic cycle than you were before. As a faculty member you are certainly bound by the routine of semester-winter break-semester-summer-repeat. But as chair, much more of your responsibilities will be directly tied to specific times of the year. As chair, your attention at any given moment will be dictated by the budget cycle, course scheduling cycle, annual review cycle, assessment cycle, recruitment cycle, and advising cycle. In each of these cycles you are project-managing a task that requires different skill sets.

In our reflection on imposter syndrome, we focused on the number of cycles you are now implicated in as one of the reasons you might feel overwhelmed. Just when you feel like you have a handle on one responsibility another pops up, demanding a different kind of attention and mastery. This ongoing juggling act can amplify doubt about your ability to be effective. But here I want to focus on the possibilities that are unlocked by the cyclical nature of the chair position.

The pace with which cycles move may seem overwhelming at day ninety-five of being a chair. But, in time, these cycles will have a familiar rhythm to them. It may seem hard to imagine at this point, but you will get an intuitive sense of how your attention and focus must shift between cycles. In short, you will pick up the pattern. This is one reason why I have always felt like three-year appointments are too short. You are just starting to sync to the repetition and then your time is up.

One of my favorite movies is *Groundhog Day*. I love the entire genre of entertainment about reliving the same day (*Edge of Tomorrow*, *Source Code*, *Russian Doll*, *Happy Death Day*, *Palm Springs*). These films are fun because we can see the framework of a day play over and over with the protagonist making small changes that can yield big results while all other variables are held steady. The goal is usually for the protagonist to learn something valuable or to get the day right.

Like the character Phil Conners in *Groundhog Day* waking every morning to his alarm at 5:59, each cycle is an opportunity for you to tweak. As chair, you are reliving the same cycle over and over. For the first two-thirds of the movie, Phil is stuck. The repetitiveness is a curse. It leads to boredom and depression. He loses meaning. It is when Phil adopts a goal to learn from each cycle and approaches each with a new perspective that he finds value in the repetition. He transforms from an obnoxious narcissist to a caring friend. The movie serves as a testament to the power of repetition in the process of change (Daughton, 1996).

You need to start now in finding value in the repetition. You are new to the position at this moment, so is not yet repetitive. But it is not too early to begin to lay the groundwork for meaningfully engaging with repetitive academic cycles. Cycles start somewhere, and now you are in the first chapter of a series of iterative loops.

Do not simply let the cycles wash over you, responding to them as they come at you. Skip the beginning-of-the-movie Phil Conners and jump to the transformed character. Do not wait for the cycles to become routine before learning from them. As you familiarize yourself with each cycle, begin to introduce small innovations or improvements. These early interventions will help you understand the impact of changes within a stable framework, providing insight into more effective management strategies for future cycles. Your adjustments can be driven from curiosity rather than certainty. Try something different because you are curious what will happen. If it does not work, then you always have a reset coming when the academic cycle starts again.

Maintain a playful sense of experimentation with each cycle. Approach the tasks associated with each cycle with an ethos of curiosity rather than a rigid sense of duty. Doing so will make space for innovative solutions to emerge. Through this shift in perspective, you can make every cycle an opportunity not to simply complete your tasks, but to discover something. As with any experiment, keep track of what works and what does not. This can become a valuable learning tool to ensure that each iteration is more rewarding and informed than the one before it.

REFLECTIONS

1. Reflect on the claim that you should start learning from the cyclical nature of the chair position now. What does that mean to you? How can you do that?
2. How might this approach help you grow as a chair? What does Phil Conners ultimately learn, and how might that apply to your time as chair?

REFERENCE

Daughton, S. M. (1996). The spiritual power of repetitive form: Steps toward transcendence in *Groundhog Day*. *Critical Studies in Mass Communication*, *13*(2), 138–154. https://doi.org/10.1080/15295039609366968

Chapter 96

Performing as Chair

"Just be calm and professional. Act like you know what you are doing. Pretend you are not nervous." I reminded myself of this as I looked at my face in the bathroom mirror mustering the courage to walk into James's office and give him the news. I was dreading this conversation. James had been completely MIA for weeks in his online class. I had received multiple student complaints that nothing was happening in his class. No instruction, no grades, no engagement. When the dean asked IT to investigate the situation, we were told that it had been five weeks since he had even logged into the learning management system. "We will not be renewing his contract for next year" my dean declared when he learned this. The responsibility to inform James of this development fell on me. Although I knew this was a consequence of his own actions and I agreed with the decision, the thought of having to tell James he needed to find employment elsewhere next year was nauseating. I'm not naturally inclined to find joy in firing people. Yet I knew it was necessary. As I attempted to pep-talk myself in the bathroom, I framed the conversation in my mind as a role I had to play, that of a decisive manager. As I stepped into James's office, I shifted into character. My tone was firm, yet empathetic, mirroring the balanced delivery of a veteran actor. "James, we need to discuss your recent absences and its impact on your online class."

I come from a performance studies and theater background, so I find comfort in framing the chair role as a kind of performance. The similarities can provide some useful insight. An actor in a Shakespearean play does not own the role of Hamlet; they instead borrow it and put their own twist on it. Similarly, you do not own the chair position. You are occupying it and performing the role for a period. You should work to leave a lasting impression and to make it interesting for yourself.

As chair, you face many of the challenges that actors do when playing a role (Rose, 2019). Actors can suffer from a lack of connection with the role they are playing. This can make it hard to create a believable and lived-in performance (Donnellan, 2005), which can lead to an overreliance on technique that renders performances mechanical and uninspiring. Similarly, as chair you may feel detached from the role. We have elsewhere discussed how difficult it is for many chairs to feel comfortable transitioning from faculty to administration. In their heart they are faculty, and the administrative responsibilities do not feel natural. This kind of detachment can make your time as chair feel procedural rather than genuine. Donnellan (2005) suggests that an actor explore the reasons behind a character's behavior rather than simply portraying emotions. You can do the same as chair. Connect to the underlying motivations that drive the chair character you are playing. When you do faculty evaluations, remember that they may be rote for you as you plow through each one. But every single faculty member (audience) on the other side of the evaluation cares very much about the task you are slogging through.

Another challenge actors often face is how to keep performances fresh. Actors often repeat performances over and over in rehearsal and in theatrical shows. This can lead to stagnation. They say the lines so often that they become habitual. To overcome this, an actor can remember that performance is a dialogue with an audience (Alfreds, 2007). Every audience is different, so each dialogue can remain fresh and spontaneous. The same can be said for you as chair. Remember that your performance impacts an audience, and they impact you. While a play may have the same lines every night, each performance is different. Think about a football game. In every game the rules are identical, but a different game script emerges each time two teams step on the field. Your performance as chair is the same. Embrace the differences and openness in each performance as chair. Department meetings may feel stale, but if you approach them as an open dialogue rather than an agenda checklist, you will find more meaning.

Finally, approaching your role as a performance can also provide you some armor. Imagining yourself an actor playing the role of chair can protect you in those moments when you feel uncomfortable, anxious, or inadequate. If you understand that you are playing a role, you can focus on performing what your audience needs rather than what you feel. If you are not up for the task, remember that you are playing the role of competent and confident chair and perform as such. As in the example I started this chapter with, understanding myself as a performer in a role went a long way to helping me do what needed to be done, although I felt very uncomfortable in the situation.

As we started this chapter with, remember that every role is temporary. Someday you will not be playing this role. What will your legacy be then? How will you be remembered? Some actors were born to play certain roles and are remembered fondly for them. Similarly, you can be remembered for how you played this temporary role and the positive changes you implemented when you occupied it.

REFLECTIONS

1. Does the position of chair seem performative to you? What possibilities might this metaphor open for you in understanding how to be a good chair?
2. What do you want your legacy as a department chair to be? How do you plan to achieve this?

REFERENCES

Alfreds, M. (2007). *Different every night: Putting the play on stage and keeping it fresh*. Nick Hern Books.

Donnellan, D. (2005). *The actor and the target*. Nick Hern Books.

Rose, H. M. (2019). Chair communication as ethical performance: Embodiment, interpretation, and translation. In J. Brower & W. B. Myers (Eds.), *Critical administration in higher education: Negotiating political commitment and managerial practice* (pp. 37–47). Lexington Books.

Chapter 97

Summer and End-of-the-Year Planning

The end of the academic year can be invigorating. As the spring semester winds down, departmental energy changes, people are in better spirits, and everyone is looking ahead. As a faculty member you have been through this cycle plenty of times. But now, as chair, you should be aware that your relationship to this time of year will change. Many of the differences will be dictated by your particular contract, your dean's expectations, and your institution. You may be on a twelve-month contract and expected to continue as normal over the summer months. Some chairs are on nine-month contracts and are expected to keep the same schedule as their faculty, and others may receive a stipend to be available but not be expected to be present in the same way as during the academic year. Institutions and departments have various needs and expectations. If this was not hashed out explicitly during your contract negotiations, you should have a conversation with your dean to avoid any ambiguity. This conversation is also an opportunity to protect yourself. You may be assuming more is expected of you than is required. Clarifying these boundaries helps ensure you are not overcommitting yourself. It can also save you from the stress of wondering if you are in the office frequently enough during the summer. Also, talk to a seasoned chair in a similarly sized department about how they understand the expectations. They may be able to add some color to your dean's message.

Regardless of the summer expectations you are operating under, you need to pay special attention to how you end the academic year. As chair, you will be responsible for winding down operations. This may mean closing out budgets, working on end-of-the-year reports, ensuring all grading disputes are resolved, and preparing for summer sessions. One of the more important things to be attentive to as you wind down the academic year is that many of your faculty will be unavailable for the next three months. If you are working on any projects over the summer that require input or labor from faculty, you should prepare in advance. Ask yourself what needs to be done over the summer, what you need from faculty, and who may be unavailable during the summer months (Dettmar, 2023). Do you need data for assessments, endorsements for grant applications, or bios and headshots for an update to the faculty webpage? Have these conversations early so faculty have the option to squeeze them into the semester or work on them over the summer. You cannot reasonably expect your nine-month faculty to complete these tasks over the summer if you did not give them the opportunity to complete them during the academic year.

As you head into summer, do so with intentionality. Do not let summer just happen to you. Summer is not simply about closing out the previous academic year, but it is also a chance for you to take advantage of the slower pace. The timely emergency that lands on your desk and hijacks your day is one of the challenges we have returned to repeatedly in this volume. Summer offers you a respite. It certainly still happens, but with much less frequency. You have much more freedom to engage in uninterrupted "deep work" (Newport, 2016).

Summer is the time for you to work on a larger departmental project like curricular revisions, marketing materials, program reviews, and such. It can also provide an opportunity to engage in strategic planning for your department. Think about the goals of your department heading into the next year. Do not let your departmental obligations take all your summer though. You should also set aside time to address your own creative and scholarly projects. It can be very hard to focus on your intellectual and creative projects during the academic year. You often will not have the flexibility to engage in this kind of work during the academic year, so do so furiously over the summer months knowing you likely will not be able to catch up come September.

Put some time into cultivating your leadership skills (Mattiske & Angelini, 2022). Summer is a chance to slow down and pay attention to what you need to do to be a better chair. Attend a higher education administration workshop, read leadership books, have lunch with other chairs. Consider administrative and structural changes that might be needed. Are there policies that need to be revised or roles that need to be better redefined? Summer provides a prime opportunity to assess and prepare for discussions and implementations for the upcoming year.

Finally, take some time to recharge. Every year as chair has its challenges, but the first year is especially taxing. Take some time to set your out-of-office reply getaway. Even if you do not go anywhere on vacation, take a break from attending to your departmental needs. Do something you love that is not for your work.

None of this comes to fruition without careful planning. You need to strategically approach your summer. Have a list of intentions and plan specifically how you will use your time. The summer weeks will slip away if you do not go in with a clear plan and intention. Know what you want to get accomplished. It can be tempting to take a laid-back attitude to summer planning, but you are missing out on an important opportunity if you do. Summer is always valuable for those of us in higher education, but even more so now that you are chair. When you leverage those summer months toward productive ends, you set yourself up for success in the coming academic year. Be proactive so you can come into your second year as chair with a renewed sense of confidence, direction, purpose, and energy. Embrace the summer months as a crucial opportunity to set yourself up for success in your second year as chair.

REFLECTIONS

1. Have you clearly understood and communicated your availability and responsibilities over the summer based on your contract? Do you need to clarify your understanding with your dean? Why or why not?
2. What are the critical tasks that need to be completed over the summer, and how are you prepared to address them?

REFERENCES

Dettmar, K. (2023, May 10). *Ask the chair: "How do you get professors to respond in the summer?"* Chronicle of Higher Education. https://www.chronicle.com/article/ask-the-chair-how-do-you-get-professors-to-respond-in-the-summer

Mattiske, C., & Angelini, E. M. (2022). The SAIL Institute's Department Chair Virtual Academy, Part 1: Chairs can learn to lead. *Department Chair*, Winter 2022 Issue. https://sunysail.org/wp-content/uploads/2023/03/The-Department-Chair-Winter2022-Issue_WIley-publication.pdf

Newport, C. (2016). *Deep work: Rules for focused success in a distracted world.* Grand Central Publishing.

Chapter 98

Authenticity and Pragmatism

"We need to broaden our candidate pool," I explained, my voice hinting at some exasperation at how shortsighted my department was being. At my previous institution we employed a faculty member with this candidate's specific degree, and his contributions were a big benefit to the department. Despite explaining this, I could feel resistance in the room. I had carefully drafted the position announcement and had added this degree as an acceptable qualification for candidates. This inclusion was met with vocal resistance by several faculty members. Their objections were based not in practical concerns but instead from a deeply rooted belief in maintaining fairness. They argued it was unjust to hire a new faculty member in a tenure-track position with a degree they deemed inferior to their own. Human Resources had assured me that I had the authority in this matter—I was not required to acquiesce. I knew including the degree was the right decision, as this had potential to extend the areas of expertise we could add to the department. Regardless, I begrudgingly conceded, revising the job listing to remove the degree option. Preserving departmental harmony outweighed insisting on a point I knew was right.

When I was a new chair, I frequently got reassurances from folks that I would thrive in the position if I "was myself" and "did what I knew was right." I attended a retreat for new chairs where we spent considerable time identifying our "North Star" so we could lead our departments from a place of authenticity. Yet, after eleven years as chair, I have come to see that such advice, while well-intentioned, is often impractical. Authentic leadership, which implies a perfect marriage between one's actions and internal beliefs, can be a recipe for conflict for a department chair.

In the example above, staying true to values would have been more trouble than it was worth and would have set me up for failure down the road. The situation highlights the potential conflicts between maintaining an authentic leadership approach and the pragmatic need to adapt to the pressures and expectations of others. Sparrowe (2005) regards an authentic leadership style as a narrative construct rather than an innate leadership trait. Ironically, it is something you cultivate. I could have used the opportunity to insist on my own belief about the necessary expertise and crafted that as part of my leadership identity, but that would have ignored the need to accommodate the existing departmental culture.

Identity, especially in academic settings, is complex. Demands for authentic leadership ignore that complexity (Tomkins & Nicholds, 2017). As a new chair, you need to understand that you will sometimes need to make decisions that feel inauthentic to your personal beliefs or experiences. Always expecting authenticity is limiting and does not allow for flexibility. Given that your managerial authority is inherently limited and dependent on garnering buy-in, demanding unwavering authenticity is not just impractical—it's unfeasible.

Instead, effective chairing should stem from situational awareness rather than an insistence that everything you do conforms to your own internal values guiding your framework (Pfeffer, 2015). Different circumstances require different approaches. As chair, you bounce between various academic situations regularly. You need to prioritize adaptability rather than authenticity. Laboring under the expectation that everything you do as chair aligns perfectly with an internal compass is adding another layer of labor to an already very demanding job. It is also too much to expect and is likely to increase your anxiety.

Calls for authenticity stem from upright intentions, driven by a perceived lack of quality in higher education leadership. Stressing authenticity is often understood to infuse heart, ethics, and passion back into higher education leadership. It is meant to help us connect to the work we are doing. While these calls are well-meaning, they oversimplify the diverse and multifaceted demands that you face as chair.

I am not advocating that you be inauthentic, and this is not a license to practice disingenuous leadership. It is instead a reminder that not everything you do as chair will connect deeply with some core values. This expectation is unrealistic. Balancing authenticity with pragmatism and adaptability does not make you a less effective chair. Accepting the limits of authenticity can help you approach your leadership more effectively, allowing you to balance your own needs with those of your department.

REFLECTIONS

1. Have you faced any situations as chair where you have felt the need to compromise personal beliefs for the greater good of your department? How did you feel about this compromise?

2. How do you balance the often-competing demands of both authenticity and flexibility? Are they at odds? How do you understand the role of authenticity in your own leadership style as chair?

REFERENCES

Pfeffer, J. (2015). *Leadership BS: Fixing workplaces and careers one truth at a time.* Harper Business.

Sparrowe, R. T. (2005). Authentic leadership and the narrative self. *Leadership Quarterly, 16*(3), 419–439. https://doi.org/10.1016/j.leaqua.2005.03.004

Tomkins, L., & Nicholds, A. (2017). Make me authentic, but not here: Reflexive struggles with academic identity and authentic leadership. *Management Learning, 48*(3), 253–270. https://doi.org/10.1177/1350507616684267

Chapter 99

Effective Communication

We are winding down this volume, and these last two chapters are going to be focused on wrapping up what we have covered thus far. I have worked hard to try to frame the experiences of being chair in productive ways. I am less interested in giving answers than I am in helping you process what you have been encountering as a newcomer to the position of chair. When I have given suggestions, I have always tried to frame them as such. But I understand that everyone has their own experiences, and my advice may not always translate. What I hope *does* translate though is understanding that someone else has wrestled with the same experiences, and you can see how I have processed those experiences in retrospect. My goal here has not been to draw a map, but instead to craft a field guide.

With that disclaimer, there is one piece of advice that I feel confident about stating with certainty as we look for themes that stretch across these reflections. You need to be an effective communicator to be an effective chair. It is an absolute necessity. "Effective communicator" does not imply a standard set of practices that every chair must follow. It is instead a reminder to leverage your communication strengths while addressing your communicative deficiencies.

Some of the reflections here have focused on the formal administrative aspects of the job such as budgeting, formal discipline, and course scheduling. But a great many others center around communication issues. We have covered topics related to coalition building, advocacy, leading meetings, organizational culture, boundary spanning, marketing, feedback, gossip, and social media. All of these are related to messaging. While these explicitly deal with communication, other reflections prominently feature effective communication principles even though that is not the primary focus. For example, when we reflected on your increased legal liability, we covered how to guard your communication. When we covered bad faith demands for justifications, we explored silence as communicative response. When we covered supporting international faculty, we focused on early and open communication as key. This list could go on and on. In short, effective communication is baked into much of what we consider effective chairing.

You may accuse me of bias since I teach organizational communication. As academics, I'm sure we've all heard some version of the criticism, "When you approach the world as a hammer, everything looks like a nail" leveled at us at one point in our careers. I won't deny it, but there is research about chairs that confirms my suspicions. Bryman (2007) argues that one characteristic that effective chairs have is facilitating open communication within their departments. Keith and Buckley (2011) argued that interpersonal communication skills are key to success in the position. Ambrose and colleagues (2005) identified that basic communication skills are one of the key factors that contribute to the success of chairs. So, I am not the only one.

Effective communication is key for any managerial position, but especially so for department chairs. Early in this volume we spent considerable time discussing how important buy-in is due to your lack of formal managerial authority. You need to be persuasive and charismatic. This obviously requires competency in interpersonal and public communication.

While there is no secret formula for how to be a good communicator, there are best practices that are always a good idea to follow. First, engage in active listening. Communicating is not about doing all the talking. Active listening means not only hearing the words but also being present to the speaker. I learned the importance of active listening after reading former FBI hostage negotiator Chriss Voss's (2016) book on negotiating. Expecting to read about how to be a bulldog in negotiating situations, I was surprised when the book focused mainly on active listening. The next time there was a contentious meeting with a colleague, I decided to commit to doing very active listening in the meeting. I was shocked by the results. That sounds like hyperbole, but it is not. It was so surprisingly effective that I called a friend to report on the strangeness of how effective it was. When you engage in active listening, not only do you learn more, but the other party can tell, and it changes the energy of a conversation.

Second, relationship building is key to your success. You need to build friendly collegiality with your team. You do not have to regularly grab drinks with every individual, but you do need to have genuine connections. So much of your success will depend on whether your colleagues trust you. Connections can foster that trust.

Finally, be accessible and visible. Send regular emails with important updates. Make sure your faculty know they can come to you with problems and ideas. Ensure your department does not feel lost about policy, personnel, or procedural changes. This reduces rumors and uncertainty, and it engenders a confidence from your team that you will keep them in the loop.

Communication is essential. Being good at the clerical aspects of the job are the bare minimum you can do as chair. To truly elevate your leadership, communicate with intentionality and reflexivity. The essence of effective chairing is rooted deeply in communication. The reflections in this book have not just highlighted strategies but have also underscored the profound impact of communication on the dynamics within an academic department. Effective chair communication is not simply about relaying information, but about dialoging, building relationships, and creating cohesion.

REFLECTIONS

1. Reflecting on the three best communicative practices provided here, would you add any? Which ones?
2. How do you assess your communication competency? What are your communicative strengths and weaknesses? How can you best lean into those strengths and work to address your weaknesses?

REFERENCES

Ambrose, S., Huston, T., & Norman, M. (2005). A qualitative method for assessing faculty satisfaction. *Research in Higher Education*, *46*(7), 803–830. https://doi.org/10.1007/s11162-004-6226-6

Bryman, A. (2007). Effective leadership in higher education: A literature review. *Studies in Higher Education*, *32*(6), 693–710. https://doi.org/10.1080/03075070701685114

Keith, J., & Buckley, P. F. (2011). Leadership experiences and characteristics of chairs of academic departments of psychiatry. *Academic Psychiatry*, *35*(2), 118–121. https://doi.org/10.1176/appi.ap.35.2.118

Voss, C. (2016). *Never split the difference: Negotiating as if your life depended on it*. Harper Business.

Chapter 100

Lessons Learned and Paths Forward

By now you have probably gotten a sense of how complicated being a department chair is. Your first one hundred days have likely been a whirlwind. In this volume, I have tried to offer some guidance on how many layers there are to being a chair. You are a mediator, a strategist, a visionary, a bureaucrat, and a diplomat. We started this volume with reflections on how important the role is and why you should take it seriously. One hundred days in, I hope you can begin to see the impact you can have as chair. I believe that the challenges and frustrations of being chair are usually outweighed by the impact you can have. I hope this volume has been helpful in identifying the potential inherent in even the most frustrating of moments of the position.

The reflections in this volume should serve as a reminder that academic leadership from the chair position requires a delicate balance. Walking a tightrope between competing demands is a repeating theme in this book. You need to be an authority figure, but you have little formal authority. You need to balance the needs of various internal and external stakeholders. You must represent the often-competing needs of administration, faculty, and students. And you need to do it all while navigating change in professional identity and status, increased legal liability, and work relationships. The ability to balance everything might be one of the most important aspects of being a successful chair.

Rather than approaching this balancing as a frantic juggling act, think of it as dynamic and continuous adaptation. This can help you understand each challenge and decision as part of the unfolding story about your leadership and influence rather than as balls you must keep in the air. When the need for continual adaptation is difficult, remember that the balancing act itself is more important than each individual task.

From day one hundred on, you will still find that the learning curve is still steep. But you may find it less surprising. I hope the reflections in this volume have removed some of the surprise. I have written this book with the intent to help you expedite some of the necessary experiential learning and get to wisdom faster. As I have stressed in several reflections, effective chairing does not mean you need to have all the answers to everything. Instead, you need to know how to ask the right questions and to whom. This can foster a culture where problem-solving happens through collaboration.

I have offered advice frequently in this volume, but always with the ethos of offering friendly suggestions rather than a blueprint for success. While this volume is meant to guide you through your first one hundred days, I hope you can keep it beyond that as a reference for when specific situations arise. If you have been reading in order, many of the chapters will not sync with exactly when you need them. For example, the chapters on search committees might be scheduled to be read when you do not have an ongoing search. So return to those chapters when the time is right.

As you close this chapter, literally and figuratively, on your first one hundred days as chair, look forward with optimism. The challenges are real, but so are the opportunities for growth, achievement, and making a difference. Your success as chair is not measured by the absence of problems, but by your ability to handle them.

We opened this book by troubling the popular metaphor of department chairing as survival. I encouraged you to think about *designing* as an alternative metaphor. I hope this volume has given you some hope that you can do better than simply surviving your term as chair. As this book comes to a close, reflect on the last one hundred days as a foundation from which you can design the rest of your time in this position. Design your time as chair with intentionality, a sense of why this work is important, and an awareness of the impact you can have on your academic community and your own personal and professional growth.

All the best of luck on the next one hundred days and beyond.

REFLECTIONS

1. How would you grade your first one hundred days? What is the most important lesson you have learned during this time? What is the most surprising aspect of the position thus far?
2. Which chapters in this volume have been most and least applicable? Why? What is the biggest takeaway from these reflections?

Index

academia: autonomy in, 4–5, 14, 73; bullying in, 137–38, 142; chief officer in, 164; cycles of, 152–53; freedom in, 17; identity schism in, 2; leadership in, 281–82, 299; managers in, 281–82; minorities in, 152; provost influencing direction of, 165–66; students best fit in, 226; training in, xxiv
acceptance, of anxiety, 231–32
accessibility, 99
accommodation, 16–18
accomplishments, 35, 92–93
active listening: attentiveness and, 41; in communications, 297; feedback from, 187, 258–59; listening skills in, 62; in one-on-one meetings, 240; relationships built through, 187, 297
activity-based budgeting, 53
adjunct faculty, 113–15
administration: department chair's decisions for, 5, 8; faculty's gap with, 75; faculty's relationship with, 26; needs and limitations of, 26; saying no to, 108; task attention in, 243; tasks of, 282
adults, 20
advising, in retention, 219
advocacy: by dean, 155; for department, 158–59; by leadership, 75–76; reasonable and helpful, 76; self-advocacy and, 59; for students, 68
agenda: department chair's interruptions to, 72–73, 99; loss of control of, 72; meetings created with, 34–36; research productivity in, 243–44; scholarly success and, 242–44; time spent on, 35
Alexander, F. K., 263
AlphaGo, 19
Althusser, Louis, 273
ambiguity, 7
animosity, 267
annual reviews: of colleagues, 117; of faculty, 116–18; intentionality for, 116; managing reactions to, 120–21; misinterpretations avoided in, 119–20; strategic methods in, 119–21; transparency of, 120
anticipatory guidance, 108
anxiety: acceptance of, 231–32; during department meetings, xvii–xviii; expecting, 2; over equality, 11; about public speaking, 230–32, 251
appreciation, 162
assessments: curricular, 263; of department meetings, 38–39; direct statements in, 120; performative ritual of, 263–64; personal relationships removed from, 117;

301

self-assessments and, xviii; of students, 264; universities with culture of, 263
asset, being an, 159
asymmetry, of information, 65
attentiveness, active listening and, 41
audience, of websites, 249
authentic leadership, 293–94
authority: acceptance of, 273; approaching with, 204; of department chair, 13–14
autonomy: in academia, 4–5, 14, 73; guidance and, 107–8

backdrop, for virtual meetings, 193–94
bad faith demands, 273
bandwidth, for virtual meetings, 191
beginning-of-the-year retreat, 246–47
behaviors: in all-college meetings, 40; bullying and changing of, 140–41; culture contradicted by, 204–5; department chair addressing, 82; department meetings with disruptive, 101–3; of faculty, 84–85; faculty member's bad, 16–18; faculty's disruptive, 90; investigating faculty, 85; legal consequences from, 176–77; meetings with disruptive, 31; of parents, 280; power influencing, 47; predatory, 84–85; senior faculty with bad, 170; students with bad, 81–82
beliefs, limiting, 19
Berlant, Lauren, 73
bias: decision-making without, 174; insights without, 213–14; search committee process without, 172; in tenure-track positions, 198
Black faculty members, 206–7
blind spots, 206–8
blood pressure, xviii
Bryman, A., 297
Buckley, P. F., 297
Buddhist principles, of detachment, 96
budgeting, 7; activity-based, 53; centralized, 53; cuts in, 246;

decision-making in, 50; in department, 49–50; department chair duty of, 43; incremental model in, 52–53; leadership principles in, 50; lines and restrictions in, 55; management skills in, 49–50, 56; models used in, 52–53; responsibility-centered, 53; revenue reliance in, 53; strategies and tactics for, 55–57; transparency in, 50, 56; zero-based, 52
Buller, J. L., 258, 276
bullying: in academia, 137–38, 142; behaviors changed in, 140–41; communications mitigating, 141; disciplinary procedures against, 140; threats rendered powerless of, 142; victim, 138
Burkeman, O., 29
buy-in: communications used for, 297; from faculty and students, 14; one-on-one meetings for, 239

candidate guidance, 270–71
career goals, 219, 254–55
Carnegie, Dale, 186
Center for Collegiate Mental Health, 58
centralized budgeting, 53
checklist, of search committee, 174
checks and balances, 173
chief academic officer, 164
children, 20
The Chronicle of Higher Education (publication), xx, xxi, 4, 245
class conflicts, 126
classroom engagement, 260–61
classroom observations, 146–48
coalition-building, 239
collaboration, 159, 300
colleagues: annual review of, 117; interpersonal communications with, 184; relationships changing with, 98–99
collective policies: for department meetings, 101–3; implementation of,

102–3; personal private conversations and, 105
The College Administrator's Survival Guide (Gunsalus), xx
commercial websites, 249
committee assignments, 143–44. *See also* search committee
common sense, 50
Communication Privacy Management Theory, 65
communications: active listening in, 297; bullying mitigated through, 141; buy-in using, 297; colleagues interpersonal, 184; counterproductive, 38–39; crisis, 227–29; department chair effectiveness through, 296–98; department chair's breakdown in, xvii–xviii; department's internal, 228–29; effectiveness in, 296–98; of expectations, 174; grade disputes with skills in, 58–59; with intentionality, 298; interpersonal, 188; legal liabilities in, 296–97; major, 224; meetings with constructive, 37–39; meta-discourse as, 38–39; political awareness in, 41; skills in, 34; teaching improving skills in, 261; two-way multichannel, 228; website used for, 248
community colleges, 221–22
competence, 203
complaints, from parents, 278–80
compliance, 180
confidentiality, xxiv–xxv, 65, 267
conflict management, 156
consistency, 102, 119–20
contributions, appreciation for, 93
conversations: collective policies and personal private, 105; direct feedback through, 105; engaging in uncomfortable, 210–11; with faculty members, 62–63; faculty members having reasonable, 102; meetings with monopolized, 41; about online education, 150; worst interpretations of, 180

core values, 204
counterproductive communications, 38–39
course-correction, from feedback, 258
courses: classroom engagement in, 260–61; scheduling and teaching, 122–23; students and choices of, 5–6; substitutions of, 5–6; teaching of online, 149–50
course schedule: challenges of, 127; class conflicts in, 126; department peculiarities and, 127; experienced resources for, 125; faculty involvement in, 123–26; obligations and opportunities in, 126–27; politics avoided in, 122–24; student involvement in, 123; university owns classes for, 127
The Creative Act (Rubin), 19
credit for accomplishments, 92–93
credit loss, of transfer students, 222
crisis communications, 227–29
critical thinking, 261
culture: assessment, 263; behaviors contradicting desired, 204–5; departmental, 144, 203–5; design of department contributing to, 210; diversity and inclusivity as, 206–11; of fear, 138; healthy environment in, 203–4; from history, 209; knowledge of, 34–35; matching, 171; organization's values for, 209–11; tax on, 209–10
curricular assessment, 263
curricular development, 113–14
customer service mindset, 279–80
customer value, 213

daily devotional, xxiii–xxiv
data: decision-making based on, 126; dump, xxiii; from focus groups, 213–14
day-to-day minutia, 254, 282
dean: advocacy by, 155; all-college meetings with chair and, 40–42; department chair's relationship with, 155–56, 158–59; difficulty of

being, 254; disagreements with, 156; emails causing anger in, 257–58; partnership built with, 158; strengths and weaknesses of, 156; student behaviors and, 82
decision-making: in budgeting, 50; on committee assignments, 143–44; data-driven, 126; diversity in, 210; emotions involved in, 122–23; faculty input for, 88; legal liability in, 177–78; management explanations in, 272–74; no bias in, 174; senior faculty in, 111; unilateral and multilateral, 87–88
deep work, 291
Deep Work (Newport), 243
department: addressing needs of, 242; advocacy for, 158–59; authoritative approach in, 204; budgeting in, 49–50; committee assignments for, 143–44; course schedule and peculiarities of, 127; culture developed for, 144, 203–5; culture from design contributions to, 210; customer value in, 213; diversity and inclusivity in, 206–11; documentation practices of, 180; donations impacting, 201; don't fight every fight in, 276; enrollment for, 165; fundraising needs for, 200–201; inclusive environment in, 114–15; internal communications in, 228–29; large project planning for, 291; legal, 180–81; member vanished from, 64–65; positive environment in, 266–67; public image through social media, 132–33; relationship building in, 186–88; safe environment for, 81–82, 252–53; search committee meeting needs of, 171; shared values in, 203–4; social media in, 134–35; status-based inequality in, 196–98; student assessment good for, 264; students leaving, 219; student success contribution by, 159; summer schedule for, 128–30; website for, 248–50
department chair: accommodation by, 16–18; administrative decisions of, 5, 8; agenda interruptions to, 72–73, 99; authority of, 13–14; behaviors addressed by, 82; blind spots of, 206–8; budgeting duty of, 43; communications to be effective, 296–98; communicative breakdown as, xvii–xviii; dean's relationship with, 155–56, 158–59; designing, xxii; diplomacy of, 22–23; diversity commitment of, 171; dual loyalty of, 26; duties of, 7; emails sent and received by, 28–29, 257–59; emergencies faced by, 73; expectations of, 1; experience lacking of, 19–20; faculty members conversations with, 62–63; faculty's relationship changing with, 10–11; faculty transition to, xix, 11; goal-setting by, 43–44; identity of, 25–26; interpersonal connections of, 69–70; isolation and loneliness of, 69; learning curve for, 299–300; legal liability of, 176–78; liminality and, 25–26; listening skills of, 62; obligation to do what's right of, 68; parent complaints handled by, 278–80; passive-aggressive strategy of, 98–99; performance role of, 287–89; performative assessment ritual of, 263–64; personal growth in, 251–53; power status of, 46–47; provost's relationship with, 164–66; public speaking anxiety of, 230–32; responsibilities of, 1–2; skill set for, xxii; social media managed by, 135–36; social media strategies for, 131–33; survival of, xxi; turnover of, 233; universities with differences in, xxiv, 8; unprepared to be, xviii–xix; vulnerability of, 95–96, 152

Department Chair Survival Guide (McLure), xx
department meetings: agenda created for, 34–36; all-college and dean in, 40–42; ancillary issues in, 102–3; anxiety during, xvii–xviii; assessment of, 38–39; collective policies for, 101–3; constructive dialogue for, 37–39; conversation monopolized in, 41; cultural knowledge from, 34–35; disruptive behaviors in, 101–3; face-to-face, 191, 193–94, 215–16, 239–40, 261; issues brought up in, 246–47; organizational investment in, 31–32; as sense-making events, 32
detachment, Buddhist principles of, 96
development fund estimates, 56
devil's advocate, 38
difficult faculty, 16–17
digital strategy, of universities, 248–50
diplomacy: of department chair, 22–23; hallway, 183–84
direct statements, 120
disagreements: with dean, 156; through emails, 104–5; faculty and student, 67–68
disciplinary procedures, 140
discretion, xxiv–xxv
discrimination practices, 177
disruptive behaviors: at department meetings, 101–3; of faculty, 90; at meetings, 31
diversity: Black faculty members in, 206–7; in decision-making, 210; department chair commitment to, 171; member, 206–7; as shared values, 206–11
documentation practices, 180, 237
Donnellan, D., 288
donors: bringing in, 43; department and students impacted by, 201; fundraising and relationships with, 201
dual loyalty, of department chair, 26
Dunning, D., xviii

Ecclesiastes 3:1, 152
80/20 rule, 89–90
Ellis, S., xx
emails: chair sending and receiving, 28–29, 257–59; dean angry about, 257–58; disagreements through, 104–5; efficiency influenced by, 29; inbox of, 28–29; students with time stamps on, 67; universities discovery process of, 179
emergencies, 73
emotional regulation, 96, 122–23, 228
emotional support, 168–69
end-of-the-year strategy, 275, 290–92
engagement, student, 219
enrollment: for department, 165; goal-setting for, 43; management of, 212–14; marketing manager skills for, 213; political complications in, 224; retention strategy in, 218–20; strategic planning for, 212–13; transfer students in, 221–23
equality, anxiety over, 11
equitable campuses, 206–7
evaluation performance, 288
exceptionalism, 17
expectations: communications of, 174; of department chair, 1; unrealistic, 62
experience, chair lacking, 19–20
experienced resources, 125
experimentation, 285
exploratory mindset, 20–21

face-to-face meetings, 191, 193; one-on-one meetings and, 239–40; for recruiting, 215–16; with students, 261; virtual meetings compared to, 194
facial expressions, 193
faculty: adjunct, 113–15; administration's gap with, 75; administration's relationship with, 26; annual reviews of, 116–18; bad behaviors by, 84–85; buy-in from, 14; course schedule involvement

of, 123–26; decision-making input from, 88; department chair's relationship changing with, 10–11; department chair's transition from, xix, 11; development fund estimates for, 56; difficult, 16–17; disruptive behaviors of, 90; feedback from part-time, 114; governance, 8; grievance-oriented, 89–90; international, 167–69; investigating behaviors of, 85; junior, 107–9, 111, 129; macro trends information to, 246; meritocracy myth assessing, 210; part-time, 113–15; professional development of, 150; senior, 110–11, 129, 170, 179; student disagreements and, 67–68; students advised by, 20–21; tenure-track positions of, 196–98

"The Faculty Job (Almost) No One Wants" (Zahneis), 4

Faculty Labor Relations, 84

faculty members: accomplishments acknowledged of, 35; administration's relationship with, 26; annual reviews reactions of, 120–21; bad behavior by, 16–18; Black, 206–7; buy-in from, 14; chair's relationship changing with, 10–11; committee assignments to, 143–44; conflicts with, 61; department chair conversations with, 62–63; department chair transition from, xix, 11; diversity member and, 206–7; evaluation performance for, 288; feedback from, 32; formal discipline of, 236–38; gossip among, 62, 266–68; harassment of, 137–38; interpersonal harmony among, 62; investigations by, 104; needs and limitations of, 26; obligation to do what's right and, 68; playing devils advocate, 38; power paradox experienced by, 46–47; professional conduct of, 102; reasonable conversations with, 102; relationships with junior, 107–9; social media displeasure by, 135–36; student grades and, 59; students advised by, 20–21; success of, 2; summer schedule for, 128–30; support of, 7–8; teaching process of, 147; tenure-track position of, 293; troubling material possessed by, 64–65; unexpected medical procedure for, 242; within universities, 4–5

fair labor practices, 115

Family Educational Rights and Privacy Act (FERPA), 279

fear, culture of, 138

feedback: active listening leading to, 187, 258–59; conversations for direct, 105; course-correction from, 258; from faculty members, 32; grading as loop for, 161; from office associates, 162; from part-time faculty, 114; self-perceived identity and, 257–58; from students, 227; of teaching, 148; virtual meetings for, 190; from website, 250

FERPA. *See* Family Educational Rights and Privacy Act

Feuerstein, A., 263

final exam timing, 275–76

financial compensation, 233–34

financial security, 234

Floyd, Alan, xix

focus groups, 213–14

formal discipline, of faculty members, 236–38

four-year institutions, 222

free-speech violations, 135

French, J. R. P., Jr., 13

Full Time Equivalents (FTE's), 53

fundraising: for department needs, 200–201; donor relationships for, 201; groundwork laid for, 200

funds, spending of, 56

generosity, 93
van Gennep, A., 25
get-togethers, 69–70
Gmelch, W. H., xix, 258
goal-setting, 43–44
Go game, 19
Gonzales, L. D., 95
good faith inquiries, 273–74
Gopnik, Alison, 20
gossip, of faculty member, 62, 266–68
grade disputes, 58–59, 279
grading, 161
graduation: courses offered for, 5–6; major switching changing date of, 225
grants, bringing in, 165
grievance-oriented faculty, 89–90
grievances, 41, 61
grooming habits, 101–3
Groundhog Day (movies), 285
guidance: anticipatory, 108; autonomy and, 107–8; of candidates, 270–71; for social media, 136
Gunsalus, C. K., xx

hallway diplomacy, 183–84
Hancock, N., 23
harassment: of faculty members, 137–38; of students, 278–79
healthy environment, 203–4
Hellawell, D. E., 23
hierarchy, respect of, 165
Hierarchy of Needs, xxi–xxii
higher education: challenges facing, 245–46; cyclical nature of, 284–85; legal interventions in, 176; market pressures on, 245; online classes for, 111, 149–50; podcasts on, 245–46; students retained in, 218–19; upward mobility in, 254–55; virtual meetings in, 190–91
higher-value work, 29
high-impact projects, 200–201
hiring process: fair and thorough, 174–75; search committee for, 170

history, culture from, 209
How to Win Friends and Influence People (Carnegie), 186
Human Resources, 82, 104, 135, 293

identity: academic schism of, 2; of department chair, 25–26; self-perceived, 257–58
implementation, of collective policies, 102–3
imposter syndrome, 152–53, 284
inbox, of emails, 28–29
inclusive environment: Black faculty members in, 206–7; department with, 114–15; as shared values, 206–11
incremental budget model, 52–53
inequality, status-based, 196–98
information: asymmetry of, 65; boundary turbulence, 65; macro trends, 246; memos providing, 78–79; regulating flow of, 22; statistical, 79; variables in sharing, 23–24
innovations, 285
Inside Higher Ed (publication), xx, 245
The Intellectual Devotional (book series), xxiii
intentionality, xxii; for annual reviews, 116; communications with, 298; designing your time with, 300; research productivity, 243; summer schedule, 291
international faculty: challenges facing, 167–68; emotional support for, 168–69; value of, 168; vulnerability of, 168–69
internet, 64
interpellation, 273
interpersonal harmony: colleague's communications for, 184; communications in, 188; for department chair, 69–70; disruptions to, 92; among faculty members, 62; hallway diplomacy for, 183–84; leaderships role in, 188

investigations: of faculty behaviors, 85; by faculty members, 104
isolation, 69, 95
issues: attention lacking to, 92; in department meetings, 102–3, 246–47; upper-level management, 164–65; warranting intervention, 276

job candidates, 122–23
job-related emotions, 95–96
Johnson, M., xx–xxi
junior faculty, 107–9, 111, 129

Keith, J., 297
Keltner, D. K., 46
Kramer, R., xx
Kruger, J., xviii
Kruger-Dunning effect, xviii

Lakoff, G., xx–xxi
Lamond, Greg, 252
leadership: academic, 281–82, 299; accessibility to, 99; advocacy by, 75–76; assessment role in, 264; authentic, 293–94; budgeting showing principles of, 50; emotional regulation in, 96; interpersonal harmony role of, 188; non-negotiable responsibility of, 85; power bases for, 13–14; recognition of others in, 92–93; skills cultivated in, 291; transparency in, 23; virtual meetings and, 190–91
Leading Improvements in Higher Education... (podcast), 245
learning curve, xix, 299–300
Learning Management System, 150
learning process, 58–59
legal department, 180–81
legal liabilities: in communications, 296–97; compliance and, 180; in decision-making, 177–78; of department chair, 176–78; general practices limiting, 179–81; of questions about grades, 279; risk mitigated for, 179
legal training, 179–80
lifestyle habits, 234
liminality, 25–26
limiting beliefs, 19
listening skills, 62
loneliness, 69, 95

macro trends information, 246
majors, students switching, 224–26
management: academic, 281–82; of budget, 49–50, 56; confidentiality maintained by, 65; conflict, 156; cycles with improvements for, 285; decision explanations in, 272–74; 80/20 rule in, 89–90; of enrollment, 212–14; personnel, 89, 236–37; power of, 14, 46–47; responsibilities of, 5, 13; rights, 8; time, 260–61; upper-level, 164–65
mandatory reporter, 180
Marketing and Communications team, 215
marketing manager, 213
McLuhan, Marshall, 191
McLure, L., xx
medical procedure, unexpected, 242
meditation, 96
memos: information provided by, 78–79; for resource allocation, 79; writing of, 78–79
mentorship, 109–11
meritocracy, in universities, 198
meritocracy myth, 210
Mertz, P., xx
meta-discourse, 38–39
Metaphors We Live By (Lakoff and Johnson), xx
mindfulness, xxiii
minority academics, 152
misinterpretations, 105, 119–20
Mucha, P. J., xx
multilateral decision-making, 87–88

National Communication Association, 10
Newport, Cal, 29, 243

office associates, 161; for administrative tasks, 282; feedback from, 162
Office Space (movie), 78
one-on-one meetings: active listening in, 240; for buy-in, 239; scheduling of, 240; while walking, 240
online classes: conversations about, 150; for higher education, 111, 149–50; quality control of, 150
On the Inconvenience of Other People (Berlant), 73
open systems, in universities, 203
opportunity: personal growth for, 251–53; recruiting for, 216–17
Organizational Communication, 152
organizations: budget cuts on, 246; cultural values of, 209–11; department meetings investment by, 31–32; dynamics of, 171; goals of, 29; meetings as sense-making events of, 32
Orwell, George, 141
outsiders, transfer students as, 222

parents: behaviors of, 280; complaints from, 278–80; customer service mindset with, 279–80; recruiting targeting, 216; teacher complaints from, 279–80
Pareto Principle. *See* 80/20 rule
partnerships, dean building, 158
part-time faculty, 113–15
passive-aggressive strategy, 98–99
pedagogical process, of grade, 58–59
peer-review process, 269–70
performance role, 287–89
personal growth: for career goals, 254–55; of department chair, 251–53
personalities, 37–38
personal relationships, 117
personnel management, 89, 236–37

The Philosophical Baby (Gopnik), 20
poaching, of students, 224–25
podcasts, on higher education, 245–46
police officers, 278
policies, in scheduling, 129
politics: communication awareness and, 41; course schedule avoiding, 122–24; enrollment with complications of, 224; tenure-track aspect of, 270
positive visualization, 231
power: behavior influenced by, 47; department chair new status of, 46–47; leadership's base for, 13–14; of management, 14, 46–47; paradox, 46–47; referent, 14; search committee's dynamics of, 171; threats with no, 142
predatory behaviors, 84–85
premium class times, 126
privacy, 65
proactive approach, 281
problem-solving, 41, 162, 300
professionals: conduct, 102; development, 110–11; faculty development as, 150; growth, 260–61; identity, 2; integrity, 181; social media conduct of, 135
provost, 164–66
public-facing events, 230–32
public image, 132–33
public speaking, anxiety of, 230–32, 251
publish-or-perish mantra, 152

quality control, 150
questions, asking, 62

Raven, B. H., 13
reactions, managing, 120–21
recharging, 291
recognition of others, 92–93
recruiting: face-to-face contact for, 215–16; opportunity and outcome focus in, 216–17; parents also targeted in, 216; for potential students, 215–17

referent power, 14
reflexivity, 105
relationships: active listening building, 187, 297; administration and faculty building, 26; colleagues changing, 98–99; dean and department chair building, 155–56, 158–59; department building, 186–88; department chair and faculty's changing, 10–11; department chair and provost building, 164–66; fundraising and donors, 201; with junior faculty members, 107–9; personal, 117; reliability building strong, 156; trust and goals aligning, 161
reliability, 156
repetition, value of, 285
reputation, 267
research, 122–23, 243–44
resource allocation, 79
responsibility-centered budget model, 53
retention, enrollment strategy for, 218–20
retirement savings, 234
revenue, 53, 165
rights, of students, 104
Rincones, R., 95
risk, legal liability mitigating, 179
Rites of Passage (van Gennep), 25
ritualistic elements, xxii
Rubin, Rick, 19
rumors, 105

safe environment, 81–82, 252–53
salary raises, 233–34
scheduling, 7; of one-on-one meetings, 240; policies in, 129; summer, 128–30, 290–92. *See also* course schedule
scholarly success, 242–44
Schwartzman, H. B., 32
search committee: checklist of, 174; checks and balances of, 173; department needs met by, 171; fair and unbiased process of, 172; for hiring process, 170; power dynamics of, 171; selection criteria of, 174; universities protocol for, 173–74
selection criteria, 174
self-advocacy, 59
self-assessments, xviii
self-awareness, xxv, 14
self-disclosure, 187
self-doubt, 153
self-perpetuating cycles, 230–31
self-preservation, 276
senior faculty, 110–11, 129, 170, 179
sense-making events, 32
sexism, 64–65
shared values: in department, 203–4; diversity and inclusivity as, 206–11
sharing, of information, 23–24
skill set, 7, 34, 132
social media: department chair managing, 135–36; department chair strategies for, 131–33; in department or workplace, 134–35; faculty member's displeasure on, 135–36; guidance sought concerning, 136; professional conduct on, 135; public image through, 132–33; strengths and limitations of, 131–32
Social Penetration Theory (SPT), 187
Sparrowe, R. T., 294
spending, 55
SPT. *See* Social Penetration Theory
staff: accomplishments acknowledged of, 35; credit for accomplishments of, 92–93; power paradox experienced by, 46–47
statewide articulation agreements, 222
statistical information, 79
status-based inequality, 196–98
strategies: annual review methods and, 119–21; for budgeting, 55–57; end-of-the-year, 275, 290–92; enrollment planning, 212–13; passive-aggressive, 98–99; retention and enrollment, 218–20; social media,

131–33; universities digital, 248–50; for virtual meetings, 193–95
students: advocacy for, 68; assessment good for department, 264; bad behavior by, 81–82; best academic fit for, 226; buy-in from, 14; course offerings to, 5–6; course schedule involvement of, 123; department left by, 219; department's contribution to success of, 159; donors impacting, 201; emails with time stamps from, 67; engagement, 219; face-to-face meetings with, 261; faculty advising, 20–21; faculty and disagreements with, 67–68; faculty members and grades of, 59; feedback from, 227; grade disputes of, 58–59; harassment of, 278–79; higher education retaining, 218–19; major switched by, 224–26; objections voiced by, 227; poaching of, 224–25; power paradox experienced by, 46–47; recruiting for potential, 215–17; rights, 104; teaching creating closeness to, 260–61; transfer, 221–23; universities switched by, 222; value propositions from, 213
Student Services, 82
successes, celebrating, 108
summer scheduling, 128–30, 290–92
surplus, 55
Surviving and (Sometimes) Thriving as a Department Chair (Mertz), xx
Surviving Chairdom (Ellis), xx

teaching: classroom observations of, 146–48; communications skills improved by, 261; course scheduling and, 122–23; faculty member's process of, 147; feedback of, 148; online courses and, 149–50; parents complaints about, 279–80; quality of, 146; student closeness created by, 260–61

tenure-track positions: adjunct faculty and, 114–15; candidate guidance for, 270–71; components of, 269; of faculty, 196–98; of faculty members, 293; peer-review process and, 269–70; political aspect of, 270
threats, powerless, 142
three-year appointments, 284
time management, 260–61
to-do list, 72
Training Day (movie), 142
transfer shock, 222
transfer students: credit loss of, 222; in enrollment, 221–23; as outsiders, 222; smooth transition for, 222–23
transparency: of annual reviews, 120; in budgeting, 50, 56; of committee assignments, 143–44; in leadership, 23
troubling material, 64–65
trust: gossip undermining, 267–68; hallway diplomacy building, 184; knowing who to, 181; relationships with goals and, 161
tuition money, 50
Turner, Victor, 25–26

Uncertainty Reduction Theory (URT), 187
unfair treatment, 17–18
unilateral decision-making, 87–88
universities: assessment culture in, 263; budgeting models used by, 52–53; chair differences at, xxiv, 8; classes owned by, 127; connections built within, 76; digital strategies of, 248–50; diversity initiatives at, 206–7; documentation practices of, 180; email discover process of, 179; equitable campuses in, 206–7; faculty member's support in, 7–8; faculty members within, 4–5; formal discipline procedures of, 237–38; legal department of, 180–81; legal training at, 179–80; Marketing and

Communications team at, 215; master digital strategy of, 248–50; meritocracy in, 198; open systems in, 203; salary raises at, 233–34; search committee protocol at, 173–74; student's experiences switching, 222; tenure-track positions in, 196–98; virtual meetings in, 190–91
upper-level management issues, 164–65
upward mobility, 254–55
urgent family matters, 134
URT. *See* Uncertainty Reduction Theory

values, xxii; core, 204; customer, 213; goals set based on, 44; of international faculty, 168; organizational, 209–11; propositions of, 213; of repetition, 285; shared, 203–4, 206–11; staying true to, 293–94; work as higher, 29
victim bullies, 138
virtual meetings: backdrop for, 193–94; bandwidth for, 191; face-to-face compared to, 194; facial expressions in, 193; for feedback, 190; guidelines for, 194–95; in higher education, 190–91; platforms for, 191; strategies for, 193–95; in universities, 190–91
visa renewal, 167
visibility, 99
visionary projects, 282
visual complexity, of slides, 147
Voss, Chriss, 297
vulnerability: of department chair, 95–96, 152; of international faculty, 168–69; of junior faculty, 108

walking meetings, 240
Washington, Denzel, 142
website: audience of, 249; commercial, 249; communications use for, 248; for department, 248–50; feedback from, 250; innovative, 249–50
work, higher-value, 29
workplace, social media in, 134–35
workshops, xxi
A World without Email (Newport), 29

Zahneis, M., 4
zero-based budget model, 52
Zoom Fatigue, 191, 194

About the Author

W. Benjamin Myers is a professor of communications and chair of the Department of Communication at the University of Toledo. He has served as chair for eleven years at three different universities. He teaches classes such as Organizational Communication, Business Communication, Small Group Communication, Communication Theory, Leadership Communication, and others. He is coeditor of the book *Critical Administration in Higher Education: Negotiating Political Commitment and Managerial Practice*. He has published articles in diverse outlets such as *Text and Performance Quarterly, Qualitative Inquiry, Qualitative Health Research, The Journal of Autoethnography*, and *Basic Communication Course Annual*.

www.ingramcontent.com/pod-product-compliance
Lightning Source LLC
Chambersburg PA
CBHW050836230426
43667CB00012B/2026